Latin America in C

Latin America in Crisis

John W. Sherman

Wright State University

Westview Press
A Member of the Perseus Books Group

Published in 2000 in the United States of America by Westview Press, 5500 Central Avenue, Boulder, Colorado 80301-2877, and in the United Kingdom by Westview Press, 12 Hid's Copse Road, Cumnor Hill, Oxford OX2 9JJ

Find us on the World Wide Web at www.westviewpress.com

Library of Congress Cataloging-in-Publication Data
Sherman, John W., 1960–
    Latin America in crisis / John Sherman
        p.   cm.
    Includes bibliographical references and index.
    ISBN 0-8133-3540-X (pbk.)
    1. Latin America—Politics and government.   2. Latin America—Economic conditions.   3. Poverty—Latin America.   4. Human rights—Latin America.   I. Title.

F1410 .S554   2000
980.03'3—dc21   00-036814

10   9   8   7   6   5   4   3   2   1

Contents

List of Illustrations   vii
Prologue   ix

1 Introduction: Why Is Latin America Poor?   1

Part I   Historical Latin America

2 A People of Conquest   19
3 The Colonial Centuries   37
4 Progress and Populism   56

Part II   Revolution and Counterrevolution

5 Nationalism and the Military Response   77
6 Revolution in Central America   95
7 Christianity and Counterinsurgency   114

Part III   Contemporary Latin America

8 The Politics of Control   135
9 Big Money: Debt and Wealth Extraction   154
10 Latin America in Perpetual Crisis   173
    Epilogue: A Strange World   193

Notes   199
Suggestions for Further Reading   201
Index   207

Illustrations

Maps

1.1   Nations of the Third World   2

2.1   The territories of three ancient Latin American civilizations   26

6.1   Central America and the Caribbean   103

8.1   Latin America   134

Prologue

This book is a concise introduction to contemporary Latin America for the beginning student or lay reader. It is what I call a skeletal text, intended only to provide a framework upon which, presumably, the instructor or reader will want to build. Whereas the general practice in college textbooks is to reach a minimum level of detail that most professors would view as sufficient, I have opted here for a more sweeping albeit concise survey of economic and political topics, leaving the choice of adding weightier material, or additional readings on social and cultural history, to each instructor. The advantage of such an approach is simple: Instead of examining all topics in equal depth, the professor can skirt by some lightly and emphasize others (through his or her choice of supplemental readings), while still presenting a basic framework.

This skeletal text is distinctive in a second way: It meshes introductory history with the fundamental economic and political realities of Latin America today. It is my goal that having read this book, the reader will be able to pick up a newspaper and, presuming that he or she can find an article of substance about Latin America, readily appreciate its meaning and context. The great challenge in writing this kind of book is to synthesize exceedingly complex trends, which are taking place in an enormously diverse region, without violating the integrity of our understanding of those trends. Simply put, it was not an easy book to write. But my frustration with introductory texts made it a necessary project. Far too many, in my estimation, jump from one topic to another (most often, by jumping from one nation to another), without cogent themes or continuity. There is also a dearth of books that strike a healthy balance between history and contemporary realities.

Finally, this is an evocative text. It has a point of view. After a few years of teaching I discovered that the most common student complaint about textbooks is that they are boring. Indeed, in the process of synthesizing scholarship and reaching consensus, it seems that many authors have eschewed risk-taking and shunned fresh argumentation. Even with lively prose, our textbooks have become predictable. This makes teaching hard because students have little to say when it's time for discussion. I do not expect everyone who uses this book to agree with all of its arguments—on the contrary, I present some novel interpretations that should spark vigorous debate—but what I do provide is a thinking text that will churn minds and arouse interest. For, if the truth be told, I too find most textbooks boring.

I do not, of course, make this an evocative book by challenging conventional facts! On the contrary, I am a classic academic, wedded to notions of truth. Without pursuing the nuances of postmodernism and language deconstruction engulfing much of academe, we can say that there are those among us who believe the message changes in meaning when proclaimed by different messengers. Many now question the whole notion of absolute truth, but I am not one of them. My premise is that truth exists, and that it is our quest in the university to find it.

If you and I walk down the street and see a man with a yellow shirt on, we discover a raw fact: There is a yellow shirt. If we close our eyes and chant "the shirt is red, the shirt is red," when we open our eyes, it will still be yellow. If another comes along who is color-blind and sees the shirt as gray, it is still in reality no less yellow. If an optometrist strolls by and explains the dynamics of the lens and retina—how rays of light are screened out and create for us the image of yellow—we might want to debate the nature of light, and ask the intriguing question of whether the shirt is truly yellow. But for all practical purposes within the bounds of reason, the shirt is still yellow. I am a product of the Enlightenment in this regard: I believe that there is a practical world of hard and simple data obtainable through a universal law of reason. Facts, by definition, are unchangeable, certain, solid, and invite no reasonable contention or dispute. The first obligation of the scholar is that every basic point of fact be accurate and correct. To the best of my knowledge, everything I have written here holds to this high standard.

The second tier of knowledge, as I see it, is contention. By accumulating facts, we make an argument. On seeing that man wearing the yellow shirt, I might quip, "Ah, he is a clown" (that is, a literal clown hired as such for entertainment). And you, asking why I say so, might hear me build my case with assorted facts: "He has an oversized pink bow tie with black polka dots, and a bright green polyester jacket that looks like it's from the 1960s" (so far, this description is painfully close to the standard dress of aged alumni on Homecoming Day at my undergraduate alma mater). "He has giant rubber ears attached to his head, a foam red nose, makeup on his face, and floppy shoes, each three feet long." Therefore, I conclude, he is a clown.

By their nature, contentions or arguments are biased in their selection of facts. In building the case that the man with the yellow shirt is a clown, I of course utilize only the facts supporting my position. I do not mention, in the litany of statements, that his hat is a conventional fedora, or that he happens to be carrying a briefcase. When one is constructing an argument, this type of omission is entirely acceptable. What is not acceptable is to omit facts that directly contradict or obfuscate the core of the argument. If I state that he is a clown, in part, because he is holding a giant swirled lollipop, it would be disingenuous of me to fail to mention that he is standing beside a confectioner who sells giant swirled lollipops. *Disingenuous* is defined by Webster's as "lacking in candor." The scholar, in building arguments, must not employ such sophistry. He or she must cite hard facts to support a case; and even in neglecting those facts that do not support the case, must never cloak facts that directly contradict the case.

Such integrity is especially vital when the author speaks from a privileged position. If you are standing beside me, seeing the same images I see, you might well challenge my interpretation of the lollipop. But if I tell you about it from a nearby pay phone, you are at the mercy of my integrity. For most readers of this book, such a parallel is relevant: few will have the background and knowledge of a doctorate in Latin American history. Again, in every way, I have tried to meet this second standard of intellectual honesty.

But there is another inherent bias in any communicated knowledge, and that is the selection of thematic material. If I stand in a phone booth, and choose to tell you that I am looking at a man whom, I contend, is a clown, I have selected that issue as the topic of our conversation. A book is a one-way conversation, and every writer has an inevitable bias about subject matter. In writing this book, I made decisions on what themes I would address. But perhaps my presumptions about what my readers should learn about Latin America are all wrong. Perhaps, in the great scheme of things, nothing much matters besides soccer. There may be a host of gods above us, and at the end of our existence they might simply grill us with questions about soccer teams and game scores. Or perhaps ultimate meaning is not defined by theology, but by the future values of humanity itself. Maybe in three centuries what will really obsess people are kitchen utensils. New Yorkers might someday convert the Met into the Museum of Forks and Knives, and care little about my book except for its fleeting reference to Argentine knife fights.

These silly examples aside, the point is that no one can say, for certain, what is ultimately significant about human existence. This is a question, perhaps *the* question, that lies beyond the boundary of human reason. In critical sections of this book, I focus on economic and political patterns that bespeak inequities between different groups of people, with special attention to the related issue of what are commonly termed human rights. My interest in inequities stems from the contention that they are directly linked to the interests and activities of the United States in Latin America (significant because most readers of this book are likely to be U.S. citizens). I would argue that human rights, at least in terms of political processes, are largely tied to questions of inequity. Some of the most important facts behind this contention are, for whatever reasons, omitted from almost all academic textbooks on Latin America. They are not, however, omitted here, and make this an especially provocative text.

But if the topic matter or presentation of novel material (especially in the final chapters) suggests any particular moral agenda, let me dispel such a notion quickly. Who has the authority to say what constitutes "right" and "wrong"? The presumption of *what's important* is here, but the *moral assertion* is not (and I encourage anyone to challenge me on passages they find to the contrary). I do not evoke moral terminology in this book. I avoid words such as *good* and *bad* (as used in a moral sense, though they may be used to suggest an economic or political advantage), or *right* and *wrong*. I do not presume to say that the world should change, or even that I personally dislike it. Maybe I like the way things are. But I do believe that it is high time for scholars to really embrace what has been dubbed "value-neutral education," and allow ourselves, and our students, to think freely— even in what a majority might regard as amoral terms.

This book is written primarily for North American university students taking introductory courses on Latin America. I have opted to use some politically incorrect terms for purposes of clarity: *Indian* (or *Native*) refers to the native inhabitants of the western hemisphere, and *American* means of, or related to, the United States. I have deliberately avoided other terms, especially those with ideological definitions commonly used in political science, such as *left* and *right* (though sometimes I use them inside quotation marks). These labels, in my evaluation, are useful because they simplify—but that is also their weakness. I have edited out countless adverbs and phrases of conditionality, like *generally* and *for the most part*, which appeared all over the place in earlier editions of the manuscript. To my peers in scholarship: I am only too aware that I have had to generalize, especially with regard to some early historical phenomena, theories, and trends. That is the downside of a skeletal text, and competent teachers will surely want to delve into other topics of interest, in part to show students just how horribly complicated the world really is. Yet I stand by my overarching conclusions and believe that this book represents a solid synthesis.

The book is divided into four parts. Chapter 1 introduces the intellectual problem of Latin American poverty, and discusses some of the explanations scholars have traditionally used to account for it. It is a short chapter, with a very basic overview of theory, yet some readers might wish to skip it, and some instructors might prefer to explain these paradigms themselves. The narrative proper, beginning in Chapter 2, is divided into three subsections of three chapters each. Chapters 2 through 4 [Part I] sweep broadly across the contours of history, from its early beginnings to the mid-twentieth century. The purpose of these chapters is not to overview history for its own sake but rather to lay the groundwork necessary for understanding present-day Latin America. Chapters 5 through 7 [Part II] extend the narrative into the 1980s, focusing on the political and military dimensions of revolution and counterrevolution in the postwar era. Chapters 8 through 10 [Part III] discuss Latin America today. Chapter 8 examines the rise of what I call *media*cracy, or media-driven "democracy"; Chapter 9 traces the rise of International Financial Institutions; and Chapter 10 explores trends in human rights. This final chapter also pulls the broader themes of the book together in its analysis of Latin America's new symbiotic relationship with the United States. An optional Epilogue, more informal than the body of the text, addresses questions of sources and of intellectual discernment. If the book accomplishes its task, readers will want to learn more about Latin America and their relationship to it. Hence, a few suggestions for further reading appear at its conclusion.

John W. Sherman

1 Introduction: Why Is Latin America Poor?

Latin Americans on the whole are poor, although the region also is home to some of the wealthiest individuals in the world. Mexico, for example, had twenty-four billionaires in 1994, prior to its 1995 economic meltdown—more than Britain, France, and Italy combined. But comparatively speaking, Latin America is an economically disadvantaged land. If you were randomly born into a family in the United States or western Europe, the odds are overwhelming that you would not go hungry or lack a solid roof over your head. If you had been born into a Latin American family, however, odds are about 50–50 that you would suffer malnutrition and poor health due to insufficient and unsanitary living conditions. Why is this so? Why is there such inequity among the different areas of the globe?

Social scientists have long acknowledged the economic disparities between large sections of our world. After all, such differences are conspicuous. In the early stages of the Cold War—that is, the arms race and political rivalry between the East (led by the Soviet Union) and the West (led by the United States)—people labeled regions according to their economic strength and political orientations. The industrialized and wealthy countries of the West were known as the *First World*, which was joined eventually by rebuilt, postwar Japan. The Soviet Union and its eastern European satellites were termed the *Second World*, even though their economic muscle lagged badly behind that of the West. Most of the remainder of the globe was designated the *Third World*—a term that survived the end of the Cold War in 1991 and is still commonly used today. Such labels have proven remarkably long-lived, although they are not particularly apt: *Fat World* and *Thin World* would be far more creative—and more meaningful—descriptions of these highly unequal regions.

The Third World consists of nations that lack economic vitality, financial independence, and broadly shared prosperity. When the term was first

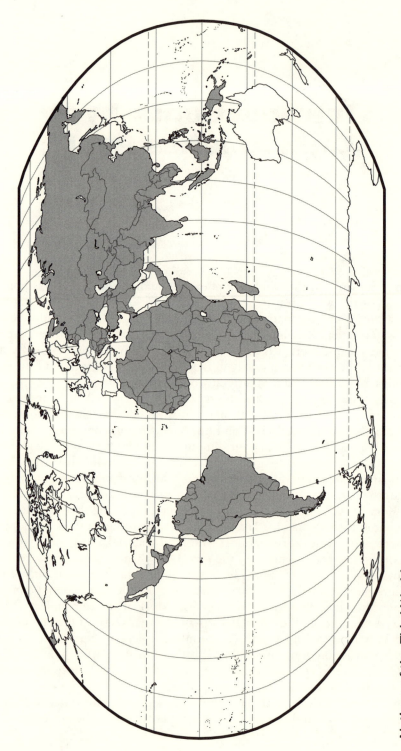

Nations of the Third World

coined, many also demarcated the region by its lack of industry. Today, as we shall see, some pockets of the Third World are heavily industrialized, yet still not prosperous. The Third World includes China, parts of southeast Asia, southern Asia, sections of the Middle East (e.g., Jordan and Turkey), all of Africa, and all of Latin America. Since the demise of the Soviet Union, most of the Eastern bloc has joined its ranks. Four-fifths of humanity lives in the Third World, which geographically dominates southern portions of the globe, prompting some to speak of a rich North and a poor South. Third World nations also, for the most part, are located on the outskirts of the historical core of Western civilization (Europe), and thus constitute what some refer to as a *periphery*.

By the late 1950s people had begun to use another term to identify the Third World: They called it the *developing* world. This description is still widely used by the media and even by many academics. In the 1980s and 1990s, a number of business interests, including major banks and investment firms, supplemented this designation with a new phrase: *emerging markets*. Both terms, with the adjectives *developing* and *emerging*, implicitly reflect a popular interpretation of why Latin America and other parts of the Third World are poor. That is, many (especially in the First World) believe they are poor simply because they are behind on the road of time. These regions are in the process of rising to First World status: They are just now emerging and developing. Someday they will be wealthy and comfortable like us.

But is that idea, which has endured in various forms for nearly two generations, well-grounded in fact? Pondering questions of poverty and calculating future global trends are formidable tasks. Yet such activities are essential to any realistic understanding of our world, since, after all, most of humanity is still poor. By identifying the origins of the notion that the Third World is developing, and by observing some basic economic evidence, we can draw a few rational conclusions. Those conclusions, in turn, will set us on our way to discovering *why* Latin America is poor.

Thinking About Latin America

Beyond the realm of hard economic data and fact-based argumentation lies *theory*. Theories are broad models, or constructs, that attempt to explain the macroeconomic and political realities of our world. Academics use theories in order to answer the "big questions," such as why there are such enormous inequities in global resource allocation and consumption. Although they are built upon arguments and facts, theories are by nature abstract, and they are usually engaged at such a level of intellectual sophistication (and verbalized by means of such unique vocabularies) as to remove them from the realm of popular discussion. They are one reason why—

some might argue—academics are marginal players in public policy debates. Yet because Latin America has been an important case study for theoreticians, a very rudimentary understanding of some theory, even for the
introductory student, is helpful. It enables one to discern the intellectual
orientation of professors and books, and explains the motivation behind
much scholarship.

Social scientists and just about everyone else who wrestles with the question of Third World poverty can be grossly divided into two camps: Some
believe that poverty is destined to disappear over time, and others do not.
Some think that in the future, Latin Americans can live just as well as those
of us in the First World; some think they cannot. The first of these two
viewpoints is frequently presented in the mainstream media. Political com-
mentators like Irving Kristol, for example, have long prophesied that
American-style capitalism will solve all of the world's major problems. This
interpretation had its beginnings, however, in the early years of the Cold
War.

Before the ascent of the United States to superpower status following
World War II, Americans—even intellectuals—were relatively uncon-
cerned about questions of poverty in the rest of the world. In the 1950s,
notions concerning development arose in the context of the new U.S. rivalry with Soviet Russia. With funding from government agencies, academics began to examine the economic and political realities of Latin America. Both the level of interest and that of financial support rose
meteorically in the early 1960s, when it seemed that the region might suc-
cumb to communism and threaten the security of the United States. Although such studies were interdisciplinary in nature—involving a range of
political, social, and economic issues—sociologists and political scientists
dominated the nascent fields of theoretical inquiry.

These thinkers saw in Latin America a plethora of "backward" qualities
that, they assumed, needed to change. First, the region relied heavily on
agriculture and had experienced little in the way of industrialization. Second, the nature of the rural sector bothered them: It was traditional, sub-
sistence-oriented agriculture, based on a peasant culture that had relatively
few built-in market incentives. Third, those peasants lived in a hierarchical
world, where status and deference were accorded to the elite owners of
large estates—a society almost feudal in its demeanor, with patron-client
relations instead of competitive and individualistic egalitarianism. This
feudal order was reflected also in archaic political institutions: strong executive branches; little in the way of functioning legislative democracy; and
loyalties that rested more on personalism, or political connections and al-
legiances, than on parties and ideas. These and other social features contrasted markedly with conditions in the United States. One of the presumptions of early theoreticians was that Latin America had to undergo a

transformation in its *political culture*—or values and ideas as they relate to politics—in order to join the modern world.

A second, important assumption was that this evolutionary process was unavoidable. In the 1950s and early 1960s, the debate over whether or not the Third World was developing was, in fact, not much of a debate. Nearly everyone agreed that the whole world was moving forward (with the possible exception of the Soviets) and that the future for all humanity was bright. At the core of this general assessment emerged a *school*—a group of scholars united around a central idea. And this school, in turn, articulated *modernization theory*. Although modernization theory featured various facets and twists of meaning, at its most rudimentary level it simply held that the Third World was already on the road to modernity. Time alone assured the development of tradition-laden, simple societies. The process was unavoidable, argued scholars like Walt Rostow, who compared the process to a train rolling down a track.

Modernization theorists linked economic evolution to political change. If economic problems and political instability went hand in hand, then the opposite proposition must be true: Economic growth and well-being would fuel tolerance and a healthy exchange of ideas. In this evolution, John Johnson of Stanford University, among other academics, emphasized the role of what he termed the "middle sectors." He foresaw that prosperity would fuel the rise of an urban middle class comprised of small businessmen, bankers, professionals, lawyers, and salesmen. Entrepreneurial and profit-oriented, these citizens, in turn, would embrace First World political values, insisting on rights similar to those found in the U.S. Constitution. The long pattern of authoritarian and often arbitrary government in Latin America would end as political institutions matured in harmony with economic and social advances.

The element of harmony was also important. Modernizationists drew on long-standing anthropological notions about society, including what is known as *functionalism*. Adherents of this notion believed that complex social structures, like interlocking gears, moved together in natural unison. Change in one area made change probable—even certain—in others. Thus, not surprisingly, theorists also linked economic and political transformation with culture. Indeed, they believed that much of the backwardness of the Third World was cultural. They held that modern man, in contrast to his intellectual and social predecessor (and Third World counterpart), was individualistic, efficient, resourceful, confident, and achievement-oriented. Traditional man, in contrast, was a slave to superstition, hierarchy, obedience, and fate. Latin Americans were destined to become sophisticated, modern people.

These notions of intellectual and social evolution were drawn from earlier, nineteenth-century ideologies, including positivism and social Darwinism. Positivism exuded great confidence in the rationality of humankind and in its ability to scientifically solve social ills. Social Darwinism adopted Charles Darwin's evolutionary theory (survival of the fittest) to humans and civilizations. Both positivism and social Darwinism had influenced the works of Max Weber, which in turn inspired the modernizationists. Weber had argued, at the turn of the twentieth century, that Western progress was attributable to a collection of traits embedded in the "Protestant work ethic." Liberated from irrationality and fatalism (such as that supposedly found in Catholicism and Eastern religions), Western man had obtained the correct mind-set for advancement. Weber-influenced books, such as Edward C. Banfield's *The Moral Basis of a Backward Society* (1958), paved the way to modernization theory. Building on Weber's faith in Western man's rationality, American scholars anticipated the rise of new cultural values in underdeveloped lands.

One modernizationist especially indebted to Weber and Banfield was Walt Rostow, who published *The Stages of Economic Growth* in 1960. Rostow argued that societies passed through five distinct periods on the road from backwardness to full modernity. After an era of tradition, a critical second stage followed, in which "preconditions" for modernity emerged, often taking centuries to come to completion. Then, at some point in time, a "leading (economic) sector" would grip a land and launch the third stage, a period of "takeoff"—when a nation rushed forward into modern maturity, and eventually, mass consumption.

Rostow and the modernizationists were optimistic. One reason for their confidence about the inevitability of Third World development was their faith in previous First World experience. Had not England once been primitive? Had not France and Germany, and even Soviet Russia, modernized? Rostow argued that England's textiles were its "leading sector," catapulting it into wealth and power. Railroads, he said, did the same for the United States, and military hardware was sparking the Soviet economic engine.

Modernization theorists, then, assumed that the poorer, "backward" regions of the globe were on a trajectory to prosperity and stability. They believed that the world was changing, prospects were bright, and the future favorable for all. If you venture into used bookstores, you can still find old atlases and travel guides that echo the refrains of modernization. Titles speak of progress and advancement. Photographs show new highways and factories, neatly dressed businessmen and modern office towers—images long associated with the First World but used to demonstrate that the Third World was coming of age. Modernization theory's assessments and verbiage filtered into the standard high school and college texts of the 1950s and 1960s, as well—such as in the classic *Latin America: The Development of Its Civilization* (1968), by Helen M. Bailey and Abraham Nasatir.

The dicta of modernization also found expression in popular culture. For example, in the early 1960s, as television sets appeared in American and European homes, the Summer Olympic Games became a major international sporting event, linking all of humanity in a supposed community of equal nations. That idea of global community was reflected in 1964, when the Tokyo Games ended with a salute to the spectacle's next host: Mexico City. Yet, since 1968, neither the Summer nor the Winter Olympics have returned to the so-called developing world; poor countries simply do not have the economic resources with which to outbid rich nations that covet the prestigious and lucrative games.

Of course, television not only covered the Olympics; it also beamed images of American wealth into the living quarters of Third World residents. Whether they watched *Leave it to Beaver* in the 1950s or *The Simpsons* in the 1990s, viewers could not help but note that nearly all Americans seemed to own cars and live in spacious, two-story suburban houses. Television has largely instilled in Latin Americans the myth that all North Americans are rich. It has revealed some of the stark realities of global economics, if only by default. Shortly after television arrived in the Third World, popular impatience with such inequities began to grow. In the 1950s, Cuba—a Latin American nation plagued by stark rural poverty (and significantly, possessing one of the continent's most sophisticated television industries)—exploded in revolution. By 1958, rebel forces led by Fidel Castro had toppled the U.S.-supported dictatorship, startling policymakers and modernization theorists alike.

Modernization theory resonated with U.S. government officials in the early 1960s, and some of its proponents helped design a response to the Cuban revolution: the Alliance for Progress. Many believed that although modernization was inevitable, it could be accelerated by technical assistance and aid packages. Rostow's proverbial train was on the rails to prosperity, but the United States could increase its momentum by granting loans and launching nation-building programs through new organizations such as the Peace Corps. The motive for doing so, of course, was to undercut unrest and prevent more revolutions. John F. Kennedy's administration initiated the Alliance for Progress, but also accompanied it with increased military aid. Fearing the expansion of Cuban communism (Castro turned to the Soviet Union for aid within a couple of years after acquiring power), the United States initiated counterinsurgency training programs and military collaborations with other Latin American nations.

The Alliance for Progress, established to pacify Latin America, had many mixed and unforeseen results. Stipulations required that most of the loans be spent on goods produced in the United States; heavier debt and some inflationary pressures ensued. Increased direct U.S. involvement, through a range of developmental programs from agriculture to health care and education, disrupted social relations and traditional practices, creating instability. The so-called Green Revolution, for example, begun years earlier in Mexico, accelerated crop yields (through fertilizers and chemicals), but undercut many small farmers, driving them out of business. Middle-class demands for political reform, sometimes sanctioned or encouraged by the United States, sparked fears among elites, who were ready to use their newly improved militaries to suppress any early signs of "communism."

Despite (in part, because of) U.S. policies, there were more revolutions in Latin America in the 1960s, but none of the kind experienced in Cuba. On April 1, 1964, a momentous day for both Latin Americans and modernization theorists alike, the military in Brazil ousted the elected president from office and took control of the government. For observers the coup was not the only surprise: The new regime largely enjoyed the support of the emerging middle class! This was the very opposite of what most had predicted. Brazil's generals dubbed their takeover a "revolution," but there was nothing revolutionary about it. They strengthened economic policies that favored the rich and suppressed politically active, poorer Brazilians. The United States, which previously had established close ties to the military, supported the new regime. But modernization theorists in U.S. universities were puzzled. Latin America was supposed to be headed toward democracy; Brazil's coup unexpectedly reversed a trend so many had thought they could see.

In the short term, most academics, though disturbed, concluded that Brazil was an isolated case—only a temporary setback in modernization's progress. Many predicted that the military would restore civilian rule by the end of 1964; to their surprise, Brazil's generals stayed in power for a quarter century. Even more shocking was that Brazil's situation was but a harbinger of similar events elsewhere: In 1966, Argentina underwent yet another in a series of coups. In 1973, Chile, a nation with a history of relative political openness, experienced a violent takeover. By the mid-1970s, almost all of Latin America was under military rule, and the very middle classes that had been expected to promote U.S.-style democracy were, for the most part, supportive of the coups.

These unexpected developments spawned academic debate. Modernization theorists stuck to the most obvious lines of intellectual defense: Despite the militarization of Latin American regimes, they clung to their earlier predictions and downplayed evidence suggesting fundamental flaws in their theories. Some even became apologists for the new regimes. Textbook authors Bailey and Nasatir advised American college students that "undemocratic and high-handed procedures were perhaps not all bad."[1] Yet as military governments multiplied and human rights conditions worsened, intellectual evasion became all the more obvious, in the general failure to explain stark reality.

Nor was the collapse of democratic openings the only embarrassment for modernizationists. By the mid-1970s it was increasingly clear that the economic prosperity so long forecast was also not forthcoming. Real wages under military governments declined as inflation took hold and independent labor unions were dismantled by security forces. Living standards, as measured by malnutrition, child mortality rates, life expectancy, and illiteracy, flattened out and in many cases began to slide in the other direction. Something was horribly wrong with the prognosis for the Third World. Why was it not developing?

Political scientists and others began to provide a whole range of new and adjusted theses. Some examined Latin American society, and argued that resistance to modern capitalism and pluralistic democracy was ingrained due to the medieval Hispanic heritage. Spain, so the argument went, had nurtured authoritarianism and military order for centuries after the conquest. Fatalism, violence, and subservience to hierarchy were inbred cultural traits from which the region could never escape. This argument, supported by some historians, was exceedingly static—that is, it did not account for change over time. Furthermore, when the maternal country (Spain) itself replaced a conservative dictatorship with modern political institutions in the late 1970s, these events did much to undercut the currency of this explanation.

A second, more plausible answer came in the scholarship of Samuel Huntington. The Alliance for Progress had rested on the premise that poverty bred political instability; but Huntington, by comparing poor countries, argued that the premise was not necessarily true. His influential *Political Order in Changing Societies* (1968) contended that the poorest of the world's peoples were actually politically docile. Those experiencing change and entering the political arena for the first time were more prone to generate social conflict. If a modernizing state lacked adequate civic structures (such as political parties), unchanneled political energy could bubble up into revolution. Under Huntington's rationale, U.S. policies under the Alliance had raised expectations and aroused political forces rather than taming them. Increased instability, and consequent military intervention, was thus the order of the day.

Critics Respond: Notions of Dependency

Many scholars found Huntington's argument no more convincing than those made under the rubric of modernization theory—a paradigm increasingly in disrepute, having itself been subjected to critique. Several Latin American academics posited a counterargument for why the region was not becoming like the First World. They contended that the economic playing field between disparate regions was not level: Latin America could not develop because of certain structural disadvantages that created what they called *dependency*.

Dependency theory, a critical response to modernizationists, seemed new and exciting when it first appeared in the late 1960s. Its antecedents, however, were many. An Argentine economist named Raúl Prebisch had long argued that neoclassical economics, with its emphasis on trade as the means of development, was insufficient for understanding the complexities of global wealth. As the director of Argentina's Central Bank in the 1930s, he had urged his nation to industrialize. After World War II, Prebisch headed up the United Nations Economic Commission for Latin America (ECLA), where he and others again pushed for deeper structural change. These men distinguished between economic growth and "development." They held that the latter necessitates technology and economic diversity, only then assuring a nation of self-sustaining growth. Like a child that matures physically but is mentally impaired, they saw Latin America as a region with rising economic output but fundamental incongruities.

Two of Prebisch's postwar colleagues at ECLA, Brazilians Enzo Faletto and Fernando Henrique Cardoso, later published *Dependency and Development in Latin America* (1969). A rebuttal of modernization theory, the book offered an explanation of why developmentalist models were not working. It posited that underdevelopment was not a product of backwardness but a consequence of commercial capitalism. After all, as Cardoso and Faletto noted, Latin America was hardly an isolated region. It had gained independence from colonial rule in the early nineteenth century and had traded with advanced nations ever since. But it could never catch up with the First World because of the unequal nature of its partnership in finance and trade.

Others followed Cardoso and Faletto's lead. Although few dependency thinkers were historians, almost all attempted to use history to excoriate modernization theory. Development, they argued, has not taken place because the First World enjoys a historically favorable position with regard to industrialization, capital, and commerce. Because Europe and the United States industrialized first, Latin American nations emerged just as they began to produce nearly all the manufactured goods the world needed. Industrial powers shipped their goods (almost always on their own ships) into the colonized Third World, thus undercutting the process of industrialization and producing a lopsided balance of trade. Latin American countries soon found themselves exporting raw materials, such as wool and cotton, and importing finished products, such as cloth.

Not only was there an immediate trade imbalance, but the emerging First World soon accumulated a disproportionate amount of capital, since importing nations had to pay the difference between the value of raw materials and manufactured goods. Ironically, much of the gold and silver that backed various European currencies had originally come from the mines of Spanish-exploited Latin America. After Independence, in a quest to modernize, Latin American states borrowed money from European and U.S. banks at high rates of interest. Many slid into debt and were unable to foster their own diversified economies in order to compete with the nations that had gotten the jump on them in the critical process of industrialization. By the twentieth century, all they could hope for were enclaves of industry and development—not vibrant domestic production and markets. Rather than a "natural" process of modernization, Britain and other First World countries had experienced unique historical evolutions that could not be repeated.

One of the apparent loopholes in this line of argumentation was the obvious fact that much of Latin America was heavily industrialized by the early 1970s (due in part to the economic policies of the military regimes). Yet dependency theorists provided answers to this problem by pointing out differences between the First and Third Worlds' industrial growth. André Gunder Frank, for example, referred to the "development of underdevelopment"; by examining pockets of industry, he analyzed their ties to the First World via multinational corporations. Unlike those in Europe and the United States, where unions helped unskilled workers organize, Third World regimes cooperated with corporations in keeping wages low. Ownership stayed in foreign hands, and profits were remitted to stockholders instead of being invested in Latin America.

Dependency theorists not only addressed trade and industry; they also pointed to critical patterns in agriculture. They noted with chagrin that many Latin American nations engaged in monoculture—the growing of a single crop for export, on which economic growth heavily depended. Whether coffee in El Salvador or bananas in Honduras, these *commodities* went abroad and tied local economies to First World markets. One of the drawbacks of such a link has been the fact that any sudden drop in prices spells disaster for the exporting nation. When coffee prices sank precipitously during the 1930s, for example, El Salvador's economy collapsed and hunger swept the countryside.

Dependency certainly made more sense, in attempting to explain conditions in the 1960s and 1970s, than did modernization theory. But like their intellectual opponents, dependency theorists were all over the place. They were never able to systematically unite their ideas into a cogent, complete explanation. In fact, there were profound divisions. Orthodox dependency theorists, such as Frank, questioned the ultimate efficacy of capitalism. Other, more unorthodox dependency thinkers, including Cardoso, believed in the fundamental structures of Western-style capitalism but thought development in the periphery had been distorted. The different sub-schools were reflected in politics: Frank fled Chile in the wake of its military coup, had difficulty reentering the United States (although he was a citizen), and settled into an academic career in western Europe. Cardoso, in 1994, became president of Brazil.

Both currents of dependency theory had garnered the allegiance of many Third World scholars by the early 1970s, when dependency theory entered its heyday. It was not as well received in the United States, for obvious reasons. At its heart was criticism of the First World—as partly responsible for Third World troubles, rather than a benign agent of modernization seeking to advance humankind. A number of U.S. scholars began to vigorously critique dependency theory, and by the 1980s, a flood of books had largely discredited it. There was a political dimension to the process: Well-funded anti-dependency theory scholars resided in the First World, whereas the theory's die-hard protagonists labored abroad. The rejection of dependency theory coincided with a revived U.S. patriotism under President Ronald Reagan but also reflected the fundamental repugnance of a theory tying Third World woes to First World policies.

On the front lines of the intellectual assault were a number of historians who, until the late 1970s, had largely remained on the sidelines of theoretical debate. Even in its most sophisticated expressions, dependency theory was disappointingly simple. Few of its early proponents were historians themselves, and they often made sweeping generalizations about the breadth of Latin American experience. Critics pointed out that contrary to conventional wisdom, some nations had once accumulated great wealth: Argentina, for example, at the outset of the twentieth century, had a per capita income comparable to that of the United States. A historian of Brazil, Warren Dean, showed that an export economy based on a single commodity could fuel broad growth and diversification (a rebuttal of dependency theory that was dubbed *staple growth theory*). Others noted the role of corruption in sidetracking advancement: Subject to very little public accountability, military and nonmilitary governments alike have often squandered Latin America's wealth. In sum, dependency theory was attacked for failing to address a wide range of cultural and political questions—even though its creators were essentially concerned with economics.

The tendency to simplify centuries of complex history continued in an offshoot of the dependency school, called *world systems* analysis. U.S. sociologist Immanuel Wallerstein launched world systems theory with the publication of his multivolume *The Modern World-System* (1974–1976). Arguing that Europe generated a capitalist world economy around the beginning of the sixteenth century, Wallerstein and subsequent authors posited that core nations structurally dominate peripheral states through economic dynamics. Noting the pervasiveness of slavery and other forms of coercive labor in the periphery, they contended that labor relations and even many social conditions stem from an entrenched and systematized global economic order.

The idea of an overarching, global economic structure might have merit in today's world, but its projection over the distant past is a serious blunder. Historians have had a field day critiquing the world systems approach. Evidence demonstrates that labor conditions and social relations in Latin America have not been determined by the consequences of commercial capital, and instead of consistent patterns of coercion we find that Indians and other subservient groups often helped define the parameters of commercial exchange and even sometimes enjoyed its benefits (although, admittedly, conditions immediately after the Conquest were harsh).

More damning is the fact that much of the historical record refutes the notion of long-term economic integration. In the nineteenth century, for example, large portions of Latin America fell into isolation—the exact opposite of what should have happened in an emerging system. Silver mines closed down, the money supply shrank, deflation took hold in some areas, and trade declined. With the exceptions of Brazil and parts of the Caribbean, which continued to import African slaves, the commercial economy of the entire area was in profound regress. For decades, from roughly the 1810s through the 1850s, there was no serious foreign capital investment in the whole of formerly Spanish America. The walls of a supposedly rising global structure simply did not exist.

Marxists and other theoreticians have attacked the world systems approach on the basis of methodology—how data are collected and analyzed. One of their primary complaints is that a focus on nation-states is oversimple. World systems theorists use nation-states as their units of analysis, classifying states as *core*, *semiperipheral*, or *peripheral*. This classification is inadequate because it fails to account for the complexity of factors at work in societies. Marxists, in particular, dislike it because it neglects the orthodox analytical tool of class. World systems theorists, largely spawned within the ranks of dependency theorists, were trying to gain acceptance for their ideas at the very moment when much of the academic world was starting to move in the other direction. World systems theory came into vogue among some sociologists but failed to transcend disciplinary lines.

After Dependency: History and Theory

For all their skill at debunking other people's theories, historians have been slow to offer alternative constructs for explaining the economic disparities in the modern world. Why is Latin America poor? Exploring that question and concomitant political issues from a historical angle into the present is the primary purpose of this book.

Yet unfortunately, a theoretical framework for our economic and political introduction to the region is lacking. The last decade has seen theoretical debates in Third World studies splinter and disintegrate. Many political scientists now dabble in statistical analysis, fusing their discipline with economics, while parting company with sociologists and historians. Anthropology entered the twenty-first century in a state of flux. Scholars in various fields continue to espouse variations of world systems and dependency theories, while others search for new alternatives.

The past twenty years have brought a revival of modernization thought. Many academics reembraced some of its tenets, believing that with the advent of new democratic regimes and more transparent free-market economics, Latin America had finally turned the corner. This neomodernizationism was aided by the fact that many earlier proponents had become senior professors with status and influence (there is no penalty, in academe, for promoting dumb theories). The inbred optimism of modernization surged on good news: After a dreadful era of economic and social decay, in the late 1980s and early 1990s, prospects for Latin America did, briefly, appear to be looking up.

Yet the weight of statistical evidence continues to belie optimistic predictions at the outset of the new century. No matter what one thinks of the theoretical paradigms of debate, there is no denying that—for the world's poor—conditions have steadily worsened. Today, nearly a quarter of the globe's burgeoning population of 6 billion lives in extreme poverty: 1.4 billion people struggle to survive on the equivalent of less than US$1 a day (and contrary to myth, a dollar in the Third World does not buy much). Half of the world's population suffers at least some degree of malnourishment. And perhaps more significantly, key macroeconomic trends are headed downward: Both in real numbers and in percentiles, malnutrition and related preventable diseases have increased over the past two decades and now account for an average of 40,000 (mostly child) deaths per day. Real wages in the Third World are, almost without exception, in decline. The world's literacy rate is numerically stagnant and proportionally shrinking; two-thirds of humanity cannot read at an adult level. Third World life expectancies have, depending on the region, remained steady or modestly declined. Poor nations are proportionately much poorer now than they were just a generation ago. The fifty poorest states—most of which are in Africa—have just over 1 percent of the world's total income but nearly 20 percent of its population. The richest fifth of the world's populace had thirty times the average income of the poorest fifth in 1960, sixty times by 1990, and seventy-five times more income by 1998. In comparison with the rest of the Third World, Latin America is relatively well-off. With a per capita income six times higher than that of Africa, Latin America has only about one-half the population Africa has (240 million people) who are living in severe indigence, on less than US$2 a day. Per capita Gross Domestic Product (GDP) declined from US$2,850 in 1980 to US$2,700 in 1992, leveled off through the mid-1990s, and more recently resumed its decline. The entire region's GDP is much smaller than the U.S. government's budget. Cholera, a poverty-related disease once largely eradicated, has reappeared in many countries of the Third World, including several in Latin America.

All of this has occurred in the context of rapid industrialization—the panacea of modernizationists, which was supposed to answer many of the Third World's most persistent economic problems. In fact, Mexico and Brazil are nearly as industrialized now as the United States (combined, they account for 75 percent of the region's manufactures). A large chunk of the First World's auto industry, for example, is now south of the U.S. border. Mexico is one of the world's largest producers of 4-cylinder engines, and its car production has soared from 18,000 vehicles in 1980 to more than 500,000 today. But—as was not supposed to happen—almost all of Latin America's industrial products are exported to the First World. Ninety percent of Mexican-made cars end up in America, since the vast majority of Mexicans cannot afford them.

How can modernization theory remain a viable explanation in the face of so much contradictory evidence? One line of defense is the theory's "escape clause" of cultural factors, which persists largely through the writings of Lawrence E. Harrison. Harrison, who worked for twenty years in the U.S. Agency for International Development (USAID, the main organ for distribution of U.S. foreign aid), continues to argue that cultural factors account for poverty, and that if Latin Americans and others can just be taught modern Western values, then their living conditions will rapidly improve. Many of Latin America's elite are receptive to this message. For example, Peruvian novelist–turned–political aspirant Mario Vargas Llosa anticipates new growth any day now, as the twin features of democratic stability and market economics kick in and begin to solve all the problems of underdevelopment.

Yet if one refuses to rest the basis of one's case on the unknowable future, modernization no longer provides a viable alternative for understanding the global realities of our world. The Third World is not developing. Things are not getting better. Why aren't they?

In January 1995 an internal memorandum produced by Chase Manhattan Bank, which has close financial ties to the Mexican government, argued that a group of Indian rebels along the Guatemalan border should be "eliminated." When Mexico's army went into the region with U.S.-supplied helicopters and weaponry the following month, a Mexican television actress of native descent stood before 150,000 protesters in Mexico City and chided North Americans. "Tell them," Ofelia Medina said, "that their consumer lifestyles come at the expense of Mexican Indian blood." This is a potentially disturbing message to those of us who live the "good life" in the First World. Could it be true?

Theoretical constructs for explaining Third World poverty are necessarily complex, and readers should not be troubled if some nuances slip past them. This introductory chapter, too, is reductionist and simple—intended only to provide a necessary shell for the remainder of the book. Suffice it to say, there is a long-standing scholarly debate about the nature of Latin America, its poverty, its political structures, and how and why (or whether) things can change. The debate itself, however, is significant. It directly speaks to what professors teach in the classroom. Theory-influenced ideas filter into the media, politics, diplomacy, and even religion. An understanding of the lines of debate, even at a rudimentary level, will help us perceive reality and think clearly about our world.

One of the fundamental problems for scholars, which is certainly evident in this overview, is the gap between disciplines. Sociologists, political scientists, and others have long dabbled in history-based explanations without much help from historians. Similarly, because of the traditional academic divisions, few books have attempted to breach the gap between the past and the present. But if modernization and dependency theories have left many of us intellectually dissatisfied, what—in the context of such a broad sweep—might constitute an alternative reply? How deep are the historical reasons for Latin America's persistent poverty? What is history's relationship to today's world, and what are realistic prognoses for the future? This book addresses these questions.

PART I

Historical Latin America

2 A People of Conquest

As the sleek *METRO* train dashes underneath Mexico City, a small boy walks up to a businessman, kneels down, pulls out a rag, and begins to polish the man's shoes. The subway in the world's second-largest city draws citizens from all walks of life, and though both the man and the boy are authentically Mexican, they appear starkly different. The dapper businessman, dressed in a fine suit, has skin so light that he looks Caucasian. The boy, in contrast, has the dark skin and physical features of an Indian, and his ragged clothes suggest acute poverty. After wiping the shoes for half a minute, he rises and stretches out his hand in hopes of payment, just as the train pulls to a stop at the next station. The man gives him only a glance of disdain as he steps onto the station platform and disappears into the crowd.

Ofelia Medina, a Mexican television star who recently accused Americans of living at the expense of Mexican Indians, is also of Indian descent. But what is an "Indian" in the late twentieth century? And what has been the historical experience of Indians in Latin America? In order to understand the region's diversity, we must go back centuries into its past. Although there are not many obvious continuities between the distant past and rapidly changing, present-day Latin America, some seminal features of Latin society are displayed in the era of dramatic encounter and conquest.

The New World Before 1492

The first humans in what is commonly referred to as the New World likely arrived tens of thousands of years ago, during the ice age, from across a land bridge that then linked Alaska to Asia. Waves of migrants slowly wandered south. Given the geographical shape of the North American continent, it is not surprising that their descendants eventually began to concentrate in the areas that make up today's Mexico. Mexico itself is something like a geographical funnel, with the steep mountains of the

Sierra Madre gradually narrowing upward and encircling a high, central plateau. Here, not far from present-day Mexico City, some of the greatest early concentrations of New World inhabitants coalesced.

Around the second century B.C., one such population center emerged at Teotihuacán. The name of this now famous archaeological site comes from the Aztecs, who referred to its ruins as a "Place of the Gods." Indeed, in some ways even to the modern eye it almost seems that a superhuman race must have conceived and built Teotihuacán, popularly known to Mexicans today as *las pyramides.* At the center of the grand city stood two enormous pyramids, eventually given the inaccurate but poetic names of the Sun and the Moon. The larger of the two, the Pyramid of the Sun, rises 215 feet from a base that is larger than that of its famous Egyptian counterpart, the pyramid of Cheops. In 1908, amateur archaeologists who were intrigued by the possibility of inner chambers blew up a quarter of it with dynamite. Others dug a tunnel through the dirt-filled structure in the 1930s, only to be disappointed. Despite the damage wrought by these and other misadventures, the Pyramid of the Sun, in recent times illuminated by giant floodlights, has remained a mecca for tourists.

Stretching away from the pyramids is a series of plazas that form something akin to a great boulevard—again dramatically but inaccurately christened the Avenue of the Dead. These plazas, situated on a gradual incline toward the Pyramid of the Moon, form a line that diverges slightly from due north. Given that other major archaeological sites in central Mexico have the same orientation, some scholars have hypothesized that various stars and constellations dictated the initial outlay of this gridlike metropolis. Both the avenue and the two pyramids were completed around the time of Christ, and during subsequent centuries Teotihuacán continued to spread outward. Palaces and temples in the heart of the city housed a nobility that governed a tiered society of artisans, craftsmen, and farmers. Apartment-like structures sprawled out in nearly all directions. Today, their stone foundations are nearly all that remain.

Despite the fact that Teotihuacán is one of the most thoroughly and methodically analyzed archaeological sites in the world, we still know relatively little about its builders and inhabitants. No written language has survived to tell us the names and exploits of its great kings. If royal tombs exist, we have not found them. In its heyday the city was plastered with colorful murals, and these drawings have provided many clues about life in Teotihuacán. Other answers have been garnered from the archaeological record. By studying the ruins themselves, as well as factors such as the surrounding timber, food, and water resources, we can safely speculate that when Rome was at its height, this urban center may well have been the largest city on the face of the earth. Pottery shards tell us that the Teotihuacanese traded widely. It appears that their society was governed, at least for a time, by a fairly benign and farsighted leadership that maintained peace with distant peoples.

But after centuries of glory, the city declined. Evidence of a crude eighth-century wall suggests fears of invasion, and radiocarbon dating shows that much of Teotihuacán was at one time sacked and burned. The culprits, presumably (though some fires may have been initiated by the inhabitants themselves), were waves of wild tribes migrating in from the north. These diverse peoples, collectively termed the Toltec, mingled with the more civilized inhabitants that they conquered, and apparently absorbed the practices of some sophisticated Indians from the southeast. A Toltec empire eventually emerged, smaller and less centralized than that of Teotihuacán, but still vibrant, and in places, urbanized. Tula, a Toltec city that was home to some 50,000 persons in the eleventh century, was still inhabited by modest numbers at the time of the arrival of Europeans in Mexico in 1519.

The Toltecs floundered in a fashion similar to that of their predecessors, as new bands of violent invaders swept into their domains. Various nomadic hunting tribes, collectively called the Chichimec, mingled with sedentary Indians in central Mexico and continued to help populate the chamber-like valleys on the central plateau. Over centuries the human population rose into the millions, with one unusually attractive highland valley growing the most crowded. The Anáhuac, as this valley was known, was blessed with a group of lakes, the largest of which was named Texcoco. Lake Texcoco attracted not only people but varied animal life, including fowl. Indians learned to build dams and irrigation canals, and even developed what the Spanish later mistook as floating gardens—beds of mud and seaweed that yielded multiple harvests. On the shores of the lake rose a prosperous new city-state, also named Texcoco, led by a reputedly wise king, Netzahualcóyotl (Hungry Coyote).

Netzahualcóyotl's mid-fifteenth-century rule coincided with the ascent of yet another lakeside city. Tenochtitlán was the capital of the Aztecs, a late-coming people that had a reputation as fierce fighters. For awhile, Texcoco and Tenochtitlán joined in an alliance; but under a powerful lord named Moctezuma, the Aztec expanded their empire, and shortly before the arrival of the Spaniards, gained control over their rivals in Texcoco.

There are many colorful stories and myths about the Aztecs, who like people the world over, loved to extol the accomplishments of their ancestors. They claimed, for example, that the site of their great capital was predestined by a sign from the gods: an eagle devouring a serpent while sitting on a prickly pear cactus (an image emblazoned today on Mexico's flag). A militarized society, the Aztecs were especially prone to exaggerate their accomplishments and brutality in battle. War was central to Aztec religion; and Huitzilopochtli (Hummingbird-on-Left), their god of war, held a prominent place in a pantheon of deities. Human sacrifice to Huit-zilopochtli, which involved inserting an obsidian blade swiftly up and under the rib cage in order to extract a still-pulsating heart, was a feature of Aztec religion, though the numbers of victims appear to have been greatly inflated by historians. The often grotesque and sensational tales of the pre-Contact Aztecs, part of an oral tradition recorded by sixteenth-century Spanish friars, were a means of elevating a culture in the wake of devastating humiliation and defeat.

In reality, most of the Aztecs of Tenochtitlán lived lives of work and routine. Large portions of the populace engaged in artisanal work, commerce, and farming. The large population of the Anáhuac valley necessitated the importation of foodstuffs—a process complicated in part by the city's location on an island in Lake Texcoco, linked only by manmade causeways to the shore. The Aztec capital's comfort and survival depended heavily on tribute-paying peoples in distant valleys. Aztec armies were formidable, and they had subdued much of central Mexico by the end of the fifteenth century. But the Aztec empire was not a tightly defined political entity: As long as non-Aztecs honored Tenochtitlán with tributary payments, they were often left alone. Other, sizable tracts of central Mexico remained completely free of Aztec control. For example, Tlaxcalans, in the mountains to the east, passionately resented the lords of Tenochtitlán and successfully resisted their domination. Thanks to support from a number of independent tribes as well as those who were only too happy to sever their tributary links to Tenochtitlán, the Spaniards would have no trouble bringing the Aztec capital to its knees.

Scholars' estimates of Mexico's population at the time of the Spanish arrival vary wildly. There is no doubt that the central highlands were home to millions of human beings by the early sixteenth century; but just how many millions remains a matter of conjecture. Tenochtitlán and its environs housed well over 100,000 persons, yet only here did Aztecs numerically dominate; they remained a small minority of the total population of the highlands—no more than 10 percent. Central Mexico's rise to political and commercial prominence is understandable; the tropical lowlands of the great isthmus were not as heavily populated, and peoples nearer the coastlines were not as advanced as were those in the central highlands and valleys.

A major exception to this rule, however, were the Maya, an ancient people that dominated the tropical southeastern peninsula known as Yucatán. Mayan origins lie primarily in Guatemala and present-day Honduras, where for centuries several grand population centers flourished. Although recent advances in deciphering hieroglyphs are helping us understand the ancient Maya, scholars still struggle to articulate the contours of this civilization in its so-called classic age, prior to 1000 A.D. The great city-states that emerged among the Maya, including Tikal and Copán, enjoyed cultural, though not political, unity. Around 900 A.D., many of these magnificent sites were gradually abandoned, for a variety of reasons, in favor of migration northward to the Yucatán peninsula of present-day Mexico.

Although the postclassical Maya crafted a great culture in the jungles of Yucatán, that culture was in decline by the time of the Spanish arrival. This New Empire, as it is sometimes called, featured large city-states and ceremonial sites such as Chichén Itzá—whose spectacular ruins remain immensely popular with tourists bused in from Cancún. The site, though well-studied, still intrigues scholars for a number of reasons. For example, there is puzzling architectural and cultural evidence of a Toltec presence at Chichén Itzá. Scholars have theorized that a small number of Toltecs, perhaps led by the legendary historical figure Quetzalcóatl (Feathered Serpent), helped build the great city, or that Mayan architectural ideas were used in the construction of Tula, having reached central Mexico through intermediaries such as the Nonoalca—a group that came from an area in present-day Tabasco. It is also at Chichén Itzá that we find one of the intriguing Mayan ball courts. The rules of the game are still debated, but it is fairly certain that the Maya endowed this competitive event with religious significance.

Mayan thought about existence hinged largely around cyclical notions of time. For an agricultural people dependent on the sun, rainy season, and harvest times, such a preoccupation is not surprising. Many of the Maya's nearly 120 known deities were tied directly to the concept of time. Astronomy and mathematics also loomed large in their investigations of the world. The Maya developed an excellent calendar, and studied the patterns of the stars with considerable skill. But the image of the Maya as a wise and peaceful people—intellectual Indians in a jungle paradise—has been dashed as scholars have translated more of their writings. Although Mayan culture was advanced in many ways, it was also militaristic, ensnared in civil wars, and fragile. Chichén Itzá itself fought a war with another city-center, Mayapán, and lost. After a couple of centuries of glory, Mayapán in turn succumbed to internecine strife and was abandoned in the mid-fifteenth century. When the Spanish arrived a century later, the Maya were dispersed, living in small, remote villages.

The Maya, like the Aztecs, are well known. Ancient jungle cities-turned-tourist sites, and myriad television shows, often emphasizing the more "mysterious" and evocative features of ancient life, cater to a general interest in pre-Columbian peoples. The third great Indian culture that readily, and rightly, attracts our attention was not based in Mexico but in present-day Peru. This is the culture of the Inca.

In some ways, given the proximity of the equator and difficulty of life in tropical lowlands, the advent of a great people high in the Andes mountains is comprehensible. Yet the accomplishments of the Inca, given the incredible mountain terrain, are nothing less than astounding. A precursor culture in northwestern Peru, that of the Mochica, flourished from roughly 300 B.C. to 400 A.D., amalgamating various valley peoples and producing beautiful pottery, much of which has been preserved in burial sites, thanks to sandy soils. Still, the Mochica are so distant to the Inca that we have relatively little knowledge of what lies in between. As in central Mexico, not until the fifteenth century did a grand consolidation begin to take place in the Peruvian Andes.

The meteoric rise of this empire, unfolding largely under the ambitious rule of a lord named Pachacuti, is, like that of the Aztecs, only partially understood. Quechua, the predominant tongue of the Inca, was not converted into writing. Although a powerful emperor came to dwell in the ceremonial center of Cuzco, he oversaw a realm that was heterogeneous and decentralized. The empire was a mosaic of diverse peoples, eventually stretching 1,500 miles from present-day Ecuador, into Chile and Bolivia. It was not only vast but also divided, by the steep mountains of the Andes. Hence, the famous transportation and communication networks of the Inca are particularly impressive. Young runners dashed messages along roads from Quito to Cuzco, reputedly crossing the thousand-mile stretch in as little as eight to ten days. Rope bridges, with cables sometimes several inches thick, spanned rollicking rivers in narrow gorges far below.

The Inca are known also for many other accomplishments. A religious and polytheistic people, they venerated natural landmarks and tied their various cults to ancestral lineages, exercising great care in preserving and honoring the dead. They were masters of embalming. When the cadaver of one mummified emperor was unwrapped by Spaniards in the sixteenth century, an observing priest noted that his body was "as hard as wood." Architecturally, Inca stonework continues to baffle scholars intent on explaining their techniques, given a lack of mortar and the sheer size of the boulders that were presumably transported from distant quarries. The mountaintop ruins of Machu Picchu, discovered in 1911 and today the most famous archaeological legacy of the Inca, amaze visitors with their grandeur. On countless other mountains the Inca terraced the land so as to conserve the topsoil while farming. The Spaniards were so struck by this that they called the mountains *Andenes*, or platforms—a term that eventually mutated into the name *Andes*.

Those terraced mountainsides were just part of a great agricultural tradition. Natives in the Andes developed a diverse diet, in part because of the vertical variation of the terrain. They gathered tropical nuts, fruits, and berries from the humid coastal plains, and mountain rice, rich in protein, from fields in the highlands. The Inca developed some forty varieties of cultivated plants, including various types of squash, pimiento, haricot beans, and their staple, the potato. Transformed over centuries from a wild tuber that was bitter and small, the potato helps account for the upsurge in population in the Andes; much later, after the Conquest, it worked the same miracle in Europe.

Another reason why the Inca were well fed was the efficiency of their empire. In addition to a road system, imperial authorities established storage cities in an attempt to insulate society from cycles of famine. Provincial elites helped manage the empire and addressed local concerns. Newly incorporated peoples received help and instruction in, for example, utilizing the llama, the Andean region's timid beast of burden, primarily useful for its wool. All governing officials were subject to strict moral codes, and even the old proverbs of Incan sages reflect the expectation of clean government: "Judges who secretly receive gifts are lowly thieves."

Yet the existence of such proverbs also suggests that, in fact, plenty of Incan officials *did* accept bribes. As they have the Aztec and Maya, some historians have tended to idealize the pre-Columbian Inca, with early accounts portraying an advanced, socialistic empire of peace and happiness. Even recent historians have crafted overly generous tales; one has even argued that idyllic gender relations provided Incan women with a modicum of social justice until white European males came along. Yet the more discerning students of history naturally question such conclusions. The Aztecs, Maya, and Inca established great empires because they were violent, militarized, and aggressive peoples. And there was no shortage of violence in these large and diverse societies. Had the Spanish not arrived, the Aztec and Inca systems nonetheless might soon have fallen to internal divisiveness and rebellion.

Beyond the heavy concentrations of people in the Mexican highlands and the Peruvian Andes, millions of others occupied or roamed almost every corner of the vast New World. Generally, population concentration coincided with advancement. Semiadvanced cultures, such as the Muisca in the heart of what would become Colombia, numbered perhaps a million or so, with moderately sized urban centers. Many of the sparsely settled areas were home to more primitive peoples, and nomadic tribes wandered huge tracts of land in the Argentine pampas and the North American plains. Because of the gradual nature of European exploration and conquest and the cataclysmic collapse in the Indian population—largely due to disease from contact with Europeans—it is difficult to say how many people lived in the New World in 1492. Yet certainly there were several tens of millions of inhabitants in the Western hemisphere when Columbus sailed the ocean blue.

Iberia and the First Encounters

The Europeans who conquered most of the New World were primarily Iberians—people from the southwestern peninsula that today is home to

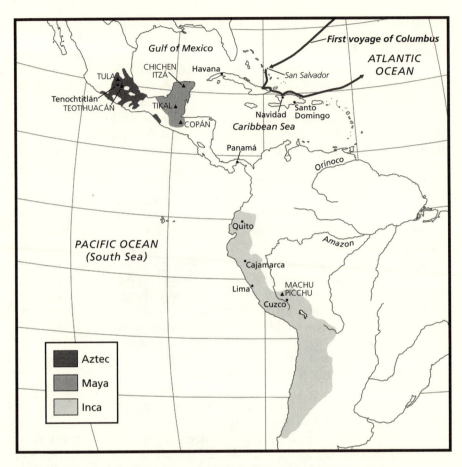

The territories of three ancient Latin American civilizations

Portugal and Spain. Iberia had a unique pre-1492 history, the contours of which are helpful to understanding what transpired after first contact; for Iberia itself was a land transformed by multiple invasions and the intermingling of conquerors and conquered. Romans explored and colonized "Hispania" over several centuries before yielding the territory to successive waves of Visigoths that invaded beginning in the fifth century A.D. In 711, Muslims from northern Africa (also known as Moors) swept through Iberia and even crossed the steep Pyrenees Mountains that separate the peninsula from France.

The Moorish invasion was most significant, and it left lasting impressions on the lands that would eventually become Spain. Moors were independent conquerors, and remained in Iberia on their own terms, without answering to a distant metropolis or state. They shared many advances with the less sophisticated, Christian peoples that they subdued. The city of Córdoba, at the heart of Islam-saturated southern Iberia, reached an era of splendor around the tenth century as a center of religion and culture, boasting libraries, a vibrant intellectual community, and eight hundred mosques. The Moors gave Iberia a distinctive, airy, and colorful architecture; transmitted several important mathematical and scientific concepts to the West; and helped shape a distinctive culture—in language, for example, by donating thousands of words to the still-evolving Spanish tongue during the middle centuries. But popular adherence to Christianity persisted, especially in the north, and intermittent war erupted, especially after the tenth century.

Christian Iberians termed this military struggle the *Reconquista*, or Reconquest. Despite the fusion of cultures, religion remained distinctive, and a belligerent brand of Christianity attracted a knightly class of warriors who rallied to the faith under the banner of St. James—whose reputed bones were conveniently unearthed on the eve of the fighting. The Christian prototype was El Cid, the legendary eleventh century knight who helped free Valencia from the Muslims. By the thirteenth century, the Reconquest was largely complete, with Moors retaining control only in the southern stretches of the peninsula. Feudal kingdoms emerged in the north, with assemblies of nobles, and eventually, a royal lineage of kings.

These small kingdoms in the north slowly moved into the same orbit. In 1469, Spain was unified through the marriage of eighteen-year-old Isabella of Castile to the sixteen-year-old Prince Ferdinand of Aragón. Ten years later, the two simultaneously inherited and effectively united their respective thrones. So devout that they earned the title "most Catholic monarchs," Ferdinand and Isabella soon resolved to complete the Reconquest. In January 1492, their armies triumphed at Alhambra, the last of the great Moorish fortresses in the south to fall to the forces of Christendom.

Centuries of warfare had equipped Iberians with ideas that in turn influenced their conduct in the New World. To Spaniards, war was a holy crusade. It involved devotion to God, not solely allegiance to political entities. Infidels, who resisted the faith, could rightly be punished or even enslaved (had not the Pope, after all, specified that certain types of cruel weapons should be employed only against nonbelievers?). In Iberian culture, concepts of manliness revolved around fighting and war. In the Spanish psyche, real men did not till fields and plant wheat; they were brave, loyal, and when necessary, violent—in the spirit and tradition of El Cid.

As Spain emerged and finished the Reconquest, the small nearby kingdom of Portugal, which had remained politically independent, was busily engaging in sea exploration. Under Prince Henry "the Navigator," ships under the Portuguese flag skirted the coast of west Africa. In 1488, just four years before the fall of Alhambra, Bartolomeu Dias rounded the Cape of Good Hope, opening a direct albeit rather difficult route to the spice-laden Far East. It was the East that captured every sailor's imagination, and the quest for a sea route was related to the fight against the Moors. Spices from the East came to Europe by way of Muslim middlemen, who marked up prices by several hundred percent. Handing their wealth over to infidels great frustrated Christian Europeans, though the coveted spices, used primarily for food preservation and flavoring, seemed worth it. Many seamen, including the devout, Italian-born Christopher Columbus, who sailed with the Portuguese for nine years, dreamed of finding a route that bypassed the Muslim world.

The Portuguese, who lived on the western coast of Iberia, could not help but notice that the sun sank in the sky over the seas each night and then reappeared in the east on each following day. Contrary to historical myth, most sailors and thinkers confidently believed the world was a sphere. But how large was it? The Greeks had calculated the earth's circumference accurately, but their figures were endlessly debated. Columbus reasoned that the Asian landmass was enormous—much larger than it was in reality. He theorized that a direct route westward, near the equator, would land him in the spice islands, some three or four thousand miles away.

Columbus's reasoning was unexceptional, but as everyone who sailed knew, it was one thing to hug the coastline of Africa and another to head out into uncharted, open seas. Still, Columbus's name is etched in Western history largely because of his persistence. For years he sought the support of a major European crown, facing rejection after rejection, until 1492, when in the wake of the triumph at Alhambra, Ferdinand and Isabella decided to back Columbus and grant him the title Admiral of the Ocean Sea.

From the northern Spanish port of Palos, Columbus set sail with three small ships and ninety men at the beginning of August 1492. Within a couple of months, the arduous journey and fears of never finding land nearly sparked a mutiny; but on October 12 the Admiral and his elated crews thanked God as they sighted an island in the Bahamas. They were greeted by friendly yet frightened Arawak, people whom Columbus wrongly termed "Indians," thinking that he was somewhere near India. He sat down and penned his first impressions in a diary for the King and Queen:

> The islanders gathered round us. I could see that they were people who would be more easily converted to our Holy Faith by love than by coercion, and wishing them to look on us with friendship I gave some of them red bonnets and glass beads which they hung round their neck, and many other things of small value. . . . All the men I saw were quite young, none older than thirty, all well built, finely bodied and handsome in the face. Their hair is coarse, almost like a horse's tail and short. . . . They must be good servants, and intelligent, for I can see that they quickly repeat everything said to them.[1]

Convinced that the spice islands must be nearby, Columbus continued southward, coming upon the northern coastline of a much larger island that he christened Hispaniola. It was here that he wrecked his largest vessel, the *Santa María*, on coral reefs, and opted to leave its 39-man crew on the shore in a hastily constructed fort in late December. Appropriately naming the site Navidad (Christmas), the explorer and his men unwittingly established the first European settlement in the New World, though they still assumed themselves to be somewhere in the Far East.

Columbus returned to Europe with his remaining two ships, and reported his findings to the pleased monarchs of Spain. As was the custom, Ferdinand and Isabella asked the Pope—who was, conveniently, a Spaniard—to certify their ownership of the new lands. When the Pope did so in 1493, an indignant Portuguese crown threatened war. Thus, the following year, Spain signed the Treaty of Tordesillas with Lisbon, assuring the Portuguese monarch that any lands east of an arbitrary line drawn through the Atlantic would belong to Portugal. The Spanish had inadvertently given away much of Brazil, though at the time no one knew it existed. The Portuguese realized the scope of their holdings only after a 1501 voyage by Amerigo Vespucci, an Italian sailor commissioned by Lisbon, who also ended up giving the entire land mass his name in the feminized form of *America*.

In fall 1493, Christopher Columbus made a second voyage to the New World, this time with a small fleet of ships and fifteen hundred colonizers—all males. The Spaniards also introduced important animals to the New World, bringing along hogs, cattle, and horses, the latter of which were being reintroduced to the Americas after a ten-thousand-year hiatus. When the Spaniards arrived at Navidad, however, they made an awful discovery: The settlement was gone, its inhabitants having been massacred by frustrated Indians. The crew of the *Santa María* had apparently dominated and abused the surrounding Arawak at will, eventually triggering a bloody revolt. European-Native relations were off to an inauspicious start.

During subsequent months, the Spaniards pillaged the Arawak yet again, requiring that they bring food and spend long days panning small rivers in search of gold. The demands of these strange newcomers must have perplexed and angered the Indians, who predictably rebelled, were defeated, and soon lived in conditions akin to those of slavery. Columbus, as governor of the island, presided over an increasingly chaotic colonial experiment. By all reliable accounts he was a poor administrator, and after his return to Spain in 1496 his fame slowly declined until he eventually died in relative obscurity.

There was little gold to be found on Hispaniola, and as Columbus himself pointed out, the only real wealth was the labor of the native population. Within a few years, the institution of *encomienda* was firmly established. Encomienda was a grant of Indians (not of land, which was plentiful) to a Spanish *encomendero*, who would see to their Christianization in exchange for their labor and tribute. It was an obviously unequal exchange. On Hispaniola, though not legally chattel slavery, encomienda effectively functioned as such. Widespread savagery broke the spirits of the Arawak; childbearing all but ended, and some even left their living hell by way of suicide. Brutal physical abuse was common.

So few Spaniards questioned the morality of their practices that when one eventually did so, his name became renowned far and wide. Antonio Montesinos, a Dominican friar, delivered one of the most famous sermons in history on Christmas Sunday, in 1511, when he compared his Spanish parishioners to Moors because of their treatment of the Indians. His cry for justice was embraced by a former encomendero, fellow Dominican Bartolomé de Las Casas, whose name eventually became synonymous with the struggle for Indian rights. Las Casas argued in behalf of the New World's Indian masses for the duration of his life, regretting, on his deathbed, that he could not have done even more. He wrote graphic accounts of Spanish cruelty, which were so effective that they gave rise to what today is called the "Black Legend"—the belief, especially among northern European Protestants, that there was something uniquely fanatical and sadistic about the Spanish psyche. Las Casas's most famous book, *The Destruction of the Indies*, was widely circulated in England. But although, as Charles Gibson—a prominent historian of Spanish-Aztec relations—contends, the Black Legend was fundamentally accurate in its portrayal of abuse, it was flawed in linking those abuses to the Spanish character. History is replete with tales of mighty nations exploiting the weak; rarely do we find humankind collectively exercising restraint in profoundly unequal power relations. At a completely different time and place—for example, in nineteenth-century Tasmania—British abuses of natives were comparable to those of the Spaniards on Hispaniola.

Conquests

The collapse of the Arawak population in the Caribbean helped drive the Spaniards to further exploration. Shortly after Columbus's second voyage it became obvious that the Spaniards had stumbled onto a vast new world, and that no easy passage to the East was available by this route. But by the 1510s, a steadily rising white population on Hispaniola and Cuba was struggling to collect adequate provisions from a sharply declining Indian base. Voyages to the south and west led to the establishment of the first settlement on the mainland, in present-day Panama, under Vasco Núñez de Balboa. Other exploratory ventures skirted the coast of Mexico, where Spaniards made first contact with mainland Indians and generated rumors of a great inland kingdom.

The governor in Cuba—which had surpassed Hispaniola as the center of Caribbean colonization—authorized an ambitious Indian fighter, Hernán Cortés, to undertake the conquest of Mexico in 1518. Cortés was a remarkable man. Born into the lesser nobility in Spain, he had dropped out of the university, and at age nineteen, decided to seek his fortune in the New World after his lover's husband resolved to kill him. He had a knack for getting ensnared in scandalous romances, and his strong personality, which seems to have initially attracted people to him, sometimes led to even longer-lasting alienation. A forced marriage in Cuba gave Cortés little reason to stay there, and by the time of the expedition he was ready to move on. But in early 1519 his benefactor, the governor, appeared poised to reverse his decision and remove Cortés from the Mexico assignment. And so on February 10, when he prematurely left the port of Havana with eleven ships and several hundred soldiers, Cortés did so under cloudy circumstances, and also as a man bent on success, since little of value lay behind him.

It was this all-or-nothing attitude, in part, that explains Cortés's energized and reckless leadership. Once on the shores of Mexico, he made the strategically unconscionable decision to burn all of his ships save one, which he sent directly to the king of Spain with a message. His men, some of whom grumbled in fear of the difficult campaign to come, now had no choice but to follow him and recognize his authority as a *Conquistador.* In order to satisfy any legalities, given that he had departed Cuba under questionable circumstances, Cortés founded the coastal city of Veracruz, appointed its town council, and had it in turn grant him authority to undertake the conquest of the interior.

Some two hundred miles away, in Tenochtitlán, couriers delivered the disturbing news of strange men, riding "mountains on the sea," to then-emperor Moctezuma II. Uncertain about what to make of these reports, the Aztec lord opted to send gifts of gold to the strangers. Instead of inspiring the Spaniards to leave, the gesture had the opposite effect. Speaking through interpreters, including La Malinche, an Indian princess given to Cortés by a coastal tribe, the Conqueror assured Moctezuma's messengers of his good intentions and vowed to march forward and meet the emperor himself. Thus began an intriguing process of deft Spanish diplomacy and discernment. Moctezuma could not know who, exactly, Cortés was, or what he and his men wanted. Though anthropologists have demonstrated the unlikelihood of Moctezuma's having seriously confused Cortés with the legendary god Quetzalcóatl, there is no doubt that the emperor and his advisers were perplexed and indecisive. They botched several opportunities to ambush or dissuade the invaders, and Cortés and his army marched into the great Aztec city unopposed.

For six months the Spaniards stayed in the heart of Tenochtitlán and acquired wealth while living as guests of Moctezuma II, whom they effectively made their hostage. Yet they were clearly in a precarious position, dwelling in the middle of a metropolis situated on an island in Lake Texcoco with 100,000 Aztecs increasingly suspicious of the political nature of their situation. In May 1520 the Spanish position deteriorated further when news reached Cortés from the coast. A new army of Spaniards, loyal to the Cuban governor whom he had offended, were in Veracruz. The Conqueror took a bold gamble: Leaving half of his men in the Aztec capital, he raced to the coast with the other half and defeated his fellow countrymen in battle. The detachment that remained in Tenochtitlán, however, panicked during Cortés's absence. It massacred much of the Aztec nobility, and an incensed populace rose up and besieged the Spaniards in the central palace compound.

Cortés, meanwhile, now reinforced by many soldiers at Veracruz whom he had defeated (his ability to woo the losers to his side is striking), returned to Tenochtitlán and united with his forces in the palace. He sent Moctezuma out onto the rooftop, ordering him to deliver a speech to pacify the crowds. But Moctezuma's efforts at persuasion did not go well. Aztecs threw stones at their own emperor, refusing to believe that he was a friend of the newcomers and that all was fine. Struck by a stone, Moctezuma II died of head injuries shortly thereafter. With no hope of regaining control in the capital, and with limited supplies remaining within the palace compound, Cortés and his men prepared to fight their way out of the city. On June 20, 1520, in what Spaniards refer to as the *Noche Triste* (Sad Night), Cortés lost nearly half his army in a bloody, running battle across the causeways on his way out of Tenochtitlán. Once safely in the mountains to the east, he reputedly sat down at the base of a tree and wept.

During the next year Cortés, ever the skillful diplomat, rallied a massive army of non-Aztecs to his side. Many welcomed the opportunity to rid themselves of the hated, tribute-collecting Aztecs. In May 1521 the Spaniards, with tens of thousands of Indian allies, sought revenge against the inhabitants of Tenochtitlán. They laid siege to the city, greatly aided by the fact that a smallpox epidemic simultaneously ravaged its populace. Cutting off the water supply, they eventually forced the Aztecs to surrender in August. The young, last emperor of the proud people, Cuauhtémoc (Falling Eagle), was subjected to torture and execution. Aztec temples were leveled, and Spaniards began to rebuild the capital as their own, renaming it Mexico City.

Disease played a crucial role in the conquest of the Aztecs. Smallpox and several other infectious diseases came into the New World from Europe, and Indians had almost no resistance to these new viral strains. The ensuing epidemics not only debilitated native societies through death but also left a deep psychological imprint on those who survived: What force could explain why so many Indians perished, even while Spaniards (who enjoyed relative immunity) remained healthy? Surely the gods favored Cortés and his men. The Christian God must be vastly superior to Huitzilopochtli and other native deities.

Disease often advanced in the New World more quickly than the Spaniards themselves. In the mid-1520s a dreadful smallpox epidemic swept through Central America, decimating Indians in the environs of Spanish-occupied Panamá. From there, the virus (or perhaps a mutant of it) spread to the Inca. The emperor in Cuzco succumbed to it, and his death triggered a civil war between rival sons that shattered the harmony of the empire. One son, named Atahualpa, slowly gained the upper hand in the bloody civil war; he was on his way south to the capital in 1532, when news of a band of strange newcomers reached his ears.

The newcomers were a small army of Spaniards under the command of Francisco Pizarro, a Panamanian colonist who had reconnoitered along the Peruvian coast and received the authorization of the crown for an expedition inland. They arrived at the perfect time. Decimated by disease and weakened by civil war, the Inca were vulnerable. Undoubtedly mindful of the details of Cortés's success, Pizarro persuaded the new emperor, Atahualpa, to meet him in an abandoned village on November 16, 1532. At Cajamarca, he and his men lured the unsuspecting emperor and his lightly armed entourage of hundreds of servants and choristers into the center of an enclosed town square. After giving the signal to attack, Pizarro took Atahualpa hostage, and the Spaniards massacred the remaining Indians. A huge Inca army, camped nearby, panicked in the wake of the news, as Spanish cavalry harried and slaughtered its stragglers.

It was like a fairy tale: The captured Atahualpa promised to fill his cell once with gold and twice with silver in exchange for his release. The Spaniards readily agreed, and the word went out to all the empire that its wealth should pour into the hands of Pizarro and his men near Cajamarca. Although the Spaniards amassed a great fortune, it technically fell short of the promised amount; Atahualpa's usefulness having reached its limit, the Spaniards killed him. In a series of follow-up battles, they easily defeated the demoralized Incan armies, aided by divisions within Indian ranks from the recently concluded civil war. As in Mexico, a remarkably small number of Spaniards had triumphed over millions of Indians—by dividing their adversaries, utilizing brilliant diplomatic and military tactics, and deriving the advantage from the devastating effects of epidemic disease.

After the conquests of Mexico and Peru, hopes of similar exploits inspired myriad expeditions into the remote backlands of the Americas. Rumors of golden ponds, fountains of youth, and Amazon women inspired Spanish males to march hundreds of miles through thick brush and over flat plains. In retrospect, such wild rumors seem outlandish; but at the time, who could doubt them, given the wonders of Cuzco and Tenochtitlán? One large expedition wandered out of northern Mexico into the present-day American southwest. Here Spaniards found no gold and no empires, though they did stumble upon what they called the "divine abyss"—a canyon like nothing known in all of Europe. After trying to send his soldiers scaling down its sides, the commander decided such efforts were worthless. His forces turned back. Another detachment marched all the way into the vicinity of Kansas before deciding that the heart of North America consisted merely of buffalo, impoverished Indians, tall grass, and "endless sky." In South America, an army cut a swath from Peru down into the jungles of the Amazon, again only to end up on a maddening expedition to nowhere. It seemed by the mid-sixteenth century that all the important places in the New World had been discovered.

In the vicinity of the Aztecs and Incas, however, there were clearly peripheral and inferior native societies to plunder. In central Mexico, Cortés himself marched northeastward to subdue the low-culture Huastecas, doing so with a mammoth army of Aztecs (Indians were easily bribed and cajoled into fighting each other). An especially cruel conquistador, a lawyer named Beltrán Nuño de Guzmán, terrorized much of western Mexico. Another march by Cortés, southeast out of Mexico City, revealed only difficult mountainous terrain and convinced most Spaniards subsequently to ignore the area. In Peru, expeditions northward and southward extended Spanish dominion, easily conquering the semiadvanced mountain chiefdoms of the Muisca, among other societies.

In the late 1520s an army of Spaniards began the conquest of the Maya in the Yucatán. In contrast to the relative smoothness of consolidation in central Mexico, the venture did not go well. In the thickness of the jungle, horses and cannons were of little use. The Maya themselves proved incredibly tenacious. Hiding in thick brush, they ambushed columns of Spaniards with arrows and ran away before the clumsily armed invaders could pursue them. Most disheartening for the Spaniards, who had marched inland, away from the reasonably prosperous towns on the coast, was the realization that the Yucatán offered little of apparent value, and certainly no significant caches of silver or gold. The initial invasion force packed its bags and sailed away. Only years later did a second army, determined to dominate and enslave the Maya themselves, reappear. This time, using light cotton armor (like the Indians) and "total war" tactics (e.g., the wholesale burning of villages), Europeans prevailed. Most Maya fled southward or died of malnutrition after their crops were destroyed; others were rounded up and put to hard labor, with some being enslaved and sold to colonists in the Caribbean.

The initial success of the Maya resistance is telling: High concentrations of sedentary Indians made for relatively easy conquest, but politically independent natives living in small villages often caused problems for whites.

Even more difficult to subdue were nomadic hunter tribes. Naturally violent, accustomed to killing wildlife for food, and freely roaming large tracts of land, these Indians offered stiff resistance. The Araucanians on the southern fringes of the Incan domains (what would eventually become Chile) are a case in point: Wild and mobile, they resisted Spanish encroachment with verve. They overran the small Spanish outpost at Santiago, forcing a retreat to the coastline. When a young Araucanian named Lautaro was enslaved at age 15, he escaped and rejoined his people, becoming a warlord. He captured his former master, the conquistador Pedro de Valdivia, and put him to death. Though he was killed in battle at age 22, Lautaro became the subject of legends after an admiring Spaniard wrote an epic poem about him. Three centuries later and thousands of miles to the north, Araucanian stubbornness was matched by the resistance of the Apaches. Facing extermination by a well-equipped American army, the Indians fought to a bitter end. Ironically, U.S. Army helicopters dubbed *Apaches* became critical weapons in the continued pacification of natives in southern Mexico and elsewhere at the close of the twentieth century.

Latin America's Indians Today

Roughly five hundred years after the Spanish conquests of the New World, most of Latin America can claim at least a fraction of the region's Indian past. Yet *Indian* is not a neatly defined term. Centuries of miscegenation have clouded the physical and cultural characteristics of native peoples. Although an overwhelming majority of Latin Americans have at least some Indian ancestry, *mestizos* (people of mixed heritage—i.e., most Mexicans) are quick to deny that they're the least bit Indian. Many Latin Americans of direct native descent have gone to great lengths to adopt non-Indian ways. They speak Spanish, wear jeans and T-shirts, and reject native religious and cultural traditions. But of course, blood and race cannot be changed: About twenty-five million Latin Americans today are full-blood Indians, whether or not they embrace the cultural identification.

And many do. Indian culture has been resilient, especially in the Andean domains of the once-powerful Inca, and among the Mayan peoples of Guatemala and the Yucatán. Native languages and dialects, distinctive clothing, religious ceremonies, and cultural practices such as the use of herbal medicines continue to denote *Indian*. Concern for Indians among human rights activists in the First World even generated a modicum of media attention to their plight during the 1980s, when the destruction of the Amazon rainforests in Brazil and repression in Guatemala killed tens of thousands of natives. The Nobel committee's decision to award the Peace Prize in 1992 to a Maya woman, Rigoberta Menchú, stunned much of the world—and left the light-skinned elites who rule Guatemala aghast.

Menchú has remained an outspoken advocate of Indian rights, although interest in her cause has dimmed considerably in recent years. The informal destruction of Indian life continues, as television reaches more homes in remote villages and as alcoholism, crime, and outward migration of youth disrupt Indian communities.

Pure-blooded Indians live primarily in the same regions heavily occupied before the Spanish Conquest: Mexico and the Andes. In Mexico, Indians populate a tier of mountainous states south of Mexico City (centuries of racial mixing have left a predominantly mestizo populace in the central highlands around the capital). Indians constitute more than 40 percent of the populations of four countries: Bolivia, Guatemala, Ecuador, and Peru. Two of the four, Bolivia and Guatemala, are among the poorest nations in the hemisphere. In several other countries—e.g., Mexico—areas dominated by the descendants of native peoples are impoverished. In contrast, the three overwhelmingly white nations—Argentina, Costa Rica, and Uruguay—enjoy some of the region's highest levels of wealth. Money and power have followed skin color in Latin America for centuries—one of the region's deeper historical continuities.

3 The Colonial Centuries

In 1970 two Latin American scholars, Barbara and Stanley Stein, published a short book that provided an explanation of the purported historical dimensions of dependency theory. *The Colonial Heritage of Latin America*, which was widely read in North American universities, argued that economic and to a lesser extent social and political dynamics inherited from the colonial era persisted in the nineteenth and twentieth centuries, in the form of "neocolonial structures" that inhibited change. Succinctly put, the Steins believed that Latin America's lack of development had deep historical roots.

The interpretation offered by the Steins was incorrect. In fact, there is relatively little historical context to the structures of power that dominate Latin America today. Hence, the following overview of the distant past is necessarily brief. From the era of the conquests until the early nineteenth century, Portugal colonized Brazil, and Spain governed nearly all of the remainder of Latin America. These three centuries are historically fascinating and complex; but for those wanting to understand present-day Latin America, a cursory review of the critical institutions of African slavery, the church, and the state will suffice.

The Forced Migration of Africans

The racial and cultural complexity of contemporary Latin America is a product not only of the fusion of native and European peoples but of the introduction of black Africans into the New World. During the colonial era, roughly 3.5 million Africans were forcibly relocated. Evidence of this great diaspora remains, especially in Brazil and the Caribbean, to this day.

The enslavement of Africans was tied to the production of a unique agricultural crop: sugar. It was during the crusades in the eastern Mediterranean that west Europeans first encountered sugar—for a people whose sole natural sweetener had been honey, a wonderful discovery. Early in the twelfth century, Europeans attempted to grow the strange cane for the first time themselves, and within a few decades fairly substantial fields were under cultivation on the large island of Cyprus—a location safe from Muslim armies, thanks to Western naval superiority. But Europeans were plagued by a perennial problem: Nobody wanted to perform the hard labor involved in growing and harvesting cane sugar. With the opening of the Bosporus in 1204 due to the capture of Constantinople, the obvious answer was "Slavs." Slavic peoples (from which we inherit the derivative word *slave*), Tatars, and Mongols began to be shipped to Cyprus, where they worked sugar fields under coercion. During the fourteenth century, these groups of forced laborers were joined by a lesser number of Africans, as sub-Saharan peoples were traded into bondage through Egyptian intermediaries. When Constantinople fell into Turkish hands in 1453, closing the Bosporus, Africans became the slaves of choice. Over time, sugar, in the European mind, became nearly synonymous with African slavery.

As wonderful as it tastes, sugar is a crop produced by the sweat of the brow. It is labor intensive, and work is required nearly the year 'round. Cane also saps the soil of its nutrients, and eventually, additional humid, wet, tropical lands must be acquired for planting, to maintain robust harvests. When the Portuguese began to advance down the African coast just as Constantinople fell, it was only logical to move sugar westward, nearer to this new source of slaves. Production subsequently soared on a number of small eastern Atlantic islands, where volcanic soil and frequent rain made for ideal conditions. The tiny Madeiras came to dominate the sugar industry in the late fifteenth century, and produced more than eight hundred tons of the "white gold" the year Columbus sailed past on his way to the New World.

But although growing conditions were ideal, the Madeiras and other Atlantic islands were small, and production there eventually declined due to soil exhaustion. The Portuguese founded new sugar plantations on a larger island just off the coast of Africa, which they christened St. Thomas. Sugar production here eventually surpassed that of the Madeiras in the early 1500s. The African slave laborers escaped into the interior mountains of St. Thomas, however, where they waged war so effectively that the Portuguese eventually abandoned the island. By the mid-sixteenth century, sugar was crossing the Atlantic to a new, spacious home in northeastern Brazil.

With sugar, Africans came into the New World. Lisbon's merchants, anxious to continue in their lucrative slave trading, linked up with colonial planters who had failed to find an adequate alternative in Indians, given the sparse coastal populations. Capturing and shipping hundreds of thousands of Africans out of their homelands was a formidable task. Contrary to what one might expect, whites did not venture deep into Africa in search of slaves. Instead, they established trading posts along the west coast and bartered rum, tobacco, and light manufactured goods for slaves delivered by other Africans. The arrival of whites sparked an increase in tribal violence in the interior of Africa. Warring parties turned their captives over to the Europeans, and individuals used enslavement as a means of ridding themselves of despised enemies and rivals. There was no shortage of human produce in the trading posts of coastal Africa.

For the slaves themselves, the initial branding marked the beginning of a long hell. Crossing the South Atlantic in what was called the "Middle Passage," they were stuffed below deck on overcrowded vessels and deprived of sufficient food and water. Often chained in positions allowing for little mobility, their limbs went numb or muscles cramped up, while seasickness and defecation produced a nauseating stench. About the slave ship, one eighteenth-century African later wrote:

> Its horrors, ah! who can describe. . . . We were thrust into the hold of the vessel in a state of nudity, the males being crammed on one side, and the females on the other; the hold was so low that we could not stand up, day and night were the same to us, sleep being denied us from the confined position of our bodies, and we became desperate through suffering and fatigue. . . . The only food we had during the voyage was corn soaked and boiled. We suffered very much for want of water, but was denied all we needed. A pint a day was all that was allowed, and no more; and a great many slaves died upon the passage.[1]

Motivated by profit, slave traders calculated that it was more cost effective to fill their ships with humans and let some die than to sacrifice cargo space to supplies of food and freshwater. The best evidence indicates that about 10 percent of African slaves perished in transit. Those who arrived in the New World were badly malnourished and depleted, prompting Portuguese sugar planters in Brazilian marketplaces to probe, jab, and thoroughly inspect new arrivals in order to gauge their remaining strength and durability.

Plantation life was predictably harsh. Slaves worked in the cane fields from dawn to dusk. Planters routinely failed to supply adequate food, insisting instead that Africans grow their own vegetables on small plots of marginal land, which they were permitted to work on Sundays. This practice, which infuriated many priests (who wanted slaves to attend mass instead of laboring on the Sabbath), rarely yielded sufficient harvests. Malnutrition, coupled with physical abuse, produced a high mortality rate, with an average life expectancy of about twelve years for newly arrived Africans in Brazil. Death was so frequent, and church burials so expensive and inconvenient, that many whites disposed of slave bodies by discarding them in nearby forests or unmarked common graves.

Most of the Africans imported into Brazil (75 percent) were young males. But a smaller, female slave population took hold in the colony's port cities, where many African women were put to work as domestic servants. For quite some time, historians assumed that their lives contrasted greatly with the brevity and brutality of those of their male counterparts. Newer scholarship counters this assumption. Under the supervision of rich white women, female slaves were subjected to frequent abuse. The *palmatoria*, a paddle-like device with holes, was applied to all parts of the slave's body, including her breasts. Legal documents reveal that even killing female slaves was not uncommon; one enraged and imaginative mistress chained her slave's face to a stove and cooked her alive.

Given the severity of a slave's life, it comes as little surprise that many risked death in an attempt to regain freedom. In northern Brazil, colonial planters had an ongoing problem with runaways. Fleeing into nearby jungles, blacks congregated in small villages, or *quilombos*—an African word for a war camp—where they reinvented African ways of life and fought tenaciously with slave-retrieving expeditions. Excavations were undertaken at the site of the most famous quilombo, Palmares, in the mid-1990s. At its height, in the seventeenth century, Palmares was home to nearly ten thousand inhabitants. It was so powerful that it negotiated treaties with surrounding plantations, in which both parties agreed to forego raiding and mutually coexist.

Despite their occasionally effective resistance, Africans made the Portuguese rich. They turned Brazil (more properly, isolated sections of its northern coast) into a grand sugar colony. Most of the refined cane, however, was sold to foreigners, as the wealth, population, and power of Protestant northern Europe rose during the colonial period. Eventually, some sugar-importing nations entertained ideas of growing the wonder crop themselves. The Dutch, whose enormous merchant marine plied most of the world's oceans during the seventeenth century, coveted the cane fields of northeastern Brazil and eventually took them by force. From 1630 to 1654, Holland occupied Pernambuco, with its port of Recife. Though they were eventually driven out by planters loyal to the Portuguese crown, Dutch entrepreneurs learned from the experience of occupation, and took their knowledge about sugar planting with them as they moved elsewhere in search of wealth.

Where could northwest Europeans grow their own crops? A number of Protestant nations eyed the Caribbean in the seventeenth century, where Spanish naval and colonial authority had badly deteriorated. Their navies seized small islands in the Lesser Antilles, where sugar planters found near-perfect conditions. But the depopulated islands lacked a workforce. Inspired by the Iberian example and already heavily involved in the slave trade, the Dutch and other north Europeans continued to subject Africans to the whip. Slavery under the French and the north Europeans was as brutal as that under the Portuguese and Spanish. Savage working conditions and an acute lack of sustenance marked the treatment of slaves in the Caribbean, many of whom perished or resisted. Runaways, or *maroons*, as they were called (from a Spanish word meaning "people of the hills"), had few options on the small islands, and they were often recaptured. Many French masters employed three tiers of punishment: The first capture resulted in the loss of an ear; the second, in the severing of a foot; and the third, in death—by creative methods such as burying the African up to his neck, covering his head in cane sap, and allowing fire ants to gnaw at him until he expired.

Despite their ruthlessness, French planters lost control of their largest slave colony, Saint Domingue, located on the western third of Hispaniola. The smaller islands of the Lesser Antilles had been great for sugar, but some were too mountainous, and many of those under cultivation suffered from soil depletion within a few decades. Hence, north Europeans shifted their operations to the Greater Antilles. In 1655, Oliver Cromwell engineered the English capture of Jamaica, and large plantations that met Britain's sugar demands were eventually developed there. The French, in contrast, only gradually absorbed western Hispaniola, decades after its pirates, called *buccaneers*, had explored its inlets and used them as hideouts.

During the eighteenth century Saint Domingue blossomed as sugarcane flourished in its central valley. But by 1790, the colony's white population was outnumbered eleven to one, and harried by a sizable maroon population hiding in remote mountains. The political instability of the French Revolution divided colonists and compounded their vulnerability, and in August 1791 the heart of Saint Domingue erupted in race war. One thousand whites, or about 3.2 percent of the French population, were killed in short order, and others fled from the interior to the ports, where many boarded ships for Louisiana or France. Napoleon, the French Emperor, attempted to pacify the Africans with a portion of his Europe-conquering army. But the determined former slaves would have none of it; they offered a relentless resistance. French warriors were stupefied. In one early battle, the French field commander even waved a flag of truce so that he could cross the battle lines and commend his worthy opponents. Prolonged fighting sapped French morale and turned the insurrection into a bitter contest marked by atrocities; but eventually, it culminated in freedom for the world's first black republic, Haiti, in 1804.

Today, Haiti is the most visible reminder of the colonial institution of African slavery. After breaking free, it lapsed into poverty and isolation, with sugar production plummeting by two-thirds and only nominal trade and contact with the outside world during much of the nineteenth century. Europeans shunned it, and southerners in the United States feared the ramifications of even recognizing its sovereignty. America did appreciate Haiti's strategic importance, however, in the age of steam and steel. The U.S. Navy, which dominated the Caribbean at the outset of the twentieth century, transported an occupation force of Marines into Haiti during World War I. Black Haitians and mostly southern-bred, white Marines did not get along well. Insurgents resisted the occupation, and only the fear of swift punishment quelled the Haitians. Charlemagne Péralte, the foremost Haitian guerrilla leader, was betrayed into the hands of Americans by a corrupt associate and was executed. His body was tied to a door and defaced with a Haitian flag and a large crucifix. A famous painting of his corpse helped turn him into a legendary figure—one that inspired Haitians decades later, when Haiti again posed difficulties for the United States.

Haiti's ruling elite are light-skinned, reflecting a blend of white French and black African ethnicity (commonly called *mulatto*). Although in Haiti this pigmentation is rare—less than 3 percent of the population have it—in Brazil, since the colonial era, a large mulatto population has emerged. In coastal areas around Recife and Salvador live millions of mulattoes and blacks—the descendants of slaves. In fact, roughly half of Brazil's massive population can claim some degree of African heritage. And although most Africans were shipped primarily into Brazil and the Caribbean, tens of thousands, especially during the sixteenth century, ended up in colonial Spanish ports. Some African communities thoroughly assimilated into the general population over time, so that in Buenos Aires, for example, there is almost no black presence left today. But others were perpetuated—for example, in Venezuela and Panamá, where the descendants of African slaves have contributed unique qualities to the national cultures, in music, dance, and cuisine.

Their most noticeable contribution is no doubt in religion: African-based spiritualism has not only survived but has won many new adherents. In northeastern Brazil, Candomblé and Umbanda are major religions; and almost all Haitians, even though they consider themselves Christians, continue to practice voodoo. These African religions involve a pantheon of gods, or spirit-beings; feature highly emotional services and "possessions" by spirits; and have a mystical element that often strikes outsiders as bizarre. Honor is accorded to ancestors, such as Zumbi—the warlord of Palmares, who is now venerated in the Umbanda faith. Haitians pay homage at the tomb of Baron Samedi, a Lord of the Dead who is believed to possess his still-living followers. In contrast to caricatures fueled by images in film and on television, voodoo practitioners do not spend their nights sticking pain pins into dolls and chopping off chicken heads. As in Brazilian spiritualism, they primarily attend festive ceremonies that feature loud drum beating, distinctive music, and emotional excitement. Spiritual possessions, if they come, are not much more transcendent than the "slaying by the spirit" experienced by some U.S. Pentecostals. And although superstitions such as the Haitian belief in zombies (the enslaved dead) persist, they rarely fuel practices more dangerous than, for example, the poisonous snake handling practiced by fundamentalist Christian sects today in some areas of rural Appalachia.

The Colonial Church

At the same time as millions of Haitians and Brazilians embrace African spiritualism, most also profess Christianity. This may at first seem contradictory; the mixing of diverse traditions, however, is central to Latin American religious experience. For the majority of the population, the descendants of whites and Indians, it is a process borne of the era of conquest. When Columbus sailed the Atlantic in search of the spice islands, he was driven by a desire both to enrich himself and to promote his religion. Similarly, a foot soldier in Cortés's army wrote that Spaniards came to "serve God and get rich." Although the history of early encounters, especially the harsh abuse of Indians, suggests that greed ultimately predominated in the range of motives, Spaniards of all backgrounds understood and often justified their actions through their faith. Religion was an integral part of the Conquest.

As in the Caribbean, mendicants (vow-taking clerics) followed their countrymen onto the mainland of the Americas and soon were interacting directly with their new Indian charges. Who were these millions of natives, they pondered, and why had God put them in a world of their own, apart from the saving message of the Gospel? Questions about the discovery of the New World and its peoples perplexed many thinkers and provided fodder for decades of discussion back in Spain. To Las Casas, the Dominican heir of Antonio de Montesinos and tireless "defender of the Indians," the answer was simple: Indians were fully human and capable of saving faith, although in the short term, at least, they warranted treatment as childlike junior brothers in Christ. To others, most notably a lawyer named Juan de Sepúlveda, who opposed Las Casas in a series of famous mid-sixteenth-century debates, they were naturally reprobate: evil, homosexual, stupid brutes, inherently lazy and best enslaved for their own good. Sepúlveda's position enjoyed considerable popular support; but much of the Church hierarchy favored Las Casas's view—a view that sanctioned clerical expansion, and in time, helped make the Catholic church a major institution in colonial society.

In the sixteenth century, after Spaniards conquered Indians with the sword, priests bent on a conquest of their own arrived with the cross. In Mexico a Franciscan friar, Toribio de Benavente, walked barefoot with eleven brothers from Veracruz to Mexico City. This open embrace of hardship was telling: With a missionary zeal, Spanish priests had resolved to win this vast new world to the Christian faith. Their passion for souls was compounded by a sense of urgency: Surely the discovery of the Americas was apocalyptic, portending the imminent return of Christ! The rapid spread of fatal diseases among the Indians signaled impending judgment, making the work of salvation vitally important. For many Indians, post-Conquest change also evoked a special spiritual longing. Many Incan peoples, for example, anticipated returning deities and new epochs in a manner that enabled them to accept the idea of universal finality. Such common theological threads facilitated the fusion of native and Catholic religious practices. This mixing, or syncretism, greatly aided the church in its spiritual conquest of the New World. Getting Indians to fully abandon their polytheism, however, was difficult. In venerating myriad saints, Indians retained a theological commonality with their ancestors even while accepting basic Christian dogma.

Syncretism was both a calculated and an informal process. In an example of its most strategized form, the Church hierarchy encouraged devotion to the reputed appearance of Mary, the Mother of God, in central Mexico in 1531. A Christianized Indian named Juan Diego, so the story goes, encountered the Virgin on a hill north of Mexico City. Knowing that there would be skeptics, she gave him a bundle of flowers, which he carefully wrapped in his serape (cloak). Upon conferring with the archbishop, Juan Diego unfolded the cloth—and discovered inside it an image of the Virgin with significantly dark skin. The syncretic cult of the Virgin of Guadalupe that was founded on this myth has since flourished, particularly in the seventeenth century, wooing many natives to the Catholic faith: They could understand the Virgin of Guadalupe in the context of traditional female goddesses such as Tonantzin, who was believed to protect the people.

For many Indians, then, adoption of Christianity did not translate into a complete break with the past; the Church understood the need for continuity. The shrines and pyramids of natives were often leveled by the conquerors and replaced with churches. To the Spaniards, these buildings symbolized the triumph of Catholicism over heathen cults. To Indians, they simply honored a still-holy place. Sometimes the builders shrewdly used the same stones that had once supported altars and pyramids, even with native script facing outward, so that Catholicism's continuity with prior beliefs would not be missed.

Yet despite the syncretic nature of post-Conquest Catholicism, some features of native and European religious traditions could not be reconciled. Both the dynamics of the conversion process and the extent of Indian subversion of church doctrine continue to draw the interest of scholars. On the first, the evidence cuts both ways: Studies of baptismal records indicate that families were not uniformly converted—and that differences of opinion and volition were honored. Conversely, historians continue to find coercive dimensions to conversion in Peru and elsewhere. Economic and social benefits enticed Indians to convert, but lapses in faith often resulted in severe punishments.

Even decades after the Conquest, many priests expressed frustration with the stubborn "waywardness" of their Indian charges. Many natives simply refused to abandon their gods. Pre-Contact rituals persisted. The Inca, who venerated their mummified ancestors (whose remains were stored in caverns) and rejected Christian concepts of underground burial, sometimes dug up corpses in church cemeteries to free their ancestral souls from the "weight of the earth." Practices starkly different from those of Catholicism, such as blood sacrifices and erotic forms of dancing, continued in secret, away from the eyes of zealous Catholic priests. The discovery of native rituals among Maya in the Yucatán in 1562 triggered a small-scale inquisition, during which Franciscan friars tortured thousands to elicit confessions and "purge the body of Christ" of rekindled paganism. Many Indian revolts during the colonial era were deeply tied to religious tensions as well as economic and political ones.

The mendicants—that is, the Franciscans and Dominicans—dominated the evangelical work in the populated areas of the New World. Differences of opinion and even rivalries between these two arms of the Church were not uncommon. Dominicans, with their emphasis on education, favored baptism only after instruction, whereas the Franciscans tended to preach and baptize at a faster pace. By the late sixteenth century, both were joined by the Jesuits, who earned a reputation as scholars and established some of the premier institutions of learning in Latin America. As latecomers on the mission scene, Jesuits ended up doing much of the most dangerous field work among remote and very primitive peoples on the imperial fringes. They pacified the Guaraní, in present-day Paraguay, and scoured desert lands in northern Mexico in search of souls.

In time, mendicants were eclipsed by "seculars," or non-vow-taking clerics tied directly to the Church hierarchy. Less zealous and more accustomed to comfort, these priests saw to the worldly needs of the Church, managing a slowly accumulating fortune. The Church was growing wealthy on donations from repentant conquerors—some making amends on their deathbeds—as well as on profits from its own prosperous farming and mission operations. By the end of the colonial era, the Church was the largest landowner in Latin America, and despite Biblical invectives against usury, behaved much like a bank in extending credit and lending money. Handcrafted gold and silver work decorated the elaborate interiors of countless baroque altars, and the carefully plastered exteriors often rivaled those of the houses of worship in Europe.

Seculars also largely supervised the Holy Office of the Inquisition, which arrived in most of the New World during the late sixteenth century. An often misunderstood institution, it preserved social and moral norms and was rarely feared or resented by the majority of the population. In many ways it functioned as a censorship board, preserving the dominant cultural and intellectual assumptions of the societal mainstream. A plethora of lesser offenses, mainly blasphemies, filled much of the Inquisition's routine docket. When, for example, one colonial used a big cross in his front yard as a drying rack for chiles, Inquisitors were not amused. A medical doctor who repeatedly compared the Pope's pronouncements to toilet paper also suffered fines and clerical queries. Most cases of blasphemy were mundane and resulted in mild punishments, such as public recantation or penance. Much more serious, however, were those involving heresy. For this small group of cases, the Inquisition is infamous: This institution persecuted Jews, many of whom had come to Latin America in order to practice their faith quietly, as well as Protestants and wayward intellectuals. The number of persons burned at the stake was minuscule; and in these cases, too, a decided majority of colonials appear to have appreciated the social control provided by the Holy Office. Autos-da-fé, or public rituals of penance, were in fact occasions for celebration.

One of the most famous women of colonial Spanish America—a woman who often flirted with danger vis-à-vis the Inquisition and Church authorities—was Juana Inés de la Cruz, commonly known as Sor Juana (Sister Juana). Juana was a nun who wrote beautiful poetry and ever-so-subtly questioned societal assumptions, especially regarding the place of women. In one famous verse, nicely translated into English, she asked:

> *Which has the greater sin when burned*
> *by the same lawless fever:*
> *She who is amorously deceived,*
> *or he, the sly deceiver?*
> *Or which deserves the sterner blame,*
> *though each will be a sinner:*
> *She, who becomes a whore for pay,*
> *or he, who pays to win her?*[2]

Sor Juana, like many women of wealthy backgrounds, found refuge in the convent, which provided the only means by which she could achieve an intellectual life. Convents flourished in colonial Latin America. The only viable choice for light-skinned women other than marriage, they enjoyed popularity despite steep entry fees and long waiting lists. Nuns acquired a modicum of social responsibility and influence by running charities and administering assistance to the poor.

Convents, as well as the Church itself, fared poorly after Latin Americans achieved independence in the early nineteenth century. Today, although the vast majority of Latin Americans still view themselves as Catholics, the influence of the Church in everyday life is greatly diminished in comparison with colonial times; and although many still habitually cross themselves as they pass by a church, many also rarely go inside. Since the mid-twentieth century, Protestant missionaries, inconceivable in colonial times, have roamed Latin America with few constraints. Aided by radio and television programs beamed in by American evangelicals, they have won converts by the millions in recent years. In 1960, all of Latin America had only 5 million Protestants; by 1990, there were more than 45 million (a period of growth coinciding with the rise of television). Large Protestant movements, often Pentecostal in nature, have begun to rival the Catholic church in Argentina, parts of Brazil, Guatemala, northern Mexico, and elsewhere. The emotional fervor and rigid morality of many fundamentalist sects have proved surprisingly appealing to a range of Latin Americans, from highly Americanized, middle-class suburbanites to impoverished Maya Indians still living in remote villages. Religious bonds fulfill a need for community in an increasingly insecure age, in which traditional ethnic and familial ties have weakened; and charismatic emotionalism provides the poor an escape from their difficult daily lives.

The Colonial State

The second great colonial institution in Spanish Latin America was the government, or state, which worked alongside the Church. Just as the Reconquest wedded faith with warfare in the Spanish psyche, so it linked the crown with the cross. The practice of royal patronage allowed the king (instead of the Pope) to appoint high church officials in the New World, and usually there was little tension between the twin symbols of Spanish authority: the Palace and the Cathedral. The state collected the mandatory church tax, the *diezmo*, which linked the two institutions together financially.

With the average journey between Spain and the American mainland taking well over three months, Spain's direct governance of its vast colonies was impractical. Realizing this, the crown established assistant kingships, or viceroyalties, in the New World. In the mid-sixteenth century, viceroyalties were formed in Peru and Mexico, the two most populous regions. In the mid-eighteenth century, recognizing the rising importance of peripheral areas, the crown designated two additional viceregal districts in Colombia (New Granada) and Argentina (La Plata). The arrival of viceroys, or assistant kings appointed by the crown, occasioned much pomp and fanfare in these colonial centers.

Back in Spain, a panel of bureaucrats called the Royal Council of the Indies was formed in 1524. Given the task of drafting laws and issuing decrees for the New World, the Council inspired an enormous bureaucracy and generated much paperwork. Yet even early on, some viceroys realized that many of its instructions were imprudent or irrelevant. Thus was coined the most famous phrase in the political history of colonial Spanish America: *Obedezco, pero no cumplo* (I obey, but I do not comply). Viceroys sent this message back to the Royal Council and king, which testified to their loyalty at the same time that it signaled that they would refrain from implementing unwise instructions.

When the first viceroys arrived in the New World, there were tensions between them and the conquerors. The men who had subdued Indian kingdoms, mostly from the lower classes, resented the arrival of nobles and lawyers, who above all else, had come to obtain some wealth of their own and to collect taxes. When Peru's first viceroy tried to enforce crown directives, colonists killed him. From 1544 to 1547, Peruvian Spaniards were on their own, ceding anew to royal authority only with amnesties and promises of less interference. In Mexico the son of conqueror Hernán Cortés involved himself in a similar antiviceregal plot, the discovery of which forced him into early political retirement. Spain's governing representatives took control of New World realms slowly.

By the late sixteenth century, however, the power of the viceroy and crown was firmly established. Government permeated to the corners of empire, and equaled the Church in its social and economic significance. A web of offices and lesser bureaucracies emerged below the viceroys. Panels of judges, called *audiencias*, functioned as a second tier of royal authority and oversaw far-flung subregions. Multiple tiers of other posts, including governorships, had lesser geographic parameters, with the smallest unit comprising the *municipio* (municipal district). *Cabildos* (town councils) managed municipios, and depending on the importance of the town, had only a few or more than a dozen members. Cabildos kept public order, regulated the marketplace, maintained roads, and served as civil courts of first instance. The oft-recognized *cabildo abierto*, or open council, was an invitation-only forum for making important decisions, and usually involved only the town's elite.

Colonial government favored the rich, and its administration of justice was partial. Spain did not provide its colonies with clean or efficient government. One reason for this was the overlapping nature of offices and functions. Each tier issued decrees and heard appeals—there was no separation of powers—making for a mess of laws and vying bureaucratic interests. In one sense this worked to the benefit of the crown, which frequently stepped in as the final arbitrator in disputes. It was not, however, a system conducive to smooth administration. Furthermore, during the breadth of the colonial era, the quality of officeholders deteriorated. The New World became less important and less attractive to the Spanish over time, and the best and brightest preferred to pursue careers at home. Even more damaging was the crown's practice of selling colonial offices to the highest bidder as a means of raising money. By the eighteenth century, even viceregal posts were up for sale. Bureaucrats who bought their offices for high prices did so with the intent of recouping the expense by graft and by doling out political favors.

Over time, predictably, elites born and raised in the New World had more to gain by holding office than did Spaniards. These *criollos*, or colonials born of white-skinned, Spanish-descended parents, came to dominate offices by the middle of the colonial era. For nearly two hundred years, little about the structure or style of colonial government changed (though its quality declined); but in time, the Spanish crown realized that an overhaul of the system could revitalize it. Criollos were very disappointed with this reorganization when it came, under a new Spanish dynasty, in the eighteenth century.

The House of Bourbon acquired the Spanish throne at the outset of the 1700s and determined to initiate reforms to reinvigorate the empire and replenish royal coffers. Both political connections and trade between the mother country and its colonies had slackened. Mindful of new ideas about mercantilism and enlightened rule, Bourbon kings set out to try and restore Spain's wealth and glory.

The Bourbon reforms stretched over decades, though the most meaningful restructuring took place in the 1760s and 1770s. Economically, the Bourbon crown attempted to revive Spain's moribund economy by increasing trade with its colonies. Since the mid-sixteenth century, when pirates frequently raided imperial ships on the open seas, the monarchy had closely controlled shipping by organizing large fleets—more easily protected by naval escort—and routing its merchant marine into specific ports. This tightly managed system facilitated trade monopolies, and in each major entrepôt a powerful group of merchants had arisen. By the eighteenth century, however, Spain's naval might had withered, and smuggling was so widespread that the old restrictions no longer made sense. The Bourbons opened new ports, lowered duties, and shelved monopolistic restrictions. Shipping costs declined, more ships visited ports legally, and tax revenues rose.

When it came to trade, the Spanish Bourbons were especially interested in importing more silver. A second area of reform thus involved New World mines. Once tremendously productive, the silver mining operations of Peru and Mexico had lapsed into disrepair over time. Bourbon kings sought to reinvigorate them. They opened a mining school in Mexico City, sent teams of mostly German technicians to solve drainage problems, and adjusted the tax code to encourage new exploration and production. Mercury (or "quicksilver"), used during the colonial era to process silver ore, became more readily available and served the crown as a lucrative monopoly. All of these efforts on behalf of silver mining helped account for production increases, though Latin America's mines never returned to their sensational mid-sixteenth- and early-seventeenth-century levels that had funded European wars and had made Spain rich.

Beyond economic reforms, the Bourbons reorganized colonial government. In addition to the two new viceroyalties, they created new *audiencias* and consolidated lower bureaucratic offices into powerful regional posts called Intendances. Intendants received extensive tax-collecting, auditing, and administrative authority; most significantly, to the chagrin of criollos who had become accustomed to purchasing offices, they were overwhelmingly *peninsulares*, or Spaniards (literally, those from the peninsula), appointed by the king. And even worse for colonials, the Bourbons increased taxes. Duties on a range of local products and imports rose sharply, generating resentment and even sparking occasional riots and rebellions. A bloody Indian uprising in Peru in 1780 was, in part, inspired by new taxation and mine labor drafts; and new duties on alcoholic beverages triggered riots in New Granada.

Colonial mistrust of Spain's intentions increased as those tax revenues began to be used to finance standing armies in the Americas. Spain's primary concern was the expansion of French and English holdings in North America and the Caribbean. The crown recognized that its empire was vulnerable, and it had new fortresses constructed at major ports and on the frontier of northern Mexico in order to deter encroachment. By the 1790s, more than half of Spain's expenditures on behalf of its colonies went for defense. But the presence of troops under the command of peninsulares spawned new suspicions among colonials and heightened criollo distrust of Spaniards.

With a mind toward consolidating its rule and raising revenue, the Bourbons also expelled the powerful Jesuit order from the New World in 1767. The Jesuits, who answered directly to the Pope, had been materially successful in the colonies, amassing property, managing lucrative missions, and educating sons of the criollo elite in prestigious schools. The expulsion enriched the crown and weakened a potentially disloyal wing of the Church; but it further annoyed the wealthy criollos, who appreciated the Jesuits' work. Many of the twelve hundred priests expelled were criollos themselves, and some became outspoken critics of the Bourbons. In a second sense, too, the crown may have weakened its position with the expulsion: The Jesuits and the Church were bulwarks against new ideas filtering in from northern Europe. Enlightenment notions of limited monarchy, constitutionalism, and natural rights, which inspired revolutions in France and (North) America, also found their way into criollo heads, primarily through books made more available through the weakening of the Church.

All told, then, the Bourbon reforms effectively drove a wedge between whites born in the New World and those from Spain. After nearly three hundred years of colonialism, elites in the late eighteenth century had little loyalty to the Spanish king. The arrival of Bourbon bureaucrats made them receptive to new ideas—ideas of governing themselves and creating their own national identities.

Independence and Its Aftermath

Latin America's wars of independence were triggered by events in Europe. After the French Revolution of 1789, a series of conflicts ensued that weakened links between the colonies and the motherland, and demonstrated Spain's second-rate military status. In 1796 the British warred against Spain and blockaded its ports, effectively shattering the Bourbon system of mercantilist trade. In 1806, without authorization, British Admiral Sir Home Popham seized the viceregal capital of Buenos Aires, again causing chaos and revealing the vulnerability of the Spanish empire. Although ousted by Spanish colonials, the British had unwittingly helped set in motion forces for independence.

All-encompassing chaos ensued in 1807–1808, when Napoleon sent an army into Spain in order to attack Portugal, which had refused to abide by his continental system prohibiting trade with Britain. The French invasion put the Portuguese crown to flight: Boarding British naval ships, the royal house and thousands of subjects sailed to Rio de Janeiro and made it their temporary imperial capital. Napoleon, meanwhile, refused to withdraw his troops from Spain itself. He removed the new Bourbon king, Ferdinand VII, and placed his own brother on the throne. Castile's religious peasantry soon rebelled, bogging French troops down in a protracted and difficult war.

Throughout Latin America, Spaniards determined to rule in the name of Ferdinand. But the uncertainty of political events in Spain caused peninsular and criollo divisions to explode. In almost every important colonial city, rival cabildos and juntas, or governing bodies, formed. Each claimed authority to rule in the name of the king. Nowhere was this divisiveness more acute than in Buenos Aires, where the criollo-dominated militia that had ousted the British reassembled to usurp Spanish authority. Backed by rich merchants who wanted to liberalize trade policies, the militia soon became an army of independence, and in 1810 a new "United Provinces of La Plata" was formed.

Buenos Aires sent its army inland to clear other areas of Spanish rule (and to exert its own control). Yet although Latin Americans could drive the Spaniards away without much difficulty, criollo unity proved elusive. Regional interests predominated, and it was soon apparent that an independent South America would feature many nations. Inland elites wanted nothing to do with the new leaders in Buenos Aires. They raised their own army and soon declared Paraguayan independence (1811). Uruguay, too, broke away, and even the area that today is known as Argentina was not fully integrated until the mid-nineteenth century. Despite this, Argentinians played a prominent role in liberating the southern half of the continent from Spain. José de San Martín, a criollo who had studied in Spain and fought the French until 1812, returned home, organized a tightly disciplined army, and marched it across the steep Andes into Chile and Peru. He helped found these new nations with the aid of local insurgents, although elites, especially in Peru, were badly divided and suspicious of his intentions.

San Martín is recognized as one of two great independence heroes in South America. He met the other, his northern counterpart, in Guayaquil, Ecuador, in 1822. Símon Bolívar was the criollo son of a well-to-do merchant. During much of the 1810s he waged relentless and bloody warfare against Spaniards in New Granada (areas that would become Colombia and Venezuela). At the Battle of Boyacá, in August 1819, his forces finally turned the tide, mopping up remaining resistance with the help of foreign mercenaries during the next couple of years. At their 1822 meeting, San Martín deferred to Bolívar for the final operation inland—to an area that adopted the Liberator's name, Bolivia.

Although sometimes compared with revolutionaries and other national heroes, such as America's George Washington, neither San Martín nor Bolívar were visionaries or sons of the Enlightenment. Although they were certainly cognizant of Enlightenment ideas, both men favored monarchism and remained staunchly conservative. As criollos, they viewed whites as superior, and Indians and mestizos as incapable of self-rule. Indeed, they and others who waged the wars of independence struggled for equality at the top—between Spaniards and criollos, not for all citizens. And even though San Martín decreed changes in the status of Indians in Peru and elsewhere (decrees uniformly ignored by local elites), he spent the remainder of his life where he felt most comfortable: Europe. Independence movements in South America brought no meaningful social change. In fact, for most mestizos and Indians, it was as though nothing had happened.

In Mexico, however, a genuine social revolution briefly exploded. In 1810 a criollo priest, jealous of peninsular Spaniards and longing for criollo equality, inadvertently launched a race war. Miguel Hidalgo, as every Mexican schoolchild knows, rang the bells at his church in the small town of Delores on September 16, and rallied his Indian parishioners with a moving speech. Under the banner of the Virgin of Guadalupe he led an "army" (it was more like a mob) in sacking a nearby city and killing its Spanish inhabitants (including an intendant), who had barricaded themselves in a granary. In October his rebel forces, now seventy thousand strong, approached Mexico City. Although he could have easily defeated the small Spanish force that stood in his path, Hidalgo inexplicably ordered a retreat at the Battle of Monte de las Cruces, and his insurrection disintegrated as quickly as it had coalesced. He was hunted down, tried, and executed by the Inquisition.

Hidalgo's revolt is evidence of the deep rifts that defined colonial society. Whites could not conceive of dark-skinned peoples either as citizens or as equals. To the educated, wealthy "people of reason," the Indian-blooded majority was brutish, irrational, and dangerous. It was to be feared and controlled, not liberated. When Hidalgo's dark-skinned legions began to kill both peninsulares and criollos, all whites united in order to suppress the rebellion. Mexico's long struggle for independence subsequently mutated. New, small guerrilla forces were mustered under mestizos, and continued to face the opposition of both local and Spanish whites. In 1820, when Spain's government did a volte-face and embraced liberal constitutionalism, a criollo army officer, Agustín de Iturbide, switched sides and marched his troops into Mexico City to establish a new empire.

Iturbide's break with Spain, unlike that attempted by Hidalgo, was anti-revolutionary. He issued a pronouncement, called the Plan of Iguala, in which he guaranteed the legal privileges and status of the rich, his army, and the church. In an elaborate coronation he was named Agustín I, Emperor of Mexico. Criollos supported him in large part because of his fiscal policies, which favored them. They displaced their peninsular rivals, who a few years later were thrown out of the country. Like independence in South America, then, Mexico's independence brought change only at the top.

Brazil obtained independence from Portugal in a similarly conservative fashion, and without bloodshed. Government in the plantation-dominated colony had always been weak, and late-eighteenth-century reforms under the Marquis de Pombal were a faint echo of the Bourbon restructuring in Spanish domains. Discoveries of gold and diamonds in the south-central region of Minas Gerais (General Mines) had shifted the population and made Rio de Janeiro an important city. When the Portuguese royal family arrived from Lisbon in 1808, they soon transformed the city. An influx of Portuguese migrants and money provided reason and resources for an urban face lift. In 1816, when many in Europe expected King João to return, he opted to remain in Brazil and elevate the colony to a status equal to that of the motherland. Brewing discontent on both sides of the Atlantic forced his hand, however, and the royal court departed for Lisbon in 1821, leaving

João's son, Pedro, as regent. During the following year, colonial planters persuaded Pedro to have himself crowned as emperor of a fully independent Brazil while British naval might prevented a Portuguese invasion.

New nationhood early in the nineteenth century may have changed little in terms of how people lived in Latin America, but it denoted a sharp break with the institutional past. Strong government disappeared, and the Church also lost a great deal of its influence. When scholars attribute today's formidable executive branch powers to a distant colonial history, they are reaching. In the wake of Independence, state authority wilted and Latin America lapsed into regionalism. Many factors were involved in this process. The central one was that the rich took Independence as a reason to quit paying taxes. In nearly every new nation, after the Spaniards departed, tax revenues plummeted and government coffers ran dry. In the 1820s many Latin American nations turned to European banks for loans. With a lack of revenues and declining exports, however, almost none of those nations could raise the hard currency necessary to repay the loans. Defaults followed, and credit dried up. From the late 1820s until midcentury, there were exceedingly few big financial transactions between Europe or the United States and Latin America. Thus, theorists who envision a "world system" lasting from the colonial epoch to the present day must also make a grand, ahistorical stretch. In mid-nineteenth-century Latin America, political instability and economic isolation were the order of the day.

Despite this stagnation and chaos, criollo elites did well for themselves. Their peninsular rivals either willingly migrated home to Spain or were driven away. Powerful merchants continued to dominate the economic life of each region or country, and under various legal mechanisms many acquired enormous tracts of land. *Latifundio,* or the concentration of land in the hands of a few, had already been well established during the colonial period. Huge semifeudal estates, called *haciendas,* dominated much of central Mexico and elsewhere. In the wake of Independence, the rich, whether liberals or conservatives, exercised political power to advance their own wealth. In Argentina, for example, a legal mechanism of Roman origin, the Law of Emphyteusis (1826), equipped merchants to buy up much of the pampas and diversify their wealth by moving into ranching. Elsewhere in Latin America, elites acquired Church properties—which were a major incentive for their allowing liberalism to triumph. In the post-Independence era, enormous loans were extended by the Church to elites, many of which were never repaid.

Because many would-be colonial continuities with the present were broken during the Independence period, most pieces of the historical puzzle that help explain contemporary Latin America originated after the mid-nineteenth century. Demographically, this should not surprise us. At the time of Independence, there were fewer than 25 million persons in all of Latin America; today there are 0.5 billion. The complexities of today's society and its political and economic structures are myriad, and differ exceedingly from those that predominated in a simpler and long-ago age. The clearest beginnings of modern Latin America rest in the late nineteenth and early twentieth centuries.

4 Progress and Populism

Although Latin America was independent by the mid-1820s, it was only after the mid-nineteenth century that the region began to redevelop close economic ties with the outside world. Trade increased and investment capital began to enter the region from Europe and to a lesser extent from the United States. The mantra of the age was "Order and Progress," as the wealthy pursued new economic opportunities, primarily by building railroads and exporting mineral and agricultural goods. Slowly, too, dictatorial regimes established political stability. These changes were striking against the backdrop of midcentury disunity and isolation.

Nation-building in the Nineteenth Century

Independence brought political instability to Latin America. Once Spanish authority had disappeared, rich criollo elites could not arrive at a consensus about who should govern, or how. A small number of wealthy, light-skinned men constituted a political class in each nation. Nearly everywhere, they split into two camps, called liberals (or federalists) and conservatives. The liberals entertained ideas bequeathed them by the Enlightenment: notions of equality, rights protected by constitutions, separation of powers, and decentralized, or federal-style, rule. Many looked to the United States for inspiration. Conservatives clung to the region's Hispanic heritage, proffering strongly centralized authority, hierarchy, and order—often by endorsing monarchism. The confusion and disruption wrought by the wars of independence weighed heavily on their minds; they feared that without strong leadership their tender nations would flounder into anarchy.

Liberals and conservatives also were divided regarding the role of the Church. Though no Latin American nation unfrocked Catholicism in favor of religious plurality, liberals sought to weaken the status and role of the Church. Predictably, bishops and priests rallied to the cause of the conservatives. In time, the Church became the foremost issue over which politicized elites clashed.

With deep divisions among the wealthy, bankrupt national treasuries, and large military forces, what transpired in nearly all of former Spanish America comes as no surprise. From Mexico to Chile, popular presidents (usually acclaimed heroes of Independence) who had held office only a few years were toppled by barracks coups. Competitive groups of liberals and conservatives plotted against each other and regularly overthrew their rivals by marching out the troops. Officeholders, certain that their time was limited, despaired of providing clean government and concentrated instead on enriching themselves. Only in Brazil was there anything akin to stability, and that was because of the continuation of a Portuguese-bequeathed monarchy.

Elite disunity contributed to a process of fragmentation in much of Latin America, as the wealthy refused to share authority. Once-unified Central America broke into pieces, and many interior regions of South America remained isolated. By the 1830s, however, a new kind of leader began to emerge: the caudillo. Neither liberals nor conservatives, caudillos were not much concerned with political ideology. They ruled by personalism—that is, by building a network of loyalties and rewarding their associates as they acquired power. Historians have long viewed caudillos in a negative light, regarding them as rank opportunists. But their rule also can be interpreted more positively: In rising above the petty rivalries and ongoing ideological debates of localized elites, caudillos expanded state authority and held nations together.

The two most famous caudillos were at opposite ends of what was once Spain's vast empire: Juan Manuel de Rosas of Argentina, and Antonio López de Santa Anna of Mexico. Rosas dominated Buenos Aires and the surrounding countryside from the early 1830s until 1852. The son of a military officer and a wealthy gentlewoman, as a young adult he saw firsthand the nearly two decades of intermittent strife that frayed Argentine society and disrupted business and commerce. Accordingly, like other caudillos, he placed a high premium on order. Rosas was, in many ways, a vintage despot—fearful of the masses and willing to hold them at bay through state terror. Known as the "Restorer of the Laws" because he made people obey authority, in reality he was a law unto himself. His often arbitrary punishment of criminals and political enemies was meted out by henchmen known as the *mazorca*—a term derived from the Spanish *más horca*, meaning "more hangings." The preferred method of slaying was a slit to the throat (predictable, given the cattle culture of the nearby pampas); and headless corpses routinely appeared in the streets of Buenos Aires, with the severed heads swaying from poles or city balconies. This controlled violence had its proponents: Rosas's regime enjoyed the support of the merchant-ranching elite, and for the most part, of the Church, both of which were fed up with the near anarchy and persistent crime.

Similarly, in Mexico, Antonio López de Santa Anna was fundamentally authoritarian, though his eclectic mix of politics defies the tidy category of "conservative." Ruling around the same time as Rosas (ca. 1829 to 1853), he dominated the political life of his country, serving as its president on eleven separate occasions. He rose to prominence when he rebelled in support of a liberal, only to overthrow the same man—in the name of conservatism—two years later. In 1836, Santa Anna abolished federalism and introduced a new constitutional order that effectively centralized power and established a military dictatorship. Shrewd and intelligent, he often played liberals and conservatives against each other to further his personal ambitions.

Santa Anna's name is generally recognized by students of U.S. history; given his failed attempts to hold Texas and his inability to defeat invading American armies in the war of 1846–1848, he is often portrayed in U.S. history textbooks as a buffoon. The 1836 rebellion in Texas was nearly inevitable, with American newcomers outnumbering Mexicans there by 7 to 1 (Texas—then a region of Mexico—was being overrun by unwanted American immigrants). Overwhelmingly Southerners and resentful of Mexican restrictions on slavery, the Anglo "Texans" revolted and confronted Santa Anna with a logistical nightmare—rebellion on a periphery a thousand miles away, with desert in-between, his army ill-trained, and the government nearly bankrupt. In many ways, it's a wonder that Santa Anna even made it into the wasteland with a viable force. Mythology has badly twisted the historical record. Many Texan heroes were, in fact, seedy characters: Sam Houston had mental problems and had attempted suicide; James Bowie was a former slave trader; and William Travis had abandoned his pregnant, teenage wife without cause in Alabama. Yet there is no denying that these men could kill; Santa Anna's demoralized army fared badly, incurring enormous losses at the Alamo and suffering a humiliating defeat at the Battle of San Jacinto, where the Mexican dictator himself was captured.

Despite the fiasco, ten years later it seemed that only the famous caudillo could save Mexico from the next threat: an American invasion. In early 1846, U.S. President James K. Polk sent an army into disputed territory, deliberately triggering a border incident that he could use to justify war. Making the dubious claim that "American blood has been shed on American soil" (a young congressman, Abraham Lincoln, tried to embarrass the warmongering leader with his "show us the spot" resolutions—for which he lost reelection), Polk authorized a three-pronged attack. Santa Anna and the Mexicans held their own against one overland invasion, but the determined advance of a seaboard army under Zachary Taylor proved overwhelming. In the climactic battle of Chapultepec, Americans stormed the walls of Mexico's Military Academy and forced final surrender (a few cadets cast themselves off the cliffside rather than face defeat—Mexico's famous Niños Héroes, or Boy Heroes). A disgusted Santa Anna, watching through his field glasses nearby, reputedly muttered, "God is a Yankee." The real goal of the American invasion—territorial expansion—was achieved when Mexico was forced to cede 40 percent of its territory to the United States, in the Treaty of Guadalupe-Hidalgo. Mexico's defeat was made more bitter by the news, barely a year later, that gold had been discovered in the former Mexican territory of Sierra Nevada, California—by a Mexican.

Santa Anna and Rosas relied on their instincts and charisma in attempting to bring their fractured countries together, yet neither fully succeeded. Although he exerted considerable influence with caudillos in the provinces, Rosas, who fancied himself the "Supreme Chief of the Argentine Confederation," ultimately broke with the interior over trade disputes. A brief civil war in 1851–1852 led to his ouster. In the wake of humiliating defeat at the hands of the United States, Santa Anna exerted regal authority over a disenchanted land. Addressed as His Serene Highness, he briefly committed Mexico to renewed militarism, bloating the size of the army and employing pageantry in an effort to rekindle national pride and patriotism.

Rosas and Santa Anna, like other caudillos, were eventually displaced by rich liberal intellectuals who resented their usurpation of the political arena and abuse of power (in that order). These equally ambitious men embraced nation-building on their own terms, crafting new constitutions throughout Latin America in midcentury and consolidating political rule through centralized government, though they often espoused federalism. In Buenos Aires, dissident intellectuals known as the Generation of 1837 gained control after Rosas, and under the auspices of an 1853 constitution, they finally and firmly united all of Argentina. Their foremost leader was Domingo F. Sarmiento—one of only a few early-nineteenth-century Latin Americans to acquire international acclaim (he had written a book, the title of which translates into English as *Civilization and Barbarism*, decrying the violence and ignorance of knife-fighting cowboys on the pampas). As president (1868–1874), Sarmiento built on his reputation and became renowned for promoting public schools.

In Mexico, a similar core of so-called liberal purists—staunchly idealistic, inflexible, and determined to remake their country—wrested power from Santa Anna. In 1857 they drafted a constitution under which the status of the army and the Church were diminished. Outraged priests and army officers inspired a popular revolt, and a bloody civil war ensued. The liberals and their flag bearer, Benito Juárez, emerged triumphant in 1861, largely by wooing rich landowners into an alliance by selling them Church property at cut-rate prices. Perceiving Mexico as vulnerable to exploitation, the French invaded; there followed a strange, interim period of rule by imperial France. Not until 1867, after a decade of warfare, was the ideological struggle resolved as Juárez restored constitutional law and began the process of forming a cogent national government for Mexico.

By the 1870s and 1880s, much of formerly Spanish America had found its way back to a modicum of political stability. Even the Andean nations, notorious for drafting new constitutions every few years, adopted long-lasting documents (Peru's ninth constitution in 1867, and Bolivia's tenth, in 1878, both endured into the mid-twentieth century). But why did the liberal model—as opposed to monarchism, for example—triumph? A large part of the answer rests in the fact that liberalism, more than kingship, sanctioned the participation of a small political class (rich, light-skinned males) that insisted on playing a role in government. A role no doubt was also played by the fact that Latin Americans lived in the shadow of the United States, and men like Sarmiento and Juárez were well aware of the rise of the American political example. Separation of powers, constitutionalism, bills of rights, and electoral politics were increasingly the order of the day.

Yet while constitutions and speeches promised equality before the law, late-nineteenth-century Latin American liberalism was a far cry from true republicanism. Mass participation in government was neither encouraged nor tolerated. There was a profound gap between liberal rhetoric and practice. Constitutions generally gave adult males the right to vote; but in elections, only the desires of well-to-do landowners counted. Rich criollos, no matter what their ideological orientation, were not about to share power or grant genuine rights to dark-skinned mestizos and Indians.

The momentum for embracing liberal ideas on paper in the late nineteenth century was, however, considerable. Monarchism in Brazil faltered as a result, although the political dynamics of the previously Portuguese colony remained distinctive. After establishing his throne with the support of the aristocracy in 1822, Pedro I governed until his abdication in 1831, when he returned home to Portugal. His son, Pedro II, ascended to the crown once of age, in 1840, and held it for nearly fifty years, until Brazil officially became a republic in 1889. The monarchy was never strong. Local sugar (and later, coffee) planters exercised power through a related parliamentary system, and regionalism was a hallmark of political life. The weak central government maintained close links with the rich and the army, which helped it suppress numerous revolts and keep the enormous country from splintering. Elites and army officers, finding little reason to maintain the monarchy (especially after the final demise of its symbiotic institution, slavery, in 1888), penned an 1891 constitution that gave lip service to political rights; however, literacy tests, land ownership, and other barriers to enfranchisement effectively preserved the political arena as their private domain.

The trappings of political modernity, as well as nascent centralization and renewed stability, coincided with economic changes that enveloped all of Latin America. As reflected in the shibboleth "Order and Progress"— which is still emblazoned on Brazil's national flag—many elite and intellectuals anticipated a new era of technological and rational social management that would alleviate poverty, bypass the legacies of "backward" Indian traditionalism, and usher their nations into a new age.

Many of the ideas related to these expectations came from positivism, the predominant late-nineteenth-century ideology that prophesied human triumph, through science, over centuries-old social ills. Positivists believed that the application of presumed scientific principles to human relationships would solve societal problems. Had not the human mind, after all, begun to unlock the mysteries of physics and disease? Why could it not also deduce the causes of sexual deviance or criminality? The father of positivism, French philosopher Auguste Comte, had taken some of the Enlightenment's ideas concerning human nature and religion and carried them beyond rational frontiers. Glorifying great minds instead of deities, he eventually declared himself to be the High Priest of Humanity. He envisioned a postmortem heaven of Holy Woods, and a hell containing— among others—his ex-wife. Comte's theories had become popular reading the world over, and Latin America's rich soon embraced the triumphant cause of human "progress."

At the same time, economic change was beginning to take place on the ground, largely without structured management. Technology was revolutionizing the world in the late nineteenth century—the age of science and steel. With the introduction of telegraph lines and steam-powered vessels, the world seemed a much smaller place. Demographics also played a role in undercutting Latin American economic and political regionalism, as the region's population quickly grew. Booming populations in the United States and Europe also required more food and more plentiful resources. The factories of the second industrial revolution created a seemingly incessant demand for a diverse range of raw materials. Between 1850 and 1913, Latin American exports rose by roughly 1,000 percent.

This was a time of commodities, when nations and regions found niches in the export economy through mineral resources or cash crops. Coffee, a well-established export crop in Brazil (which had sustained a good volume of foreign trade during the mid-nineteenth century), also was grown for export in Colombia and Central America: Americans and Europeans had come to prefer the bean over tea leaf. Sugar, which had migrated into the Caribbean during the eighteenth century, dominated the Cuban economy.

Chilean copper mines were opened, and Bolivian tin production soared. Henequén, a fiber used for rope, created an export boom in the Yucatán peninsula of Mexico until it was replaced by synthetic fibers. Mexico also became a leading oil producer, supplying a quarter of the world's crude by 1910. In the late 1920s, Venezuela's oil fields began to take off. Yet export growth was uneven; and although significant, economic change through trade was by no means all-encompassing. Some nations, such as Peru, which had been a major exporter of guano (bird droppings used for fertilizer), saw their exports decline. Others, such as Paraguay and Honduras, remained largely isolated; the latter was still a couple of decades away from becoming a "banana republic."

The nation most transformed by trade was Argentina: Its pampas became a granary for Europe. Total acres under cultivation (primarily wheat) rose from 1.5 million in 1872 to more than 10.0 million by 1895. At the turn of the century, ten thousand miles of railroad track fanned out from Buenos Aires to nearly every corner of the fertile plains. As in nearby Uruguay, wool production also flourished, though the proliferation of sheep led to oversupply by the 1880s. Fortunately for both countries, though not for the sheep, refrigeration solved the problem, after which mutton exports rose. Argentina's export economy made it rich: By 1910, its per capita wealth matched that of the United States and much of western Europe (today, it is still considerably wealthier than the rest of South America).

Argentina and (to a lesser extent) Brazil were also transformed in the late nineteenth century by what they "imported": immigrants. Southern Europeans, especially Italians, poured into both countries in search of new lives and wealth. In Brazil, immigrant labor came to dominate the workforce on coffee plantations, though exploitation kept most newcomers poor. Immigrants in Argentina generally remained in the port city of Buenos Aires, where they helped turn it into a cosmopolitan "Paris of the Americas." The tango, a dramatic dance associated with a genre of song about unrequited love, is Brazil's most famous cultural contribution. The outbreak of World War I in 1914 halted the incoming migration, and along with disruptions in trade, cast Argentina into an economic depression.

The late nineteenth century not only brought a sharp rise in commodities and exports but also the return of foreign capital to Latin America. Much foreign investment was direct, meaning that foreigners bought and built physical properties. Certainly the most significant of these were railroads. European capital (primarily British) financed the vast majority of the lines in Brazil and the Southern Cone; and Americans underwrote many of the railroads in Mexico and the Caribbean basin. Unlike the gridwork of crisscrossing tracks in Europe and the United States, links in Latin America reflected the nature of the export economy, and most lines ran from mines or agricultural areas directly to the coast. Export-related industries, such as glassworks and canning factories, as well as port facilities, were also financed by foreign capital. Governments borrowed heavily, too (especially Argentina). About a third of the capital that poured into Latin America in the late nineteenth century came by way of bond issues underwritten by European banks and purchased by private investors. And where their money went, so too did European and American businessmen. The number of foreigners visiting and residing in Latin America rose dramatically after the 1870s. They spent most of their time in cities, and interacted with rich locals who could speak French and English, and embraced the latest trends and fashions from New York or Paris.

At the beginning of the twentieth century, the United States set out to redress one of the world's most obvious spatial anomalies—the lack of a useful link between the globe's two largest bodies of water. Unable to convince Colombia to authorize construction of a U.S.-sponsored canal, Washington intervened on behalf of Panamanian separatists, and signed a treaty with the newly formed state of Panama in 1903. The Panama canal, fully funded by the U.S. government, was a Herculean accomplishment ten years in the making. In the face of mountains, mud slides, and tropical disease, American engineers managed a workforce of African-descended Caribbeans (five thousand of whom died during the project), routing the channel through a natural lake and up and down slopes through an ingenuous series of giant locks. The Panama Canal became the foremost symbol of American influence in Latin America during the twentieth century.

Vying with European powers for seafaring domination, the United States also began to intervene directly in regional politics. In 1904, President Theodore Roosevelt added a corollary to the Monroe Doctrine—the 1823 pronouncement against European interference in the western hemisphere—declaring that the United States had a right to police Latin American countries when they failed to keep their political houses in order. A lack of stability has never been good for business; and although order had largely been established in the region, in some places it did not seem to be happening fast enough. Various Caribbean and Central American nations close to the United States became the targets of U.S. military intervention during the early twentieth century. Indeed, because the presence of U.S. Marines in Haiti, Nicaragua, and elsewhere tended to only temporarily calm political storms, periodic occupations became the norm. The United States also attempted to foster hemispheric cooperation, and promote business, through the formation of the Pan American Union in 1907. U.S. concern for a country, and its willingness to take action there, was of course proportionate to its economic interests. No Latin American nation was of so vital an interest to the United States as Mexico, where the advent of trade and foreign investment triggered a cataclysmic revolt.

Mexico: Revolution and Reform

Economic changes in the late nineteenth century aggravated tensions in Mexico. In 1876, four years after Benito Juárez died of a heart attack, another liberal named Porfirio Díaz secured the presidency. Díaz dominated Mexican political life for the next thirty-five years, giving the era his name—the Porfiriato. He filled his cabinet with Mexican-trained positivists, called *científicos* (Scientists), who viewed the dictatorship as an opportunity to establish order and bring progress. It was a kind of progress, however, that produced a large underclass. Poverty in the countryside worsened even as foreign capital and technology transformed the cities.

The Porfirian elite wooed foreign investors to Mexico. Cabinet ministers overhauled regulations, dropping tariffs and standardizing currency. Awarded generous concessions, foreign (mostly U.S.) companies began building railroads during the 1880s, including the 1,200-mile Central Mexican line running from the capital to El Paso, Texas. A concomitant drop in transportation prices made large-scale industrial mining feasible, and huge lead, zinc, and copper pits soon were opened in the Sierra Madre. In addition to henequén in the Yucatán, cash crops such as rubber, cotton, coffee, and sugar flourished on reinvigorated haciendas. Changes in property laws allowed foreigners and rich Mexicans to acquire more and more land, often at the expense of Indian villages. The national police force, the Rurales, had a reputation for ruthlessness in suppressing peasant dissent and enforcing vagrancy laws, commonly instituted throughout Latin America in the late nineteenth century to discourage the poor from congregating in public spaces. Poverty, meanwhile, increased. Per capita production of corn, the staple crop for the masses, dropped from 282 kilograms at the beginning of the Porfiriato to 144 kilograms near its end. Malnutrition plagued the burgeoning rural populace.

In Porfirian cities, new services improved the quality of life for a lucky few; a small middle class and a minuscule elite were soon awash in unprecedented comfort. Like Buenos Aires, Mexico City became a world-class metropolis, with a Paris-inspired street renovation project creating the Champs-Elysées of Latin America: the Paseo de la Reforma, its broad lanes graced with tree-lined traffic islands, electric lighting, and ornate statues. The rich also enjoyed the latest Parisian fashions, being enamored with things foreign. Horse racing replaced bullfighting, boxing edged out cockfighting, and bicycling gained popularity over horseback riding among the well-to-do, who scorned the "backward" traditions of the masses. At the plush Jockey Club in downtown Mexico City, the rich sometimes entertained themselves by tossing coins from the balconies to the scrambling poor below. The image of an out-of-touch clique perched atop a volcano is not inappropriate for Porfirian Mexico. When the dictator laid plans to simultaneously celebrate the national centennial and his eightieth birthday in 1910, he must have had little inkling of the storm about to engulf the land.

Yet cracks had been appearing in the Porfirian system at an ever increasing pace since 1900. A small number of middle-class discontents had organized themselves into "liberal clubs" that were concerned primarily with limiting the role of the Church and rectifying the government's apparent disregard for the 1857 constitution's anticlerical provisions. Out of this modest movement emerged a clique of visionary and angry young men, led by Ricardo Flores Magón, who provided a much broader critique of the regime, disseminated via a small newsletter entitled *Regeneración*. After repeated incarceration and harassment, Flores Magón and his cohorts withdrew to the United States, where they continued their agitation with the help of American socialists and liberal sympathizers. Their calls for political and labor reform in Mexico struck a cord—so much so, that the Mexican government, with the aid of authorities in Washington, moved to suppress the movement by repeatedly imprisoning Flores Magón, effectively preventing him from playing a role in subsequent events.

In Mexico, financial uncertainties (especially after the Wall Street crash of 1907) and drought in the northern states fueled growing unrest. In June 1906, a strike at the Canenea Copper Company mine near the U.S. border triggered bloody reprisals from deputized American ranchers riding with the Arizona Rangers. The willingness of the Mexican government to sanction the murder of its own citizens by property-protecting gringos outraged many. Calls for change proliferated, especially from the growing middle classes but also from a minority of elites. Díaz made minor policy adjustments but moved far too slowly to stay ahead of the train. In fact, the aged dictator blundered badly in 1908, when, aware of the signs of trouble, he suggested a willingness to retire and then immediately reversed his decision.

After Díaz's sensational announcement, which he made in an interview to an American news magazine, opposition coalesced around would-be rivals, including Francisco I. Madero. The son of a wealthy northern *hacendado*, Madero, at first glance, seemed something of a joke. Short in stature and shrill-voiced, he had produced no offspring—an embarrassment in a society infused with machismo. While studying in France, he had embraced the spiritualism of Kardec, and while in the United States, he grew fond of American-style electoral democracy. He naively believed that political reforms could preserve order in Mexico; and when he toured the nation with a message of change, middle-class Mexicans flocked to hear him speak.

Taking no chances, Díaz placed Madero under house arrest in order to facilitate his own victory in the fraud-ridden 1910 elections. Surprisingly, with much to lose, after the elections Madero sought justice. He fled to

Texas, and like Flores Magón before him, issued a pronouncement inciting revolution. By winter 1910–1911, the first serious armed insurgents appeared in the mountains of Mexico. Pascual Orozco, a semiskilled hacienda worker, soon made headway with bands of guerrillas in the northern Sierra Madre. Orozco captured the imaginations of Mexicans as news of his daring raids and ambushes spread. On one occasion, after stripping dead soldiers of their clothing, he taunted the dictator with the message: "here are the wrappers; send more tamales." In fact, the limitations of the regime's military components soon became all too apparent. When the border entrepôt of Ciudad Juárez fell to the rebels, Díaz realized that his time was up. He left his nation for a comfortable retirement in France. Madero, the idol of the people, soon arrived to enthusiastic throngs in the capital, and after several months of a transitional government, assumed the presidency in the wake of Mexico's first reasonably clean national elections.

The subsequent twists and turns of the revolutionary saga read like something out of a soap opera (albeit without women). The coalition that brought Madero to power soon unraveled. Orozco was miffed at his failure to obtain high administrative office. Other rebels to the south, under the leadership of an Indian fighter named Emiliano Zapata, warily accepted Madero's hollow promises of land reform and handed in their arms. Ironically, nascent rebel forces were disarmed by a still-functioning Porfirian army under Madero—a recipe for betrayal. In February 1913, with the complicity of the U.S. ambassador, a general named Victoriano Huerta engineered a military coup that brought him to power and resulted in Madero's untimely death.

Huerta's dictatorship met with immediate opposition. Francisco "Pancho" Villa, a sidekick of the now-discredited Orozco, raised insurgents in the north. Villa's life once had been spared by Madero before a Huerta-assembled firing squad, and there was no doubt about his political proclivities. To the south, Zapata, leading Indians intent on regaining their stolen land, summarily executed Huerta's peace emissaries. The regime attempted a modicum of political and even economic reform, but its efforts to win popular approval went unrewarded, and Huerta soon turned the country into a military camp. However, even a quarter million draftees proved of little use against the burgeoning numbers of inspired revolutionaries, and by mid-1914 Huerta had to leave Mexico. Ironically, in the end Huerta had been betrayed by the United States. Woodrow Wilson, who took office just as the general assumed power, refused to recognize his government, and attempted to hasten its demise by an ill-advised invasion of Mexico's port city of Veracruz. When Huerta fell, Washington scrambled to find alternatives—for political order in Mexico was rapidly disintegrating.

Political coalitions emerged in various camps that had opposed Huerta, including those of Villa and Zapata. A third faction, largely based in the northeast, coalesced around a lawyer and former Porfirian landowner named Venustiano Carranza. Although fundamentally conservative, Carranza was a former Madero supporter who had refused, though with some hesitation, to cooperate with the Huerta regime. He enjoyed the support of many middle-class Mexicans who were alarmed at the chaos engulfing their society and the rise of Indian armies under "Attilas" like Zapata. Fortunately for Carranza, who now designated himself the "First Chief of the Revolution," both Villa and Zapata demonstrated limited interest in establishing national political order, and failed to coordinate their military activities in the face of Carranza's growing military force under the talented general Alvaro Obregón.

Using the latest technology—newly tested on the battlefields in Europe—Obregón engaged and decisively defeated Villa's army in spring 1915. Soon his forces began the agonizingly slow process of consolidating the First Chief's control over the country. The United States, preferring Carranza to the alternatives and confident of his ultimate victory, extended diplomatic recognition to his government. An enraged Villa struck back, raiding the border town of Columbus, New Mexico, where he engaged a detachment of U.S. cavalry. The confrontation prompted a second intervention by the United States: An expeditionary force under John J. "Blackjack" Pershing scoured northern Mexico in search of Villa, now characterized in the U.S. press as a "bandit," without success.

Carranza and Obregón eventually persuaded Villa to lay down his arms. The charismatic Villa remained a viable threat even in his forced retirement, and he was assassinated a few years later with the apparent complicity of Mexican authorities. In 1919, the government successfully plotted the ambush and slaying of the idol of the poor, Emiliano Zapata. Films of his corpse were displayed throughout the predominantly Indian south, helping to quell the revolts and bring order to the countryside. In 1920, when Obregón decided to oust the dictatorial Carranza and assume the presidency himself, Mexico emerged from a decade of bloodshed that had left one million Mexicans—nearly 6 percent of the population—dead.

In the mid-twentieth century, historians regarded Mexico's revolution as the harbinger of reform. The reality, however, is more nuanced. During the 1920s, Obregón and his successor Plutarco Calles centralized political power and amassed personal fortunes. A new political elite, drawn in part from the middle class, intermingled with the Porfirian rich and ensconced themselves in the leadership of a mushrooming government bureaucracy. Professional and educated, a majority of these upwardly mobile Mexicans were secularized and favored the removal of the Catholic Church from the political arena. This process, which harked back to the anticlericalism of the prerevolutionary liberal clubs, antagonized much of the devout peasantry. The Cristero rebellion of the late 1920s was a bloody affair that saw

Mexico's army wage war against guerrilla bands of zealots who fought under the banner "Viva Cristo Rey!" (Long Live Christ the King!).

Although successful in suppressing the Catholic rebellion, Mexico's supposedly "revolutionary" government enjoyed only nominal popular support. By the early 1930s, large segments of society viewed the increasingly intrusive bureaucracy with suspicion. Calles's continued harassment of the Church even antagonized segments of the middle class, and devout businessmen eventually formed a Catholic-based political organ, the Partido Acción Nacional, or PAN. The rural poor also were largely alienated by the continued lack of democracy and the regime's limited efforts at land reform. Without meaningful ballots or scrutiny by an independent press, bureaucrats were enriching themselves through shady deals and government contracts. During the early 1930s an ambitious road-building program facilitated graft not unlike that associated with the construction of railroads under the Porfirian regime.

In 1934, Plutarco Calles, who had come to control the government through a series of presidential puppets (one who failed to do his bidding learned about his own resignation by reading it in the government's newspaper), promoted Lázaro Cárdenas for president. Mexicans disinterestedly followed his ascent into the palace, and were surprised to find that this puppet was different. Idealistic and driven, Cárdenas engineered a break with his self-serving mentor. Recognizing the disappointed aspirations of the older generation of Mexicans who had fought in the revolution, he sought to undertake a series of sweeping reforms. But Calles did not go easily. The rift between the two men and their supporters became public, and only after an arduous political battle was Cárdenas able to force the dictatorial Calles into exile in the United States.

Lázaro Cárdenas is one of several renowned Latin American leaders who are sometimes referred to as "populists." Like any label, *populism* has severe limitations. However, two of its features are relevant to this discussion. First, populists appealed to the masses—a new phenomenon in Latin America. Second, they practiced economic nationalism—that is, state control of critical industries—to curtail the influence of foreign capital and enrich their own people. The two features, predictably, went hand in hand. Even under the populists many Latin Americans remained divorced from the political process—especially the isolated, rural poor. Organized labor, in contrast, provided a natural urban base on which to build political allegiance. Unionized workers were receptive to domestic-owned industries, which being protected by tariffs and aided by government subsidies, paid higher wages than those under the tutelage of foreign businessmen. Undergirding the entire populist impulse was nationalism. Latin Americans of varied stripes had caught the worldwide fever of pride and patriotism. A few of the very wealthy even aspired to make their nations great, though they rarely approved of the populists with their statist economic policies that tended to benefit workers more than private capital.

Quite obviously, populism posed a threat to U.S. and European interests. Economically independent, developed nations in Latin America could compete with the United States and Europe through new domestic consumer markets and increased manufacturing. Economic nationalism also involved taking control of, or expropriating (with compensation), significant foreign-owned businesses.

Given these dangers, how is it that a generation of nationalistic political leaders rose to the fore in several large Latin American countries without encountering stiff opposition from the United States? Much of the answer rests in the press of coinciding world events. The heyday of populism, the 1930s and 1940s, found the First World weakened by the Great Depression and distracted by war. Divisions among the industrialized powers created space in which the populists could operate. Also, First World political and economic influence in Latin America was still marginal—nothing like what the United States would enjoy after World War II, much less by the end of the century. For example, although the FBI at midcentury had an office in Mexico City, along with several hundred agents and informants, its level of cooperation with domestic security apparatuses was still primitive. Nor did American elites intermingle much with their Mexican counterparts before 1945. Hence, populism was a product and a reflection of the times.

Cardenista reforms were not simple by-products of the 1910 revolution. The gap in time and politics between the cataclysmic decade of violence and Cárdenas's regime was wide. By 1935, when he had consolidated power, many Mexicans had learned to distrust their bureaucratic government; Cárdenas was never able to mend this breach. His task was complicated by resistance from within the entrenched bureaucracy. Many local politicians were not particularly interested in reform, much less in a genuine democracy that would invite closer public scrutiny of their activities. As a result, Cárdenas left only a faint political legacy.

However, in the area of economics, this self-avowed socialist did achieve two noteworthy accomplishments: land reform and nationalization of the oil industry. In the mid-1930s, Mexico broke up much of its latifundio, distributing more than 40 million acres to nearly 1 million peasants—a delayed response to the Zapatista revolts. In 1938, when oil companies balked at government-mandated wage increases, Cárdenas seized their properties and created PEMEX (Petróleos Mexicanos), the national oil company of Mexico. A more aggressive U.S. administration might have stood its ground against this usurpation; but Franklin D. Roosevelt and his advisers opted to tolerate Mexico's move—especially given that Cárdenas had made overtures to Nazi Germany (a rare instance of the weak dividing and conquering the strong). Mexico negotiated and paid a reasonable price for the oil properties; yet the lost opportunity costs for America since 1938 undoubtedly total tens of billions of dollars. Within a short time, PEMEX became an avenue for enriching Mexico's political elite, though it also routed at least some of the nation's wealth downward, into the hands of its large underclass.

Despite land redistribution and oil nationalization—the latter of which was jubilantly welcomed by Mexicans—Cárdenas's administration failed to overcome the distrust of many citizens, and antagonized millions of others with its aggressive political program of "socialist education." Devout Catholics remained unreconciled to the regime, although they were often willing to accept plots of land; and the rich and middle classes were uniformly hostile. Industrialists in Monterrey and Mexico City could not stomach Cárdenas's moral style of government; despised his alliance with organized labor; and resented his "communistic" tendencies, which threatened the sanctity of private property. Labor unrest and inflation annoyed middle-class urbanites. It is no surprise that millions of Mexicans rallied for change during the 1940 elections. Cárdenas was forced to anoint a very moderate successor; and his personal aspirations for fair elections, which would have brought a conservative opposition candidate into office, were dashed by a bureaucracy bent on keeping power and perpetuating electoral fraud. Populism in Mexico was thus limited, fragile, and brief.

Populism in Brazil and Argentina

The large, industrializing nations of Latin America were susceptible to populism because of their more complex urban political dynamics. In Brazil during the mid-twentieth century a second example of nationalistic populism emerged, again tied to the rise and fall of a single man: Getúlio Vargas. Brazil entered midcentury with only the limited national political identity that had evolved under Portuguese colonialism, which resulted in a diffusion of power. Elites in the large cities of Rio de Janeiro and São Paulo continued to dominate a weak executive, whereas much meaningful governance unfolded at the regional or local level. Divisions arose among elites over the degree to which Brazil should centralize, and were further aggravated by the worldwide economic downturn that began in 1930. In October of that year, with the help of sympathetic military officers, Vargas gained the provisional presidency. He remained in the executive post until 1945.

Vargas was a shrewd politician. He came to power in the context of an economic crisis that aroused new political passions, especially among city dwellers. Diverse political forces emerged: a fascist movement of integralists (known more commonly as Green Shirts); and a coalition of left-leaning political parties led by communists, the National Liberation Alliance

(ANL). Vargas, in the middle, first crushed the communists and their allies in 1935, then emasculated the right. In 1937, he declared a dictatorship in the form of the Estado Nôvo, or New State. Launching his authoritarian rule with a flourish, he held a ceremony in which he burned all of Brazil's state flags—vividly symbolizing a new nationalism and the rise of the central government.

Vargas was a classic populist. He courted and placated organized labor and built a political base in the urban industrial class. He also practiced economic nationalism, dividing First World powers with acumen. Brazil's close trade relations with Nazi Germany in the late 1930s alarmed the United States, as a result of which Washington extended a number of favors to Brazil, including military assistance and industrial aid. For example, U.S. funds largely financed an enormous national steel mill, the Volta Redonda, near São Paulo. Vargas bided his time in choosing sides during World War II, but cast in his lot with the Allies and declared war on Germany in 1942, thus assuring Brazil a place on the winning side.

Like other populists, Vargas longed to convert his nation into an economic powerhouse. He used the state to promote industrialization—though the process was already underway, especially in São Paulo—and, in time, drew many rich Brazilians into his political fold. Since the Great Depression and World War II had diminished raw material and agricultural exports (especially coffee), he pursued policies that favored import substitution industries, or businesses that catered to domestic consumer needs by making light, nondurable goods. Household products, soaps, petrochemicals, and myriad other items now came from Brazilian factories instead of from overseas. These enterprises were conceived of and funded by the government and the private sector, working hand in hand. Import controls and currency policies gave the edge to domestic producers, though when the United States returned its economy to peacetime production in 1945, competition tightened.

Vargas's controversial brand of populism divided Brazil's military officials along political lines. Some officers liked industrialization, appreciating its nationalist and martial potential. Others feared Vargas's opening of the political system to segments of the working class. He had released political prisoners in the mid-1940s, including communists, and had eased restrictions on political organizing. A coup in 1945 ousted Vargas from power, though he was able to make a remarkable comeback in 1950, when he won a national election. Serving as president in the early 1950s, Vargas walked a tightrope between forces within his own coalition and the conservative, mostly rural elites who opposed him. He again pursued a mixed economy, creating Petrobrás, an oil refining and distribution monopoly, and restricting foreign investment through legislation such as profit remittance laws (which stipulated how much money corporations could remove from Brazil). His wavering between continued economic nationalism and compromise satisfied no one, and the political center evaporated in Brazil even as Vargas stood in the middle of it. In 1954, old and alone, he shot himself in the heart at the Presidential Palace, leaving a suicide note that bemoaned the rise of conservative capitalists and foreign imperialists.

Although Getúlio Vargas's flare for the dramatic made him something of a political icon in Brazil and Latin America, his legacy pales in comparison to that of a third populist, Juan Perón of Argentina. Perón, who in turn was largely upstaged by his charismatic wife Eva (affectionately known as "Evita"), governed a smaller nation than Vargas's, but one with a powerful midcentury economy. In many ways Peronism (the political movement led by the Peróns), though distinctive, is the best example of the populist state. Its colorful history is full of the contradictions between nationalist aspirations and rising global capitalism.

Like Brazil, Argentina suffered economically during the Depression, and shifted toward import substitution during World War II. Argentina's government also became increasingly authoritarian due to its fears of the increasingly disgruntled masses and of its own military officers, many of whom were attracted to the trappings of European-style fascism. Juan Perón was a colonel who had served on a training mission to Benito Mussolini's Italy and had been impressed by what he saw. He was unusual among officers in that he was the son of a provincial farmer; most of his peers came from well-heeled families. Perón never forgot his roots: He remained cognizant of the languishing countryside, and empathized with the indigent conscripted soldiers.

When Perón was elevated to the post of Minister of Labor in 1943, he began to cultivate a following among urban workers by listening to their concerns and addressing their needs. The rise of an industrial underclass, numbering nearly a quarter million by 1943, provided the ambitious Perón with a popular base. Settling strikes by decree, he often favored labor and adjusted wages upward, fostering goodwill for himself in the ranks of the booming Confederación General de Trabajadores (General Workers' Confederation). Perón eventually rode the crest of his surging popularity in the capital to the posts of Minister of War and of Vice President. With the same skill and personal dynamism that had made him popular with workers, Perón began to woo the officers' corps of the army. An anti-Peronist faction, rightly detecting his interest in becoming president, had him arrested in fall 1945, inadvertently setting the stage for his triumph. Massive demonstrations by workers rocked Buenos Aires, forcing his release and the elections in 1946 that brought him to power.

Juan Perón had used his influence during the war years to further the career of a struggling actress, Eva Duarte. Of illegitimate birth and modest means, a young Eva had left her small hometown for the lure of the big city. The two fell in love (mutual ambition seems to have played a role in their mutual attraction) and married shortly before Perón gained the presidency. Evita, with her beauty and poised charm, won the hearts of Argentinians and soon captured headlines. She was not properly bred in the eyes of socialites, however, and rich women snubbed her. They refused to admit her into their clubs, or to accept her help for their charity organization, the Sociedad de Beneficencia (Society of Beneficence). In retaliation, Evita took over their charity and rechristened it the Eva Perón Foundation.

Juan and Evita were fortunate to have come to power just as the war ended, when an accumulation of hard foreign currency reserves allowed them to take Argentina on a spending spree. The Eva Perón Foundation became far more significant than the charity from which it originated. It served as the centerpiece of a new welfare state that featured hospitals, rural clinics, immunization programs, retirement homes, and schools. Evita's compassion was well publicized, though even when the cameras were not around she worked long hours. These social programs earned public support for Peronism and adoration for Evita. Having attained fame in life, in death Eva Perón reached for sainthood. At the height of her influence, shortly after a sensational tour of Europe, she was diagnosed with cancer of the uterus. Media around the world charted her slow physical decline; when she succumbed to the disease in July 1952, a massive outpouring of grief engulfed Argentinians.

Juan Perón proved adept at using his wife's demise to buttress his waning popularity. He decreed Loyalty Day, first celebrated in October 1952, when he made Evita's will public ("I want the shirtless ones to know how much I love Perón," it conveniently read). Eva's body was preserved through state-of-the-art embalming, but plans to erect a fifty-story statue of her on the waterfront in Buenos Aires were never realized. Despite the deep sympathy her death evoked, Perón's regime was in trouble. Increasingly plagued by capital flight, inflation, and declining real wages, the economy slowed. The quiet abolition of profit remittance laws failed to woo much new foreign investment (though Italian automaker Fiat did make an entry). Strikes and unrest festered, as stalwart opponents from within the ranks of the armed forces, elite, and the Church criticized the government ever more boldly. A naval air squadron that tried to bomb the leader during a Peronist celebration in June 1955 failed; but the attempt was a harbinger of the coup that would come in September, toppling the government. Perón fled into exile.

Predictably, populism in Latin America was viewed with suspicion by many foreign interests. The U.S. State Department, for example, switched its attitude toward Peronism several times, regarding it variously as an expression of fascism, democracy, or communism. In fact, Peronism, like populism elsewhere in Latin America, had features that transcend simplistic notions of political ideology. On the one hand, Perón's Argentina was a haven for ex-Nazis—a politically repressive regime that flirted with fascistic militarism and showed little tolerance for dissent. On the other, its social programs and state economic planning caused wealth redistribution in favor of the poor and weakened the power of the entrenched oligarchy. It mobilized workers and enfranchised women, thus broadening political participation, even though it was not truly democratic. Because of the nationalist economic policies pursued by populist regimes, few First World lenders did much business with Peronist Argentina or with other populist countries in Latin America.

In the wake of the Allied victory in World War II, the United States was free again to cultivate its influence throughout the hemisphere. Populism was in decline by the mid-1950s, as signaled by the departures of Vargas and Perón; the armed forces were on the ascent, determined to root out all vestiges of populism; and the wealthy classes were poised to reassert control. At this moment, a political earthquake occurred in one of the smaller nations of the Caribbean—where dictatorships had persisted and populism had never taken hold (given the absence of such essentials as an urban industrial working class). Its epicenter was Havana, Cuba, where a revolutionary socialist government came to power in 1959 under Fidel Castro, stunning Latin America's elites and deepening the chill in relations between the United States and the Soviet Union.

PART II

Revolution and Counterrevolution

5 Nationalism and the Military Response

Mid-twentieth-century populism was a multifaceted phenomenon, and the single word *populism* is inadequate to describe all of its various and complex permutations. Nonetheless, the various kinds of populism had certain features in common, such as economic nationalism. As large Latin American nations like Brazil and Mexico continued to diversify their economies and industrialize, nationalist desires to control economic processes posed a threat to First World (particularly American) interests. If Brazilians, for example—including the rich—wished to make their nation "great," their attainment of this goal could only come at the expense of the United States and other competitors. A fully industrialized and independent Brazil could vie with America in developing and marketing consumer goods. National control of mines and agricultural resources not only would have cut American companies out of the production loop and eliminate their profits but in time would have generated enough capital to give Brazil financial independence.

The nationalism flourishing in Latin America during the postwar years posed a profound political and economic threat to the United States. American policymakers understood this, though they seem to have conflated nationalism with communism in their assessments of the danger. One reason for this confusion is the waning nationalism of Latin American elites after World War II: For the most part, nationalist aspirations were being expressed by the lower social classes. These nationalists not only wanted to make their nations great but also usually intended to redistribute wealth to benefit the poor. Washington thus found natural allies against this brand of nationalism among wealthier Latin Americans. In this sense, the fight against subversion of the political and economic order in Latin America since 1945 *has* been a struggle against communism. However, if *communism* is understood to imply allegiance to the Soviet-dominated

Eastern bloc, then there were and are very few communists in Latin America. This is borne out by the fact that the struggle against subversion has outlasted the Soviet Union, continuing to the present day.

Surprisingly, it was not in the complex society of a large, populist state that grassroots nationalism first caused America serious problems after World War II. Revolutionary nationalism exploded right under Washington's nose, in Cuba—the most Americanized of all Latin American nations, and one with close historical ties to the United States. Surely, modernization analysts reasoned, if Cuba could turn "red," then the entire region might easily be lost.

The Triumph of Cuban Nationalism

Cuba was the last of Spain's New World colonies, but by the 1890s, even though it was politically linked to Europe, its economy largely depended on an American appetite for sugar. Even many wealthy criollos, after the abolishment of African slavery in 1880, saw little reason to maintain ties to the motherland that constricted trade and kept political power in Spanish hands. A protracted guerrilla war in the 1870s failed to free Cuba; but the seeds of independence had been planted and soon matured. In the early 1890s those seeds were fertilized by the blood of José Martí, an ardent nationalist who had been exiled for his political beliefs. Martí's writings made him a Cuban hero, and his early death in the renewed military struggle elevated him to the status of martyr. The island again erupted in revolt.

Spanish military commanders attempted to pacify Cuba by establishing relocation camps for much of the rural peasantry. The disease-infested camps further politicized the poor against their colonial masters and did little to alleviate the growing insurgency in the mountains. American journalists, meanwhile, had a heyday. In the best of the Black Legend tradition, they penned graphic tales of sadistic Spaniards carrying out atrocities. Many Americans, including rich investors who owned almost all of the Cuban sugar industry, entertained ideas of annexing Cuba. As part of a show of force and as a means of protecting its interests, the United States dispatched the U.S.S. *Maine*, a state-of-the-art battleship, to Havana to oversee events.

Unfortunately, the *Maine* blew up. The U.S. government and newspapers were quick to blame Spanish authorities, although the more logical culprits were Cubans—for the last thing Spain wanted was a war with a rising power like the United States. An investigation into the circumstances of the *Maine*'s untimely explosion in the 1970s, conducted by Admiral Hyman Rickenbacker, concluded on the basis of an underwater examination of the vessel's hull that the explosion was the result of mechanical failure. But at the time, few wanted to attribute the deaths of American sailors to a breakdown in U.S.-made technology. It was better to simply "Remember the *Maine!*"

The U.S.–Spanish American War was necessarily brief. The aged and slow fleets of the once great European power were no match for America's new war cruisers (unless, of course, they blew up). Sitting in harbors in Cuba and the Philippines, Spain's ships—at least one of which could not even safely move forward and stay afloat—were easily destroyed. Enthusiasm for war raised battalions of young American recruits among a generation that had not known the horrors of the Civil War, and they routed an already demoralized Spanish Army in Cuba. In the process, however, the United States did not consult with Cuban leaders, and contacts between the two camps were kept to a minimum. Thus, when Madrid sued for peace in late 1898, Cubans were not even party to the agreement, and to no one's surprise, the U.S. army remained on the island.

Unable to colonize Cuba in the manner for which it had castigated Spain, the United States opted to gradually withdraw its troops and grant Cubans partial independence. U.S.-sponsored elections in 1900, although closely monitored and conducted only among wealthy whites (about 5 percent of the population), still produced victories for nationalist candidates. The final U.S. withdrawal in May 1902 began a period of conditional independence; however, the Platt Amendment, attached to the Cuban constitution, gave the United States important veto powers over foreign policy, banking, and financial management (Cuba's banking system was managed by the Atlanta branch of the Federal Reserve). The United States also retained the right to intervene militarily, if necessary, in the island's domestic affairs. In 1906, the Marines returned to Cuba for a few years because of political divisions and the threat of instability.

Partial independence temporarily assuaged nationalist yearnings, and many better-off Cubans even found reason to favor an American economic presence. Capital flowed in and modernized agribusinesses that catered to booming U.S. markets. Educated Cubans found jobs with U.S. firms, and a healthy middle class began to emerge in Havana. By 1905, Americans owned nearly 60 percent of the island's cultivated land, 90 percent of its tobacco production operations, and nearly all of the utilities, trading houses, and banks. Within the next two decades, U.S. investments soared to well over $1 billion. U.S. economic dominance of Cuba was so all-encompassing that a 1928 book by journalist Leland Hanks was entitled *Our Cuban Colony*. The modernization of certain areas of Cuba improved the quality of life for nearly all. On the whole, the nation's economic growth outpaced that of the rest of Latin America, especially prior to the Great Depression. When hard times did come to Cuba, however, latent nationalism revived.

A nationalist regime under Ramón Grau San Martín gained power in 1933 and ruled briefly, unilaterally abrogating the Platt Amendment and antagonizing the United States. A subsequent coup, led by a noncommissioned officer named Fulgencio Batista, restored political tranquillity. Yet for the remainder of the decade and beyond, the growth of Cuba's sugar-based economy slowed. Nationalist aspirations festered, and a restrictive political establishment failed to answer popular calls for change. By the 1950s, Batista was governing with an increasingly firm hand.

Cuban society after World War II was increasingly divided. Foreign investment had produced enclaves of prosperity in greater Havana, where a consumer-oriented middle class enjoyed electricity, appliances, telephones, and television. Cuba had the highest number of cars per capita in Latin America, and many of them were Cadillacs. But although a literate and comfortable middle class remained ensconced—and largely depoliticized—in the capital, a potentially restless, suffering underclass burgeoned in the countryside. Made up of underemployed, poorly educated, mostly darker-skinned peoples, this segment of society was a potential base for nationalist unrest.

Yet the Cuban revolution was born in the city, where disenchanted university youth thought about the possibilities of remaking their country while reading the writings of José Martí. A few of them, including Fidel Castro, recklessly attacked an army base in an attempt to spark a revolt on July 26, 1953, in honor of the hundredth anniversary of Martí's birth. Easily captured, these sons of the middle class were amnestied by Batista two years later. Castro, a gifted athlete who might have made money playing baseball, ended up in Mexico, where he recruited buddies for a return to his homeland. Among his new friends was Ernesto "Che" Guevara, an idealistic ex-medical student from Argentina. With Guevara and eighty others, Castro returned to invade Cuba by boat. Only a few of the men survived the initial landing and made it into the mountains away from the coast.

Castro's athleticism, charisma, and knack for strategy helped this very small band of guerrillas stave off the remarkably inept security forces of the Batista dictatorship. The Cuban authorities in Havana had seemingly little to fear in 1956, though they openly promulgated the lie that Castro was dead. When the *New York Times* found him in the mountains and published an interview, it spawned renewed interest in his cause. Slowly, too, Castro was winning over the rural masses. Once again, he was greatly (albeit unintentionally) aided in this by Batista and his generals, who initiated a bombing campaign that targeted villages—a strategy that outraged the vast majority of Cubans.

Two significant processes began to unfold in the revolution in early 1958: First, the middle class, which had generally supported the dictatorship, began to waiver; second, the United States, seeking to preserve order, distanced itself from the apparently ill-fated regime. An arms embargo in

March undermined Batista's position, and on New Year's Day 1959 he fled to Miami. The quick pace of subsequent events, unfortunately for U.S. policymakers, eliminated alternative scenarios that would have minimized the power of the revolutionaries. Castro's triumphant entry into Havana meant that he was in control—and even the U.S. ambassador advised Washington that it would need to work with the widely popular nationalists, offering the consoling observation that at least Castro was not a communist (the small Cuban Communist Party had opposed the revolt). In the United States, sympathetic media coverage had made Castro something of a hero: His guest appearance on the *Ed Sullivan Show* began with the host introducing him as the "George Washington of Cuba." But Castro was to America what George Washington had been to England: His deep-seated revolutionary nationalism made confrontation inevitable.

Once in power the new government attempted to hold together diverse elements of society, ranging from impoverished rural sectors to the urban middle class. The brutality of the Batista regime's rural bombing campaign prompted criminal trials of captured military officers. Castro made the televised trials a public circus when he had the defense attorneys themselves arrested. With this first salvo, the young government began to make several moves that alienated the middle class. Its nationalistic economic policies, such as mandatory reductions in public utility rates and salary increases in U.S.-owned sugar mills, signaled a fundamental lack of commitment to the sanctity of private property and market economics. Rent controls in Havana may have delighted the poor, but they offended many a landlord. Restrictions on luxury imports from the United States, aimed at controlling foreign capital exchange, also annoyed wealthy consumers.

The Castro government desegregated Cuban society, which had long resembled the southern United States—with different services for whites and blacks, mostly of uneven quality. All public venues, including hotels, nightclubs, restaurants, and beaches, were prohibited from discriminating on the basis of race, though the right to do so was retained by certain private organizations, including country clubs. Such policies outraged the well-to-do in Havana, who were almost exclusively white. They also annoyed many American southerners monitoring events from a distance, as they faced their own struggle to preserve racial privileges in the face of a growing civil rights movement.

But far more dangerous to America were Castro's economic policies in the countryside, which included an agrarian reform act in spring 1959 that divided many large, U.S.-owned estates and distributed the property to the rural poor. This was a direct blow to American interests on the island, even though some companies, such as the rum manufacturer Bacardi, were to receive government bonds in compensation (a scheme shrewdly modeled on U.S. policy in postwar Japan, so that Washington could not cry "foul" without seeming hypocritical). Soon, both the United States and the wealthy in Cuba had had enough of the economic nationalism of Castro and his cohorts. Wealthy Cubans began to leave for Miami, and the United States began to distance itself from the regime, eventually breaking off all diplomatic contact.

Washington's souring on Cuba resonated in the U.S. media, which had been generally supportive of the revolution until mid-1959. A May 11 broadcast on CBS entitled *Is Cuba Going Red?* triggered a flurry of media references to communism. The loaded term, in the wake of McCarthyism and Red hysteria earlier in the decade, spawned fear and excitement in the general public. The Soviet Premier at the time, Nikita Khrushchev, later acknowledged that the Kremlin was watching events unfold in Cuba without a clue as to which way they would go. Castro *was* a communist, however, in the sense that he did not appreciate America's economic interests in Cuba and did not commit himself to preserving the economic status quo. In fairly short order, faced with U.S. aggression, he became a communist also by the Eastern bloc definition.

The United States and Nationalist Cuba

In March 1960 the Dwight Eisenhower administration committed itself to Castro's overthrow, and the U.S. Central Intelligence Agency (CIA) began training Cuban exiles for an invasion. Meanwhile, as the pace of revolutionary economic reforms in favor of the poor accelerated, more and more middle-class Cubans left for Miami. The exodus, in turn, shifted the regime's political foundation onto radical rural sectors. This cycle repeated itself until the moderate political center was completely lost.

As it prepared to launch a counterrevolution, the main problem for the CIA was that the exiles in Miami were really lousy at keeping their mouths shut. It was soon no secret at all that an exile army was assembled and in training. In fact, when the John F. Kennedy administration implemented the invasion plan in April 1961, intelligence leaks were so bad that much of Castro's veteran army awaited the CIA flotilla at its landing point: the Bay of Pigs.

Although the invasion was a dismal failure and a public embarrassment to the United States, the infant Cuban government was worried. It tightened its bonds with the Soviets and welcomed the help of Eastern-bloc military advisers. In August 1961, "Che" Guevara—now Castro's right-hand man—approached a senior White House official during a diplomatic meeting in Paraguay. Guevara told the National Security Council's John Goodwin that Cuba was willing to break off its ties with the Soviets, if in exchange the United States would stop trying to topple the regime. Goodwin rebuffed Guevara's overture. Stung by its economic losses in Cuba and mindful of the danger the revolution posed to its interests throughout the hemisphere, Washington was in no mood to entertain such suggestions for peace.

New attempts to destroy Castro and his government failed. Focusing on Fidel's charisma, the CIA supposed that his death might undo the revolution. It soon hatched a number of creative assassination schemes. In one operation the intelligence agency, aware of Castro's fondness for chocolate milkshakes, placed an agent with poison in the ice cream parlor of a Havana hotel. Unfortunately, just as he was about to sour the leader's ice cream treat, he discovered that the cylinder of poison had completely stuck to the side of the freezer. His vain efforts to retrieve it aroused the suspicion of Castro's bodyguards, who apprehended the agent and once again saved their nation's hero.

Botched assassination attempts on Castro were of minimal consequence, however, because his death at the hands of the United States would only have served to further antagonize the Cuban populace. More effective for disrupting the revolutionary experiment was the targeting of the livelihood of the people themselves. "Operation Mongoose" was an extensive covert operation out of south Florida in the early 1960s that involved thousands of raids by small boatloads of saboteurs. Targeting infrastructure, including power stations, communications facilities, and bridges, these raiders caused new hardships for rural Cubans, who had overwhelmingly supported the revolution. However, sabotage also failed to destabilize the regime. Castro's government publicized U.S. attempts to destroy it, and in the early 1960s it continued to enjoy the overwhelming support of the Cuban people. Where invasions, assassination plots, and raids failed, an economic embargo introduced an exceedingly slow recipe for success. A July 1960 sugar embargo was gradually expanded to a total embargo by 1964, including a travel ban (though circumvented by other nations, such as Mexico, where the U.S. embassy was able to monitor American traffic in and out of the forbidden country). Only massive infusions of cash and material aid from the Soviet Union averted economic depression; when those infusions abruptly ended after the Soviet collapse in 1991, the Cuban economy foundered.

Soviet aid to the Cuban regime began in the mid-1960s. It included a military component (both weapons and personnel), which played an important role in strengthening Cuban defense. In 1962, the Russians began to install nuclear warheads on the island, a strategy that provoked the famous Cuban Missile Crisis when the United States discovered the presence of the missiles in October. From the Soviet perspective, it seemed only fair to have warheads poised for launch 100 miles off the U.S. coast, given the similar proximity of America's nuclear spears located in Turkey.

But the Kennedy administration refused to accept the direct threat of nearby Soviet warheads, and it brought the world to the brink of nuclear war in a successful effort to remove them. The Pentagon went to "Def Com 2" status, its highest state of nuclear alert during the Cold War, and put seven megatons of nuclear weapons in the air. A possible first strike against Moscow was not out of the question. The Strategic Air Command, Joint Chiefs of Staff, and Republican congressional leaders all urged Kennedy to invade Cuba with troops that could both neutralize the missile sites and take out Castro's regime. Kennedy, a cold warrior who accelerated military spending and ensnared the United States in Vietnam, uncharacteristically backed away from this confrontation (apparently due in part to the influence of Robert Kennedy, his younger brother, who was then U.S. attorney general). Instead of an invasion, JFK ordered a naval blockade to "quarantine" Cuba.

This relatively benign response proved fortuitous: The CIA had failed to detect that the Soviets had twenty-three nuclear missiles installed and ready for launch in Cuba. The targets, including Miami and Washington, D.C., had been selected. Would Russians have fired the missiles in the event of an invasion? We cannot know for certain, but it is possible they would have. In contrast, the blockade was a winner. The Kremlin had no stomach to force the issue—Cuba was not that important either economically or strategically—and the Soviets backed down. Guevara argued that Castro should throw the Soviets out and keep their missiles, but instead the Cubans deferred to Moscow's decision to withdraw. Soviet economic aid continued, and as a result, extensive health care and education programs kept a majority of Cubans faithful to their government over the next quarter century.

In the post-Soviet world of the 1990s, however, Cuba has nearly been brought to its knees. The 1992 Cuban Democracy Act, supported by elderly southern senators like Jesse Helms, who still remember Castro's desegregation, was designed by its Democratic authors "to make the Cuban economy scream." Yet the results were disappointing. The act's call for the punishment of countries trading with Cuba was a violation of international law, and enforcement proved nearly impossible. Penalties imposed on foreign businesses that had acquired properties in Cuba once owned by Americans (prior to seizure by the Castro government) also violated treaties and offended some of Washington's closest allies. Canada's parliament briefly toyed with an identical measure regarding properties in the United States, on the justification that many colonials who had fled to Canada in the wake of the American revolution had lost their lands to the victorious "patriots." In 1999 the Clinton administration modestly eased restrictions on Cuba—a slight reversal of policy that reflected a lack of policy options and frustrated anti-Castro Floridians.

CIA predictions that Cuba would fall apart after the Soviet collapse in 1991 went unfulfilled. The Castro regime's legalization of what was once the black market—coupled with its diversification of exports, wooing of European (especially Spanish) and Canadian investors, and upstart tourist industry—had stabilized the economy by mid-decade. Indeed, "communist" Cuba was more aggressively privatizing its economic sphere than was Russia under Boris Yeltsin—and the latter was being hailed by Western media as a champion of free enterprise.

Yet even though the island nation has adjusted in the post-Soviet era, it would still likely benefit from a rapprochement with the United States. An open, post-Castro Cuba could be expected to attract new capital and myriad American tourists, and its dilapidated capital city of Havana would receive a much-needed renovation. Cuba is close enough, and small enough, that the volume of U.S. wealth would net its people real benefits, especially after the hardships of post-Soviet isolation. The generation of younger Cubans who do not remember Batista's dictatorship is fairly depoliticized and seems receptive to change. Older, rural Cubans, especially people of color, have clung to their faith in Fidel; but this age group is dying off. Both generations seem hostile to the idea of Miami exiles returning to rule the land. When Florida-based Cubans broadcast promises of punishment and revenge, their threats only seem to harden the nationalist resolve still present in Cuba. Yet when Castro dies, it is likely that a healthy majority of Cubans will willingly return their nation to an American orbit. Probably only a modest level of repression will be necessary to subdue the remainder.

The Militaries Take Control

The success of Cuban nationalism in 1959 sent shivers throughout the U.S. foreign policy establishment and prompted a reevaluation of hemispheric conditions by political analysts, diplomats, and academics. If Cuba, which was such a close ally, could turn on the United States, what might happen in the rest of Latin America? When Vice President Richard Nixon's motorcade was egged by hostile demonstrators in Venezuela just a couple of years earlier, alarm bells had sounded in Washington. After Castro's triumph, America was fully aroused. It engaged policies in Latin America during the 1960s with new vigor. Fortunately for Americans, some of the forces in the region that might have threatened U.S. interests were soon detected and neutralized.

In the early 1960s, America embraced the youthful energy and charisma of its new president, John F. Kennedy. Kennedy reinvigorated the Cold War confrontation with the Soviet Union and pushed for a higher U.S. profile in the Third World. His administration formulated its policies in Latin America with a mind toward averting other Cuban-style revolutions.

Its program, the Alliance for Progress, was not ideologically different from what had come before it; the intensity of Washington's efforts to safeguard its hemispheric interests, however, was.

At the core of the Alliance for Progress was the premise that in order to stave off more revolts, a modicum of reform was necessary. The old adage, a version of which is attributed to a Russian czar, that it is better to reform from above than to experience reform (revolution) from below, echoed in the offices of U.S. policymakers. During and after the 1960s, several U.S.-influenced regimes in Latin America experimented with limited political and economic reforms—at the same time receiving abundant military provisions and increasingly sophisticated counterinsurgency instruction. In retrospect, the reforms seem not to have accomplished much, other than to heighten public awareness that change was possible. In contrast, the accelerated militarization of the hemisphere paid real dividends. It tightened links between U.S. and Latin American security apparatuses and allowed for the purging of subversive elements that sought to challenge the status quo.

One of the most important features of the new security arrangements was the establishment of the Inter-American Defense College (IADC) in 1962. Located at Fort McNair, on the outskirts of Washington, D.C., the IADC was ostensibly established under the rubric of the Organization of American States, but its direct parent is the Inter-American Defense Board, a World War II organ heavily controlled by the U.S. Department of Defense. Since the early 1960s the IADC has been a critical link between U.S. and Latin American militaries. It trains Latin American army officers and keeps them in close contact with influential and friendly American counterparts.

The economic features of the Alliance for Progress also proved beneficial to America. New loans, largely arranged through a host of rising international financial institutions, helped stimulate U.S. exports, deepen trade links, and plant the seeds of a debt problem (see Chapter 9) that led to Latin America's subservience to U.S. macroeconomic goals by the twentieth century's close. Yet in many cases, early reforms initiated by civilian governments went beyond what both Washington and Latin America's rich were willing to tolerate. Certain features of populism threatened to take on institutional form and promote a brand of economic and political nationalism clearly detrimental to vested interests. Elites were predictably nervous; after all, they lived, often quite literally, with the poor right outside their doors. What transpired in Cuba was frightening to them. Hence, the temptation to brook no dissent and intervene with newly improved militaries was naturally strong. It was both foreseeable and logical that military regimes would come to power. Although the armed forces took control in nearly all of South America, we can identify major patterns and consequences of the coups, or takeovers, by reviewing events in the "ABC" countries: Argentina, Brazil, and Chile.

The first major nation to experience military rule was Brazil. By the early 1960s, Brazilians were experiencing the benefits and contradictions of "development." During the previous decade, hundreds of millions of dollars of foreign (mostly U.S.) capital poured into the country, as corporations like General Electric, Ford, and DuPont built factories and established subsidiaries that facilitated access to the domestic marketplace and took advantage of favorable labor and raw material resources. A middle class of engineers, educators, lawyers, medical professionals, and entrepreneurs rose in cities like São Paulo—the metropolis that had already become the industry-pumping heart of the nation. The carving of a new capital, Brasilia, out of the jungles was a massive public works project designed and executed by the Brazilian government during the 1950s.

Despite apparent political harmony, Brazil faced an uncertain future. Ideas of mass participation in politics did not die when Getúlio Vargas killed himself in the Presidential Palace in 1954. On the contrary, his appeals to certain elements of the nation's large underclass spawned more grassroots mobilization. Labor unions in the cities and peasant leagues in the countryside agitated for reform. They also tended to back a rising political organ (once tied to Vargas) called the Brazilian Labor Party (PTB). Populist ideas were mutating from personalism into movements and political parties. Many wealthy Brazilians, including São Paulo's industrialists, who allied themselves with U.S. corporations and watched creeping industrial wages cut into their profits, feared the PTB and its most prominent figure, João Goulart. Goulart, known by the nickname "Jango," briefly served as labor minister before winning the vice presidency in the 1960 elections (unlike the situation in the United States, the same political party did not necessarily control both the presidency and vice presidency in Brazil).

Industrialists and others, who owned most of the mass media, promoted a São Paulo politician named Jânio da Silva Quadros for president in the 1960. Quadros, who carried a broom and roused crowds by promising to sweep away corruption, was not a man of deep ideological substance. Media, money, and flamboyance worked, however, and his campaign rolled to victory in a nation of poorly educated people. Yet, tragically for the forces that had backed him, this less-than-stable man resigned from office in the summer of 1961, elevating the PTB's Goulart into the presidential chair. The rich and the military generals, who were sometimes less than happy with Quadros, were now thoroughly beside themselves. They arranged to weaken the powers of the executive branch prior to Goulart's ascent, and at least for a brief while, the new leader seemed under control.

But Jango Goulart was not the problem. A wealthy landowner, he was in many ways a moderate who tried to hold Brazil's increasingly divided body politic together. Mass democratic pressures for change were percolating. In São Paulo and Rio de Janeiro, workers held enormous rallies. Strikes paralyzed major industries, and foreign investors cooled in their appraisal of Brazil. In the impoverished northeastern part of the vast country, peasants organized and pressed for meaningful land and wage reforms. All these cries for a new kind of mass politics reached the receptive ears of Goulart; but in many ways he was only responding to those popular cries, not inspiring them.

He did, however, respond. In 1963 his government held a plebiscite that effectively undid the conditions that restricted him. By a five-to-one margin Brazilians restored a strong executive branch to government. With this mandate, the president outlined new plans. He called for agrarian reform to reverse Brazil's centuries of latifundio by distributing plots to the poor. He urged passage of a minimum wage law, applicable both in the cities (for industrial laborers) and in the countryside. He envisioned extending voting rights to everyone—even the illiterate rural masses who were barred from participation by reading and writing tests (these uneducated Brazilians had been allowed to vote in the plebiscite, where they had overwhelmingly favored restoring powers to Goulart). But even as the president prepared to remake Brazilian society, new divisions soon racked the land. The nation seemed to be falling apart.

Business elites, fearing the future under Goulart, lampooned him in their newspapers and in radio and television media. To the amusement of many, especially in the middle class, the president's manliness was constantly under question (he was reputedly unable to satisfy his attractive blonde wife). Every major press outlet in Brazil was affiliated with one of the two major business organizations, both of which worked to destabilize the regime and combat "communism." Indeed, the specter of communism was tremendously useful in undermining Goulart. The Communist party had been outlawed in Brazil, and Goulart openly favored its relegalization. Although his intentions were largely those of a libertarian, the charge of a growing subversion aided opposition forces—for the vast majority of Brazilians rejected communist ideology.

Goulart tried to hold his own during the media onslaught. "I am not afraid of a being termed a 'subversive' for declaring the need to reform our society," he told a crowd of 150,000 in Rio, with his wife by his side. "Our political system perpetuates an economic system that is outdated, unjust, and inhumane." Many Brazilians still believed Goulart in late March 1964, when he delivered that speech (and others like it). But the clever media barrage that clouded the lines between advocacy of democracy and communism, coupled with a deteriorating economy due to capital flight, declining foreign investment, and accelerating inflation, diminished his popularity. Some Brazilians, and nearly all in the upper and middle classes, welcomed the military coup that unfolded on the first day of April. The United States, too, was very pleased. Ambassador Lincoln Gordon called the event a "great moment in the history of civilization," and Washington recognized the new authorities in Brasilia even before the former president had left the country.

The coup signaled an abrupt end to reform. Brazil, haltingly moving in one direction, now reversed course. Civil rights were curtailed and a purging of the most vocal segments of the popular forces began. Troops broke up strikes; security forces rounded up union organizers. The offices of the PTB, which had been declared illegal, were closed. Press censorship began, though most major news outlets, already sympathetic to the coup, were hardly affected.

Brazil's military regime is known for its violations of human rights, but the systematic repression of political activists did not begin immediately after the coup. From 1964 to 1968, only business-funded efforts (especially one designated Operação Bandeirantes) eliminated subversives—mostly former PTB and labor organizers, along with impoverished and vulnerable peasant activists in the northeast. In 1968 a *linha dura*, or hard line, within the military staged a so-called coup within a coup. It was only after this that the armed forces regularly engaged in torture and extrajudicial killings on a significant scale. Perhaps strangely, the regime kept meticulous records of these operations, and a sampling of the more than one million pages of documents eventually was published after the regime's demise, in a book entitled *Nunca Mas* (*Torture in Brazil*, in its English translation).

Brazilians pioneered the use of electrical shock torture, a technique popular with Third World security forces today (see Chapter 10). Military schools offered classes on methodology, complete with labs and victims, and in countless torture chambers the experimentation continued. Victims like Manuel da Soaza, a boy of age 9, were beaten soundly; others were sent flopping like fish out of water with electrical jolts to their genitalia. Luis de Vela, a twenty-six-year-old teacher, listened to the electricity-generated screams of his pregnant wife—a psychological dimension of anguish seemingly as powerful as an electrical current. CENIMAR, Brazil's naval intelligence center, housed the offices of the U.S. military attaché, facilitating American participation in torture methodology breakthroughs—though a visiting rear admiral complained that the screams of the nearby victims was a constant distraction.

Even more significant than its systematization of torture, however, was the Brazilian military's development of theories regarding internal subversion. The famous Doctrine of National Security was formulated in Brazil. The core of the doctrine is the observation that Third World threats to political and economic structures are invariably internal. Armies in Latin America in the postwar world have not existed to defend their borders but rather to preserve domestic order and keep subversive forces at bay. This insight, simple yet profound, has been a cornerstone of security doctrine in the Western hemisphere ever since.

In some ways, however, the Brazilian regime proved disappointing to those seeking pacification of the massive nation. Despite the widespread popular mobilization that had inspired Goulart, prior to 1964 there had not been any serious guerrilla activity in the country. But as the generals tightened their grip, small armed bands surfaced, carrying out annoying raids on isolated police and military posts. The regime also had a mixed record in maintaining the allegiance of the initially enthusiastic middle class. In 1968, the occupation of university campuses and repression of college students triggered mass protests, including one of nearly 100,000 demonstrators in Rio de Janeiro. Discontent among middle-class youth was more problematic than among the poor, since urbanites had access to social and legal resources that complicated their physical elimination. Yet for all of its limitations, the military government in Brazil was also innovative. It created two political parties (after abolishing all others), held procedural elections, and orchestrated the process so creatively that its "democratic" trappings gave it some international legitimacy.

Military rule in Brazil was beneficial to the rich and to the United States. Ironically, the Brazilian government banned the American Declaration of Independence, with its talk of human equality, as a subversive document. But U.S. corporations gained a great deal from the curtailment of civil liberties, especially at the expense of unionism. Real wages for industrial workers declined steadily after the coup, which brought greater profits to stockholders in America. Land reform that would have changed the economic equation in the countryside was averted. Obviously, on a number of levels, reform in Brazil as articulated by Goulart and others threatened American economic interests. That fact largely explains why the United States not only backed the coup but, as much evidence suggests (despite continued governmental secrecy), even helped arrange and execute it.

Chile and Argentina Follow Suit

Many Brazilian labor, peasant, and democratic reform advocates fled to nearby countries in the wake of the military takeover. But theirs was a world of danger, for military regimes multiplied across the continent. One of the last havens for political activists was Chile, a nation with a tradition of stability and relative openness. But Chileans themselves were increasingly divided over radical initiatives that threatened the future of capitalism in their country. A U.S.-backed government under Eduardo Frei

(1964–1970) had implemented a modest program of land distribution in the spirit of the Alliance for Progress. But these very limited efforts only aroused in the rural poor more expectations and hope. Nor had heavy U.S. investment during the 1960s translated into advances for low wage workers in the cities. Roughly a third of the nation was willing to vote for a socialist in the clean 1970 elections—just enough, in a three-way race, to deliver the presidency to Salvador Allende.

As had happened in Brazil under Goulart, the political establishment in Chile limited executive powers so as to curtail the new leader's options. Despite this, Allende forged ahead with aggressive nationalization schemes and other programs designed to turn much of the economy to the benefit of the rural and urban poor who supported him. In doing so, he fully alienated the nation's already hostile elite and portions of Chile's large middle class. Antigovernment terrorist bands began a campaign of sabotage, and the elite-owned media slandered the president. These internal pressures coincided with a covert U.S. plan to destabilize the Chilean economy. Financial credit dried up, Washington terminated debt negotiations, and CIA operatives did an effective job in agitating against the regime.

But even with these efforts, Allende's political party gained ground in midterm elections. The military trump card had to be played. Fortunately for his opponents, conditions placed on Allende prevented him in 1972–1973 from exercising civilian command over the military. During the summer of 1973, army officers opposed to ending Chilean democracy were either physically eliminated or reassigned to minor posts. Anti-Allende admirals and generals, most of whom had been trained in the United States, were poised to spring a powerful and effective coup. On September 11 they bombed *La Moneda*, the Presidential Palace. The despondent president inside apparently shot himself. During the next several days, thousands of pro-Allende Chileans were rounded up, as well as many of the foreign activists who had come to Chile from other countries. The general who led the coup, Augusto Pinochet, coordinated operations with acumen. The soccer stadium in downtown Santiago became a mass prison and torture center, and Brazilian military personnel flew in to help interrogate the captives. Only the embassies of a few west European countries provided any immediate safety for the coup's opponents; the U.S. embassy, in contrast, established a support operation that assisted the military in its takeover.

About a third of the Chilean populace openly welcomed the coup and embraced the cause of Pinochet. Even a generation later, much of the middle class (and certainly the rich) view him as a savior—one who steered the country away from its flirtation with communism. Their assessment was not unrealistic, for Allende was pursuing policies that although democratic in implementation, sought to redistribute wealth downward through state intervention instead of ensuring entrepreneurial profits and increasing capital. There is absolutely no doubt that to the United States his government posed an economic threat. The well-documented U.S. involvement in the coup was a rational choice for U.S. policymakers. As had similar governments in Brazil and elsewhere, the friendly military government in Chile brought with it a decline in labor costs, an end to disruptive work stoppages, and more favorable tax and fiscal policies for corporations.

However, Pinochet's opposition—unlike those in many military states elsewhere in Latin America—had at least a modicum of wealth, power, and international influence. Pro-Allende, middle-class Chileans fled overseas and levied a steady barrage of international criticism against the dictatorship. (The fact that Pinochet's security forces murdered Allende's ambassador in the heart of Washington, D.C. lent greater credence to the exiles' accusations.) The presence of exiled Chileans in the First World partly accounts for the unprecedented arrest of an aged Pinochet in Britain in 1998. The retired general, in London for medical treatment, was placed under arrest pending extradition to Spain, where a socialist judge was trying to hold him accountable for human rights abuses under his long rule (his regime had killed several Spaniards). Margaret Thatcher, George Bush Sr., and Pope John Paul II appealed for Pinochet's release, and in March 2000 the British government blocked Pinochet's extradition by Spain and allowed him to return to Chile. Despite this inglorious episode in his twilight years, Pinochet was successful in depoliticizing Chile in the 1970s. His efforts may even have encouraged Argentinian military planners to undertake a similar wholesale venture in their country.

Argentina had never resolved the contradictory legacies of Peronism. A series of coups had put military officers in power, but the nation remained deeply divided. An aged Juan Perón, now married to his second wife, Isabella—who dyed her hair and wore gowns reminiscent of those of Evita—resided in Spain but longed to come home. When he did so, in 1973, the military acquiesced. Nearly half a million Argentines mobbed Buenos Aires's airport in anticipation of their legendary leader's return. Some showed up with banners supporting the nation's burgeoning guerrilla movements; others showed up with guns and knives. Anticommunists abducted several suspected leftists and converted rooms in the airport's hotel into ad hoc torture chambers. Even before Perón's plane touched the ground (he was rerouted to an air force base because of the crowds), his people were at war with one another.

Perón briefly stabilized Argentina in 1973–1974, before dying of a massive heart attack. His widow, whose training as a cabaret singer provided no fiber for governance, ineptly attempted to manage a faltering economy ravaged by hyperinflation. The armed forces bided their time as conditions worsened and Argentinians clamored for change. The military consequently enjoyed considerable public support when it seized the government on March 24, 1976 and placed Isabelita under house arrest. In the wake of the coup, a thorough "cleansing" of Argentine society began. All prominent and passionate Peronists were subject to arrest. Secret detention centers cropped up in remote urban and rural settings, where thousands of *desaparecidos* (disappeared persons) were subjected to sophisticated tortures. Bodies were deposited in unmarked graves or taken by helicopter out over the Atlantic and dumped into shark-infested waters. Though the official tally of political executions is around 8,000, historians almost uniformly acknowledge a figure three to four times higher (the poor, especially, are loath to come forward and help identify lost ones).

Most politically active persons went into hiding. Grassroots organizations, including labor unions, dissolved. Recalcitrant workers at Ford Motor Company were put back onto the assembly line at gunpoint, and their strike leaders were taken out and shot. The Argentine regime is famous for its brutality (as General Luciano Menéndez prophesied, "We are going to kill fifty thousand—twenty-five thousand subversives, twenty thousand collaborators, and five thousand mistakes"); but its relatively selective eliminations did not antagonize the general populace. The urban middle class actually reaped some economic benefits from the regime. An overvalued Argentine currency allowed for the importation of consumer goods and for affordable vacations to Florida.

The Argentine military justified its tactics by claiming that it was defending itself against armed subversives; but in truth, all of the major guerrilla bands were infiltrated even before the coup, usually at the highest levels. There was never any threat of a serious insurgency, though many youthful idealists had taken up arms. The regime's ultimate claim to legitimacy rested on reviving the moribund economy, and in this it completely failed. Skyrocketing debt (up threefold between 1979 and 1981), hyperinflation, capital flight, and myriad bankruptcies undermined the dictatorship. A brief and dismal war with Great Britain over the Falkland Islands sealed its fate.

Popular opposition coalesced, in part through the visible and evocative human rights agitation of the "Mothers of the Disappeared." These bereaved relatives of political prisoners had gained international media attention during Argentina's hosting of the 1978 World Cup (and therefore could not, themselves, be easily neutralized). They silently marched around the plaza in front of the National Palace, carrying white handkerchiefs and placards with photos of their missing husbands and children. Their appeals were poignant, in part, because the Argentine regime had repeatedly stressed its commitment to preserving motherhood and supporting the family.

Massive and largely spontaneous rallies against the government in 1982 convinced Argentina's military leaders to step down. Their relinquishment of power to civilians helped demonstrate to vested interests, during the mid-1980s, that military rule was not the only option for preventing reforms. By threatening new coups and remaining influential behind the scenes, the armed forces in Argentina resisted serious reorganization as well as any serious penalties for their earlier human rights violations. Civilian rulers, even Peronists who eventually came to power, did not try to profoundly change Argentine society—a reassuring sign to elites throughout Latin America.

But Argentina's political culture has always been somewhat unique. Its military coups were backward-looking in that they were aimed at countering the dynamics associated with the long shadows of Juan and Evita Perón. Could the rich in other countries sanction a return to civilian control without again opening the Pandora's box of popular agitation for meaningful change? Brazil and Chile both set out on convoluted roads to civilian rule that finally culminated in 1989. As the armies retreated back into the barracks, it seemed that a possible cycle of repeated mass political mobilization and new coups could emerge. Fears of such a pattern, however, were laid to rest in the 1990s, when a new political synthesis took hold. Economic and political reforms that sought the betterment of conditions for Latin America's masses could be prevented in a variety of more sophisticated ways. Military regimes outlived their usefulness after people in power slowly came to understand that pacification does not always have to come at the point of a gun. Learning that valuable lesson, however, involved a decade of warfare in Central America—a topic of such consequence that it warrants exploration in greater depth.

6 Revolution in Central America

In 1994, Georgia politician and history Ph.D. Newt Gingrich, flush with Republican victories in the biannual congressional elections, quipped that anyone who had opposed aid to Nicaragua's Contra rebels during the 1980s should be required to wear an "I despise America" button. Gingrich's revisitation of the Contra aid issue was telling: Even a decade after the raucous debates on this subject in the House of Representatives, passions over U.S. policies in Central America persisted. Indeed, Contra aid was a defining ideological issue during the presidency of Ronald Reagan. In many ways it was also the last stand of a minuscule and shrinking American "left"—the tattered remnant of a political movement born in the turmoil of the 1960s.

But for the United States, revolution on the isthmus was once much more than a question for debate. Beginning in the late 1970s, momentum began to gather in Central America for political change. Because the agriculture-based small nations of the region were governed by inflexible, militarized dictatorships, meaningful change could come only through armed insurrection. Although revolutionary pressures tended to undercut low-waged, export-based agriculture, the economic threat they posed to the United States was minimal, given the modest dimensions of the Central American economy. The indirect danger, however, was immense. When Nicaraguan revolutionaries toppled a dictatorship in 1979, they began to remake their society and redistribute wealth downward. The ideas behind their reforms, including notions of human equality and responsive civil government, were exceedingly subversive in a world of haves and have-nots. Had the Nicaraguan revolution prospered, it would likely have inspired similar experiments elsewhere in the Third World.

When revolutionary sparks first flared in and around Nicaragua, the U.S. president at the time, Jimmy Carter, seemed unable to grasp this wider danger. Carter had argued for American promotion of human rights in his inauguration speech and in the early days of his presidency—a position not naturally compatible with wealth-extraction from the poorer areas of the globe. His early responses to the Nicaraguan crisis were uneven. By the end of his administration, he had ceased wavering and vigorously sought to suppress the popular forces at work south of the border. The proverbial "cat," however, was out of the bag. Only a determined and chaotic effort under Carter's successor, Ronald Reagan, restored order in Central America and averted the rise of sentiments that eventually would have generated independent governments hostile to the United States.

The Sandinistas of Nicaragua

The small and impoverished country of Nicaragua was at the center of the storm throughout much of the tumultuous decade of the 1980s. It posed no direct military threat to the United States (as *Rolling Stone* magazine pointed out, the place was so poor that it had only one building with a working elevator). In some ways, it was this very desperation and poverty that made the Nicaraguan revolution such an incredibly dangerous example: If its poorly fed and illiterate masses could take control of their destiny, what people on earth could not?

In the mid-1970s, most Nicaraguans were living in misery. Their nation was in the hands of a dictator, Anastasio Somoza, whose family had firmly governed the land since the 1930s. At the core of the dictatorship was the several-thousand-member National Guard, which used abduction and torture to terrify and isolate the regime's enemies. Somoza and his close supporters amassed tremendous fortunes worth nearly US$1 billion, largely through monopoly enterprises in construction and agriculture. Much of the country's best lands were owned by Somoza, who hogged so much wealth that he even annoyed other light-skinned elites, some of whom funded a mildly critical newspaper in the capital city Managua, called *La Prensa*.

1978 was a momentous year in Nicaragua, a year in which Somoza made several big mistakes. Firstly, either he or his confidants decided that the editor of *La Prensa* should be killed. In January, Pedro Joaquín Chamorro's assassination undermined the regime's credibility and angered the paper's supporters. Meanwhile, since the 1960s, obscure guerrilla bands had operated in the countryside, the most significant of which, the Sandinista National Liberation Front (FSLN), took its name from an anti-American nationalist named Augusto Sandino, who had been active in the 1920s. By mid-1978, guerrilla activities in the north had sparked some very modest uprisings. Somoza responded aggressively with his air force. The strafing and bombing of mountain villages—the same strategy used unsuccessfully by Batista in Cuba twenty years earlier—only alienated masses of other-wise largely depoliticized rural peasants. In August, a band of FSLN rebels led by the charismatic Edén Pastora seized the National Palace (which housed the legislature) and took fifteen hundred hostages. This remarkable display of daring captured the popular imagination and forced Somoza to cede to FSLN demands—the release of political prisoners and the publica-tion of the FSLN's vision for the country. By late fall 1978, much of the small nation was in open revolt.

The United States watched the demise of its faithful ally Anastasio So-moza with surprising detachment. The Carter administration drastically cut aid to Somoza's regime, largely because of its use of U.S.-supplied air-craft in bombing civilian populations. Military aid was halted, and U.S. economic assistance was reduced to a paltry $12 million in 1978. Carter also publicly complained about human rights abuses by the heretofore U.S.-supported National Guard. The FSLN, for its part, had no shortage of arms, with supplies coming in from multiple sources, including Cuba, Venezuela, and Panama.

A further rift between the United States and Somoza came in June 1979, when the National Guard executed ABC News correspondent Bill Stew-art. Most unfortunately for the regime, the shooting of the unarmed re-porter was captured on film by his cameraman and broadcast to a shocked American public on network television. Shortly thereafter, the United States joined the Organization of American States in calling for Somoza's resignation. The dictator fled in midsummer, taking up residence at his Miami estate until—embittered by Carter's lack of support—he decided to leave the country that had betrayed him. It was the last in a series of bad decisions. Taking up residence in Paraguay, he soon fell victim to a Sandin-ista hit squad, which blew up his limousine with a bazooka.

Back in Nicaragua, the Sandinistas had emerged at the forefront of vari-ous groups vying to lead a burgeoning popular revolution. Rural peasants and urban slum dwellers were responsive to the FSLN, in part because they correctly identified the Sandinistas as the most ardent opponents of the dictatorship. Yet initial efforts at filling the sudden void produced by Somoza's departure involved coalition-building, too. The Sandinistas formed alliances with moderates from Managua's small upper class, includ-ing the widow of Pedro Chamorro, Violeta, who had become a symbol of wealthy opposition to the regime. But in a pattern similar to that of the early Cuban revolution, most of these moderates were soon alienated from the Sandinistas, and vice versa. The fundamental question of how to run the economy was central: Would Nicaragua continue to foster private en-terprise, or implement socialist policies benefiting the majority (the poor)? The answer, under the Sandinistas, was the latter. By 1981, nearly 40 per-cent of the economy was nationalized (including large holdings previously controlled by the Somoza clan). The well-to-do were not particularly happy, whereas many of the poor were celebrating their newfound economic possibilities. Moderates resigned or were ousted from the cabinet. The elite began to flee en masse to condos and vacation homes in the United States, near Miami. The Catholic hierarchy stepped forward to oppose the new government, even while many of its rank and file, including a number of parish priests, supported the Sandinistas. A revitalized *La Prensa* also became an important forum for the opposition, and various middle-class business groups weighed in against Sandinista economic directives.

The United States was also initially divided in its response to the Sandinistas. Jimmy Carter welcomed their leader, Daniel Ortega, to the White House, and liberals in Washington flirted with ideas of working with the new regime. In 1979, Carter extended diplomatic recognition—the government's legitimacy was undeniable—and in 1980, he granted Nicaragua $195 million in economic aid. Could the United States do business with the Sandinistas without damaging its position in the world? Although such a policy appeared plausible in the short term, the lasting consequences might have been devastating. After all, much of Latin America, and even the world, was monitoring the unfolding experiment in Nicaragua. Its success might have inspired similar quests for change by oppressed peoples in Africa, Asia, and elsewhere.

Where Carter's policies would have led us must be left to speculation. Washington's willingness to dialogue with the Sandinistas abruptly ended with the January 1981 ascent of Ronald Reagan to the presidency. Although the Democrats retained control of the lower house in Congress, a shift in U.S. foreign policy regarding Nicaragua took place—a shift more consistent with American economic interests and historical precedent. President Reagan may not have fully understood the Nicaraguan situation or even, perhaps, its inherent dangers. He did, however, understand that the Sandinistas were neither good capitalists nor naturally compliant with U.S. goals. A product of the Cold War—a man who had made his mark in the anticommunist crusade in Hollywood (as part of the screen actors' guild, he fingered suspected "reds")—Reagan saw the khaki-clad Sandinistas as carbon copies of Cuba's revolutionaries—and he understood that Castro and his comrades were "bad guys." The Reagan administration's policies to rid the world of the Sandinistas were admittedly very sloppy, but they worked. In 1981, U.S. economic aid to Managua was halted, and an attempt to isolate and undermine the regime began in earnest.

With the support of a steady stream of returning Nicaraguan expatriates, military bureaucrats conceived of new ways to oust the Sandinistas from power. The product of their efforts was the cultivation and coordination of a political opposition called the Nicaraguan Democratic Force (FDN). Mustered in the north, along the Honduran border, the Contras, as they were commonly known, began a campaign of cross-border raids in Nicaragua in an attempt to inspire the overthrow of the Managua govern-ment. A second front opened in the south, out of Costa Rica, led by none other than Edén Pastora—who had grown disgruntled with his Sandinista brothers. But the Contras proved unable to rally anything even remotely akin to mass support. Part of the reason for their failure was that nineteen of the twenty-six top rebel leaders were former National Guards—mem-bers of an arm of the Somoza establishment that the vast majority of Nicaraguans hated. Also, Contra raids struck at what the CIA termed "soft targets"—bridges, schools, power stations, and health clinics—which did little to win the hearts and minds of the peasantry. Early on, too, the Con-tras proved inept in battle, gaining a reputation as losers. When opportu-nities came to engage the Sandinista army unfolded, the Contras usually scurried back across the Honduran border, where a U.S. military presence assured their safety.

Contra propaganda efforts were stymied by the goodwill enjoyed by the Sandinistas in the early 1980s. At the outset of their governance, the revo-lutionaries carried out health, education, and agrarian reforms in the coun-tryside, and issued widely publicized decrees stipulating economic equality for women (rhetoric often ridiculed by lower-class men). A vaccination campaign dramatically decreased infant mortality rates. The distribution of Somozcista lands delighted nearly 100,000 peasants; and an ambitious literacy campaign made further inroads in the countryside, though Sandin-ista claims of dramatic reductions in adult illiteracy were exaggerated. Be-cause of these reforms and a tide of optimism in the country, the FSLN rolled to victory in the first clean elections ever held in Nicaragua. Yet their adversaries could take heart: Nearly a third of the 1984 vote went to conservative opposition parties. Nicaraguans were divided, and they could be split apart.

Beyond Nicaragua's borders, the Reagan administration faced an uphill struggle in attempting to reverse the Sandinistas' fortunes. Europeans had some sympathy for the Sandinistas. France supplied the FSLN with arms until 1982, and myriad governments criticized Washington's policy—though the conservative British regime stood by its ally. The World Court in The Hague found the United States guilty of having violated interna-tional law in supporting the Contras and ordered reparation payments (a verdict that the United States simply ignored). Covert operations in con-junction with the Contra war also were not going well. In 1984, the CIA's mining operations in Nicaraguan harbors resulted in damage to Japanese freighters, antagonizing yet another important ally. United Nations con-demnation soon followed.

Even within the United States, popular opinion failed to decisively shift in favor of stopping the Sandinistas. Polls repeatedly showed the public badly split, even though Ronald Reagan expended much political capital in defense of the FDN opposition. He lauded the Contras as "the moral equivalents of our (American) Founding Fathers"; he called them "freedom fighters," a turn-of-phrase made silly by revelations of human rights atrocities they had perpetrated. Indeed, because Reagan so publicly discussed the Contras, news outlets could not help but thoroughly investigate their activities—a development not beneficial to Washington. When *Newsweek*, for example, published a sequence of photos in which a Contra forced a prisoner to dig his own grave before sticking a knife into his throat, many Americans (who thought better of George Washington) were outraged. When excerpts from a leaked CIA manual for the Contras entitled *Psychological Operations in Guerrilla Warfare* (complete with subsections on the use of terror and the "neutralization" of civilians) appeared in the press, many again condemned the U.S. role. These mishaps, linked to the doomed high-visibility approach of the Reagan administration, unraveled U.S. policy toward the Contras.

Liberals in the Democrat-controlled House of Representatives moved to cut off funding for the Contras, once public pressure to do so materialized. Nearly every major city in the industrial northern states, as well as many on the west coast, had grassroots political groups agitating against Reagan's Central American policies by 1985. One hundred thousand citizens even signed a Pledge of Resistance, in which they publicly vowed to protest or engage in nonviolent civil disobedience in the event of a U.S. invasion of Nicaragua. Coordinated largely through the Sojourner's Community, a radical Christian fellowship in Washington, D.C., this challenge posed obvious problems for the administration in the event of direct military engagement.

If the Contras had proven more effective on the battlefield, an end to their funding might have been a major disaster for U.S. policymakers. But given their ineffectiveness, the Reagan administration probably could have abandoned them altogether and banked solely on economic warfare in its efforts to destroy the Nicaraguan regime. The Contras did force the FSLN to divert resources to its army and militarize the country; and by the mid-1980s, they were inflicting enough infrastructural damage that they had become an asset for the United States. There was also the psychological factor. Nicaraguans were under stress, fearing Contra violence and an expansion of the war. Yet there was little chance that the Contras, by themselves, would force a change in government. Instead of allowing the operation to go dormant, the White House determined to move funding underground, violating congressional law. This decision was a poor one, since the subsequent operation was shoddily managed and subsequently exposed to the public.

In the White House's defense, however, few other military options existed. Panama's dictator, Manuel Noriega, offered to kill the Sandinista leadership. But although Noriega had covert connections and was on the CIA's payroll, there were legitimate questions as to whether he could deliver on this grandiose promise (U.S. National Security Adviser John Poindexter also disliked Noriega because of his drug operations). Public opposition and the Pledge of Resistance made a direct U.S. military strike impractical, although the White House drew up contingency plans for internment camps and a temporary suspension of the Constitution in the event that a military operation were undertaken in the face of widespread public discontent.

Illegal funding of the Contras was coordinated by Marine Corps Lt. Colonel Oliver North, operating largely from within the White House. Since tax revenues were now unavailable, North coordinated the sale of arms to another nation, Iran, and routed the money to the Contras. The irony of the scheme was considerable: Iran was fiercely anti-American, itself in the throes of popular revolutionary fervor; but it badly needed spare parts because of its war with Iraq. Saddam Hussein (at the time a "promising leader," according to George Bush) had invaded Iran with tacit U.S. approval. North was attempting to solve two foreign policy problems simultaneously. In selling arms, he worked to persuade Iran to pressure kidnappers in Lebanon to free U.S. hostages. The public position of the Reagan administration was that it would never negotiate with hostage-takers; so the talks had to be kept secret. The profits from the arms sales were laundered through Swiss bank accounts and then used to purchase new arms, which were in turn funneled to the Contras. The Contras also raised money through their continued sale of illegal narcotics, though it remains uncertain whether the CIA coordinated their cocaine operations. "Fourteen million dollars to finance arms," recorded North in his July 1985 diary, "came from drugs."

The Iran-Contra connection became public when a supply plane was shot down over Nicaragua and its American pilot and cargo were traced to the covert supply ring. News media gradually exposed the details of the poorly cloaked White House program, and liberals in Congress investigated matters to the point where North stepped forward as the fall guy. Television coverage helped North at this point—here was an earnest Marine in uniform, boldly stating his case, before a panel of visibly indecisive politicians. Yet despite the popularity engendered by North's appearance, Americans remained divided over the Contra cause. Evangelical Christians, who had long supported the Contras (televangelist Pat Robertson visited Honduran camps, delivering supplies and prayers for the "anticommunists"), rallied to North's defense. Old-line mainstream churches, such as Presbyterians and Methodists, opposed the Contras and lobbied the go-as-the-wind-blows liberals in the Congress. North perjured himself during the congressional hearings; but as a Democratic president later proved, perjury is not necessarily fatal to one's political career.

American public support for the Contras only began to rise substantially near the end of the 1980s, as media reportage from Central America diminished. Legal funding for the Contras revived under President George Bush, and the threat of renewed Contra raids demoralized pro-Sandinista Nicaraguans on the eve of an important second national election. It was financial and economic strangulation that ultimately crushed the revolutionary regime. During the mid-1980s, the United States pressured international financial institutions to withhold credit; blocked sympathetic businesses (such as clothing manufacturer Levi Strauss) from building plants in Nicaragua; and eventually erected a formidable embargo that gutted the small country's economy. The Sandinistas, who had succeeded in stabilizing prices in the early 1980s, watched helplessly as combined capital flight and isolation did their work. Inflation took hold and spiraled out of control—making Nicaraguan currency nearly worthless by 1989. Many poor Nicaraguans were barely able to afford food.

On the eve of the 1990 elections, the Sandinistas, gambling that good intentions could win them domestic and international support, freed Contra prisoners, sanctioned press freedom, and even authorized a U.S.-funded political opposition to form. The new UNO Coalition, made up of political groups ranging from archconservatives to the small Nicaraguan Communist Party, dominated the airwaves through the financial help of the United States. Knowing that only an anti-Somozcista candidate could win, UNO wisely chose Violeta Chamorro as its presidential contestant. The appeal of a woman candidate was tremendous, since many poor women had been politicized during the course of the revolution. The Sandinistas staged mammoth rallies featuring sympathetic foreign celebrities, such as guitarist Jackson Browne. But rock and roll was not enough; the Sandinistas lost Nicaragua's second clean election by a landslide. With the economy in ruins, popular sentiment had turned against the regime, though this did not equate with an endorsement either of the Contras or of a return to the past. Chamorro was able to serve out her term, despite a continued slide in the economy and the failure of the United States to restore economic aid at previous levels. By 1995, Nicaragua's economy was smaller than it had been in 1965, and nearly 40 percent of the population was suffering from malnourishment. Yet Nicaraguans remained depoliticized; a growing addiction to television (even on low-quality communal sets in the barrios) was more prevalent than any revolutionary inclinations. U.S. policies, though haphazard, had borne fruit. Wealthy citizens returned, and small pockets of affluence dotted the otherwise dismal landscape of Man-

Central America and the Caribbean

agua. Domino's Pizza magnate Tom Monaghan even underwrote the costs for a snappy new cathedral, a tribute to the persistent and helpful anti-Sandinista efforts of Archbishop Miguel Obando y Bravo.

Staging Grounds: Costa Rica and Honduras

The Contra war against Nicaragua could not have been prosecuted without the help of Costa Rica and Honduras, which collaborated with the United States to facilitate the Sandinistas' demise. Regional animosities as well as self-interest on the part of Nicaragua's neighbors aided U.S. foreign policy goals. Officials in Costa Rica and Honduras cooperated with the United States and were duly rewarded with money and bribes, while much of the general populations in both nations swallowed a steady diet of anti-communist media hype or remained politically ill-informed and detached from events.

Costa Rica has long been unusually receptive to American influence. Sometimes referred to as the "Switzerland of Central America" because of its relative stability and prosperity coupled with its mountainous terrain, Costa Rica entered the 1980s with a tradition of reasonably free elections and a sizable middle class. With a shallow colonial past, little racial or cultural diversity, and a minuscule Indian population, the country has remained provincial. Its conservative political culture has long resisted radical change. Given these precedents, coupled with Costa Rica's long-standing rivalry with Nicaragua and disdain for things Nicaraguan, it is no surprise that Washington found in Costa Rica a quick and willing ally for its counterrevolutionary crusade. Costa Rican authorities cooperated by quietly allowing the Contras to open a second, southern front against the Sandinistas in 1982. This front was unpredictable—not because of the *Ticos*, as Costa Ricans are called, but because the Contra forces were led by Pastora, the former Sandinista who had undertaken the memorable assault on Somoza's National Palace and had wound up in Costa Rica shortly thereafter.

Equipped with arms from Panamanian authorities, Pastora had launched a frontal attack on the dictatorship during the final stages of the uprising. He and his men were late in reaching Managua, however; and the more intellectual and politically minded Sandinista leaders who had seized power relegated him to a nominal post that involved bureaucratic paper-pushing. Pastora had always been a man of action, and he soon grew restless. The takeover of the National Palace had made him the icon of the revolution; but now, few Nicaraguans seemed to notice him. His peasant background and limited schooling made a serious managerial post unlikely. A few months later, stymied by these events and disillusioned by the newfound materialism of some of his Sandinista colleagues, Pastora decided to leave the country and explore the possibilities for initiating a second wave of revolt. He wandered off to Libya, where he sought funds from Muammar Qadhafi and talked of joining the Indian rebellions in Guatemala. He also visited Cuba and spoke with Castro, who told him to go back to Nicaragua, do his best, and support the Sandinista cause. Pastora ended up communicating with U.S. officials and go-betweens representing the CIA. In time, he was convinced that he should restart the Nicaraguan civil war and replace the Sandinistas himself. With heavy backing from the United States, he set up camp in Costa Rica.

Pastora was a problem for the United States, because although he was charismatic and a talented fighter, he was not completely malleable. For example, he stubbornly refused to work with Contras who were ex-Somoza

National Guards (a serious flaw, given the composition of the Contra ranks). He remembered his childhood, when the National Guard had murdered his father in order to seize his farm. Because of this and other preconditions Pastora set, his relationship with his American backers was exceedingly tenuous. By spring 1984, when he had several thousand men in the field along Nicaragua's southern border, he seemed to spend as much time haranguing the CIA as the government he was supposed to be fighting! In May, when Pastora was meeting with a group of reporters at his jungle hideout, a bomb exploded, wounding him. Sandinistas probably had planted the bomb, but no one on the American side was terribly sad to see Pastora go into an unanticipated retirement.

The man behind Pastora and in charge of coordinating much of the Contras' southern front was a wealthy American rancher named John Hull. Working as a CIA agent, Hull orchestrated airlifts, supply operations, and training programs for the rebels with the knowledge of Costa Rican authorities. During the administration of Luis Alberto Monge (1982–1986), Costa Rica was exceedingly helpful in these efforts, turning a blind eye to violations of sovereignty and human rights, and even allowing the United States to build a secret airstrip in a remote area of the country. Monge himself became a Reagan administration point man on Central America, flying into Washington and lobbying the U.S. Congress for more Contra and military aid. He and his cabinet members personally enjoyed the benefits of cooperation, with USAID funds and other foreign bank deposits often ending up in their private accounts. The lack of an investigative press corps in Costa Rica assured continued public docility.

Unfortunately for Washington, however, Monge's successor was not as compliant. Oscar Arias was an intellectual who was bothered by the Contras' violations of Costa Rican sovereignty and neutrality and was not easily persuaded. Arias threatened to disclose the location of the secret U.S. airfield—a ploy that prompted Oliver North to tell him he could forget about U.S. economic aid if he ever did so. Apparently even without a leak from the Arias government, American reporters found out about the landing site and decided to go ahead and report it. The newspapers that ran the story, including the *Miami Herald* and *New York Times*, pried further into the extensive CIA operations around Nicaragua—which in addition to supplying the Contras were moving shipments of cocaine northward.

Arias, for his part, did not remain idle. His government began to prosecute John Hull for kidnapping, torture, drug smuggling, and a range of charges collectively termed "hostile acts." Hull fled for home, where the intervention of Lee Hamilton and other Indiana politicians helped block his extradition back to Costa Rica to stand trial (a proceeding that, had it occurred, could have brought forth damaging evidence about U.S. covert operations). The Tico president even lectured Ronald Reagan, in a closed meeting in 1987, audaciously telling the leader of the West that he understood neither the events in Central America nor the consequences of U.S. policy in the region, and would do well to quit funding the Contras.

In 1987, the United States cut off economic aid to Costa Rica as Arias pursued a new peace initiative. Costa Ricans convinced the Sandinistas to sign a pact that sought to demilitarize the isthmus, as a consequence of which the Managua regime pursued a host of new policies that led directly to the Sandinistas' defeat in the 1990 election. They signed a peace accord with the Contras and lifted nearly all restraints on political activities, allowing for the well-organized, U.S.-funded opposition and a highly critical press. Ironically, although the United States resented Arias's peace plan at the time, the pact helped pave the way for what was clearly best for America: The end of the Sandinistas. Nor could Arias himself complain: He received the Nobel peace prize and worldwide recognition. Costa Ricans, however, rejected his party at the polls in 1990, turning the presidency over to his 1986 electoral rival and bringing Costa Rican policies back into harmony with those of the United States.

Whereas Costa Rica was a key but inconsistent ally, Honduras served U.S. interests more steadily. Government magistrates in Tegucigalpa never raised any serious objections to a profound militarization of their poor country. During the mid-1980s, enormous Contra support bases sprang up in Palmerola and elsewhere near the southern Honduran frontier, where tens of thousands of American servicemen were engaged in training or giving other support to the Contras. Honduran officers served as go-betweens in military operations, and opportunities for graft kept them happy. Most poor Hondurans seemed also to welcome the foreign presence, as the dollars flowing into the hands of restaurateurs and prostitutes aided the moribund local economy.

Despite the apparent docility of Hondurans, a small cadre of military officers and U.S. advisers who feared that unrest in El Salvador and Guatemala might spread into Honduras created Battalion 3-16. A secret intelligence unit funded by Washington, B 3-16 set up safe houses in Honduras, where political activists were interrogated and tortured. That B 3-16 operatives were digging deep in order to find subversives is evident by the identities of their prisoners: Most victims were reporters with a penchant for accuracy, or human rights and labor union organizers critical of the government. Several students who agitated for free schoolbooks and lower bus fares were also rounded up. Many victims, like journalist Oscar Reyes and his wife, survived sessions of beatings and electric shocks (though the trauma continued to haunt them). All told, when investigations by Leo Valladares Lanza and other pro-democracy advocates in Honduras systematically documented 3-16's activities during the 1990s, they could identify only two hundred persons who were "completely disappeared" (killed after undergoing torture).

Ironically, the creation of B 3-16 seems to have sparked the kind of upstart opposition it was supposed to prevent. A few guerrilla bands formed in the Honduran mountains in the late 1980s, though they never amounted to much. Perhaps their biggest score was the killing of General Gustavo Alvarez Martínez in 1989. Martínez, who helped create B 3-16, had received the Legion of Merit from Ronald Reagan for "encouraging the success of democratic processes in Honduras." After he was ousted from the army due to scandal in 1984, he resided with his family in Florida. When he returned to Tegucigalpa in order preach the gospel (like many Central American military men, Martínez was an American-influenced evangelical), the obscure Popular Liberation Movement "sent him to God" with a barrage of heavy machine gun fire. When B 3-16 and the Contras ceased operations in the early 1990s, the Honduran guerrilla cells also disbanded.

In 2000, excavations began in earnest at a former Contra camp near the Nicaraguan border, where B 3-16 victims and Contra prisoners were buried. Digging has turned up small metal prison cells, where victims apparently were held between torture sessions. Human rights investigators believed they had found damning evidence there of B 3-16's dirty war, but the Honduran military, acknowledging the find, suggested that the bodies had come from a nearby hospital.

Exterminating Indians in Guatemala

Fears of Honduran instability were not only due to the nation's proximity to Nicaragua but also to the massive repression unleashed in Guatemala, to the west. Between 1978 and 1985, tens of thousands of Mayan Indians were eliminated in counterinsurgency operations by the Guatemalan army and security forces. The scope of the bloodletting was probably unnecessary to preserve order, since Guatemala's disparate guerrilla bands never really inspired the popular support necessary for a seizure of the state. However, race was a driving factor in the repression and its excesses. It is unclear what benefits, if any, the United States expected to derive from these killings; but as is documented in the U.N. Truth Commission's 1999 report, U.S. security resources were integral to facilitating the ethnic cleansing.

With racial diversity and one of the most skewed distributions of wealth in the hemisphere, Guatemala has long appeared ripe for revolution. In fact, the Indians that make up the vast majority of the population have always been deeply divided by regional, linguistic, and cultural differences, and remote villagers in the mountains have tended to keep to themselves.

A powerful *ladino* (light-skinned elite) in Guatemala City has politically dominated the country for centuries, having usurped direct control over large tracts of land in the 1870s. Inspired by overseas demand for coffee, the rich carved large *fincas*, or coffee plantations, out of property owned by villagers or the Catholic Church, acquiring tracts through legal mechanisms provided by a classic liberal government. By the mid-twentieth century, Guatemala had both mini- and latifundio. Enormous *fincas* consumed much of the best land, with a mere twenty-two estates occupying 13 percent of the country. Surges in population growth left too many Indians on too few plots of marginal land. By 1950 most of Guatemala's nearly 3 million Indians were destitute; and more than 150,000 were barely subsistent, with less than four acres.

The political system opened up at the close of World War II, when urban unrest ousted a pro-German president. The subsequent rule of middle-class reformer Juan Arévalo laid the groundwork for land reform through a new constitution; but it was his successor, Jacobo Arbenz, who led a truly revolutionary government. Arbenz issued Decree 900, authorizing a massive redistribution of rural lands. Although well conceived, Arbenz's agrarian reform faced determined opposition from planters and triggered a chaotic process of change in the countryside. Peasant leagues flourished, even though their leaders suffered beatings and intimidation. Yet the poor themselves were divided, with different tribal groups vying for various tracts of land, and premature land seizures badly disrupting the legal processes of distribution. The United States, perceiving communist influence in the Arbenz government and annoyed by the seizure of property owned by United Fruit Company (Chiquita Brands), launched a covert operation against the regime. The conservative Guatemalan military, instead of protecting their country, yielded to outside pressures and forced Arbenz, himself a colonel, to retire. Both the wealthy and the small Guatemala City middle class, unnerved by the uncontrolled changes taking place in the countryside, rejoiced. Nearly all of the confiscated lands were returned to the rich, and a decades-long process of suppression began.

It was not so much the coup as the tightening of internal security in its wake that spawned modest guerrilla cells in the late 1950s. Guatemala found itself in turmoil during the remainder of the twentieth century. Various U.S. programs equipped and trained its security forces: Much of the officers' corps received counterinsurgency instruction from Americans; and in the mid-1960s, U.S. special forces practiced counterinsurgency operations in Guatemala's mountain highlands (we still know relatively little about these clandestine field exercises). Although the government in Guatemala City often displayed civilian features, the military firmly held the reins of power into the mid-1990s. In the late 1960s Guatemala was among the first Latin American countries to develop death squads—secretive bands of military men who carried out not-so-secret political killings in order to frighten people and squelch public dissent.

Despite the repressive environment, guerrilla groups in Guatemala never mobilized mass support like that of the FSLN in Nicaragua. Most of the early rebel leaders were educated mestizos, and the cultural and ideological gaps between them and the Maya were considerable. Living in tight communities and often suspicious of outsiders, conservative Maya resisted their overtures and turned inward. Deep-seated tribal rivalries and divergent cultural traditions also made Indian revolutionary unity unlikely. Even at the peak of their activity, around 1980, active guerrillas numbered only a few thousand.

Violence in the countryside spiraled upward in the late 1970s, when a nervous security establishment tightened its grip and sanctioned activities designed to induce fear. Fortunately for the state, not only did Indians fail to embrace revolutionary change but they also were highly susceptible to division. Military-linked death squads set out to terrorize Mayan villages. For example, in San Pedro de Laguna, on the shores of Lake Atitlán, a small band of locals, equipped with military arms, abducted and killed village leaders in the night. They operated under the orders of the military commissioner, himself a local Indian. The prospect of near-absolute power, the ability to take possessions from others, and the authority to kill one's rivals—these motivated the paramilitaries. In San Pedro de Laguna, over time, locals figured out that it was some of their own who were doing the killing (despite the death squad's practice of spraying guerrilla slogans on walls or corpses). In time, they convinced the army to intercede—making the military a kind of savior for the people.

Under President-General Romero Lucas García (1978–1982), the army itself carried out several sensational massacres in rural Guatemala. Repression accelerated during the strange presidency of Efraín Rios Montt. An evangelical Christian, Rios Montt was prominent in Guatemala City's Church of the Word, a prophetic sect that held tent revivals among the rich in the capital. Its parent organization, Gospel Outreach Ministries of Eureka, California, sent out waves of earnest evangelicals to help win souls for Christ. Rios Montt himself had long coveted the presidency and was probably deeply involved in planning the coup that brought him to power in March 1982. Surrounded by church elders–turned–political consultants, he donned army fatigues and preached Jesus on national television even as the Guatemalan army was revving up its killing machine. Rios Montt and many of his cohorts shared an apocalyptic vision of Guatemala's carnage, convinced that they were in the middle of a spiritual struggle between forces of good (authority) and evil (subversion)—a mind-set that sanctioned successive waves of assassinations. Possibly as many as 100,000 died in the Rios Montt-era purges.

Indian communities ravaged by repression sometimes found relief through conversion to Protestantism. For all of the army's savagery, under Rios Montt it began to provide the populace with a way out. Cooperation against guerrillas won communities peace, and by 1983 the army wisely began to reward such cooperation. In contrast, the guerrillas could only deliver hunger and hardship, and elicit more retribution. For years, bands of insurgents (especially under the banner of EGP, the Guerrilla Army of the Poor) visited villages and made hollow promises: If inhabitants flew their flags, they would receive protection and weapons for self-defense. After years of terror, a traumatized village-based populace longed for peace at any cost. Survival was more important than reform. Indians lined up to assist the army in tracking down guerrillas and restoring civil order. In 1982 the military created civil defense patrols, requiring every Guatemalan adult male in the insurgency zones to serve at roadblocks and report on any subversive activities. Hundreds of thousands of Indians complied; and even when mandatory service in the patrol was abolished in the 1986 Constitution, a majority continued to serve. Checkpoints greatly curtailed movement in the countryside, and the "carrot" of relative security undercut the appeal of Guatemala's guerrilla groups, which were forced to consolidate into the Guatemalan National Revolutionary Union (URNG) soon thereafter.

The visibility of state terror in Guatemala prompted Jimmy Carter to cut off U.S. military aid. However, aid was restored under Ronald Reagan, who sympathized with Rios Montt and was responsive to the evangelical lobby that supported him. Even the years when supplies were cut off posed no problem for the Guatemalan regime. Carter himself quietly approved shipments of helicopters and hardware in violation of his own public position, and other nations—in particular, Israel—routed arms and intelligence assistance to Guatemalans during the gap. An Israeli-supplied tracking system, using computerized databases, greatly aided authorities in identifying and eliminating subversives.

Still, on the downside of the repression (after 1985), multiple high-profile human rights cases damaged the public credibility of U.S. policy and of the Guatemalan regime. First was that of U.S. citizen Diana Ortiz, a Hispanic American from New Mexico who was abducted and tortured in 1989 by one of the many mercenary-infused death squads operating in the countryside. An Ursuline nun, Ortiz was stripped and burned in one hundred places with cigarettes, then dumped into a pit filled with rancid, decomposing bodies (of both the still-living and the dead) and rats. Dragged out for still more rape and torture, she was recognized as a foreigner by an American supervisor, who realized that although killing poor Indians posed no problem, the repercussions of eliminating a U.S. citizen would be formidable. Allowed to escape, Ortiz made her way back to the United

States and began a years-long fight to inform the public of her ordeal, despite considerable psychological trauma and a skeptical, corporate-owned press.

Like most Latin American regimes, the Guatemalan government hires U.S. public relations and advertising firms to promote a positive image of Guatemala in the United States. In this particular cause, the Washington, D.C.-based firm of Patton, Boggs, & Blow appears to have rendered effective service: ABC news correspondent Cokie Roberts, sister of the firm's senior partner Tom Boggs, confronted Ortiz during an interview with accusations of fraudulence. The Guatemalan government earlier had issued a public statement contending that Ortiz had fallen victim to an out-of-control, sadomasochistic lover—an explanation that no well-informed person could have taken seriously. Ultimately, the Guatemalan government's efforts to suppress reports of the Ortiz incident failed, and Ortiz's case received enough public exposure to raise serious questions.

On the heels of Ortiz's revelations came the sensational decision of the Nobel committee to award the 1992 peace prize to a Mayan Indian woman named Rigoberta Menchú. Menchú had been interviewed by a European anthropologist in the early 1980s, who recorded, edited, and published her life story, complete with grim tales of repression. Menchú and her editor took liberties—changing facts and altering details in an attempt to maximize the emotional impact of the book, which was widely read in U.S. universities. In real life Menchú and her family lost their land to other marginalized Indians in a web of local rivalry, rather than to *ladinos,* as the book contended. The facts surrounding the deaths of Menchú's relatives were also altered, as the common penchant for portraying primitive peoples as innocents won out over truth. Widely read, the account brought Menchú fame, and eventually, the Nobel prize. Some American academics were appalled. William Radcliffe of the Hoover Institution at Stanford bewailed the influence of Marxism among the members of the Nobel committee. In 1999, after Stanford Ph.D. David Stoll scrutinized the biography and revealed its errors, the Nobel laureate's name become tarnished. In the late 1980s and 1990s, however, Rigoberta Menchú's prominence did much to evoke First World sympathy for the revolutionary cause. Her influence in Guatemala, however, remained minimal.

A third disruptive case involved Harvard Law School graduate Jennifer Harbury, who had married a second-tier guerrilla leader who was abducted and tortured to death by security forces in the early 1990s. Harbury had enough contacts and influence to secure some media coverage. A particularly damaging interview on CBS's *60 Minutes* did much to elevate her cause. Attempts by the U.S. and Guatemalan governments to stonewall the investigation into her husband's death unraveled; and several major media outlets subsequently exposed evidence of CIA complicity in the case (in part because of the work of New Jersey Representative Robert Torricelli, who was in turn reputedly prodded to investigate by his friend Bianca Jagger). Although the Clinton administration issued a public promise to release classified papers on the Harbury and Ortiz cases, it repeatedly reneged on the promise, avoiding further damaging revelations.

In April 1998, Catholic Bishop Juan Gerardi was found dead in his home just after releasing a study that blamed the military and security forces for 80 percent of the human rights atrocities during the several decades of repression in Guatemala. The Guatemalan government at first tried to implicate the bishop's dog—another attempt at disinformation that evoked more public cynicism than belief. A year later, it acknowledged that the military had played a role in the bishop's death. In 2000, several suspects were arrested, including a priest. The pace and vigor of the investigation suggest that high-level collaborators will not be found. In this and other inquiries, death threats have caused lawyers, judges, and human rights advocates to stop scrutinizing the past, or even to leave their professions or their country altogether.

In the closing months of the twentieth century, Guatemalans of all stripes symbolically endorsed the official evasion of such questions by electing Alfonso Portillo to the country's top leadership post. Portillo, a former university professor and a friend of Rios Montt, admitted to having shot two indigent men in southern Mexico while on vacation in 1982—killings for which he had never been prosecuted. His media consultant-produced television ads, in the wake of the revelation, explained to Guatemala's Indians that "a man who can defend his own life can defend yours." Apparently persuaded, the poor voted for Portillo in large numbers. His nearest rival, who forced a run-off vote, was a rightist candidate of a pro-business party. In contrast, the choice of human rights crusaders and demobilized guerrillas, Alvaro Colóm, mustered a pathetic 12 percent of the tally in the well-conducted elections. Clearly the vast majority of Guatemala's poor prefer peace and stability over social justice and the risks involved in attempting social change. In 2000, Portillo's government, with excellent media relations (the presidential press secretary is a former CNN reporter), began to improve Guatemala's image abroad.

The extermination of recalcitrant Indians in Guatemala in the last decades of the twentieth century preserved social structures beneficial to U.S. national security interests. Direct American involvement under President Ronald Reagan turned back the threat presented by the revolution in Nicaragua (namely, that its delivery of equitable conditions to the poor would inspire similar experiments elsewhere in the Third World), albeit in a rather awkward manner. Yet while these operations can rightly be called victories, the true success of American foreign policy came in El Salvador, where a U.S.-supplied and -coordinated counterinsurgency campaign defeated a popular revolution. The victory in El Salvador is important for several reasons: It provides a case study of how to defeat a guerrilla insurgency; it all but assures that there will be no more "Cubas" in Latin America in the future; and it has contributed to a fundamental redefinition of the role and strategies of the U.S. military and intelligence establishments in the twenty-first century.

7 Christianity and Counterinsurgency

A philosopher in a tiny province of the Roman Empire once told a crowd, "Let the man who has two tunics share with him who has none." Not surprisingly, this advice was poorly received by his better-dressed listeners. A friend of this thinker, whose teachings were arguably even more radical, sternly warned the wealthy: "Woe to you who are rich, for you are receiving your comfort in full. Woe to you who are well-fed now, for you shall be hungry." Within a few years, both of these men were imprisoned and put to death by the governing authorities. The teachings of John the Baptist and Jesus Christ, however, remain widely read and popular to this day. Among many of the poor in Latin America, their messages have had special significance.

In the 1960s, in the wake of the social and political ferment spawned by the Cuban revolution, a second and potentially even more powerful current for change began to rock Latin America. This new revolutionary impulse came from the heart of one of the most conservative and hierarchical institutions in the region: the powerful Roman Catholic Church. It came in the form of Bible-influenced *liberation theology*. Liberation theology had its roots in several momentous events in the Church in the 1960s. By the beginning of the decade, much of the Church's world leadership had come to realize that in some ways, Roman Catholicism was becoming archaic. Attendance in the increasingly secular First World was down, and a healthy percentage of the burgeoning masses in the Third World seemed untouched by church teachings. Aware of the stagnation, Pope John XXIII convened a high church council, charging it with the task of modernizing Catholicism and reviving its social relevance. Vatican II, as this meeting of high clerics was called, met in Rome and quickly set to work, actually going beyond the expectations of the conservative Pope and his advisers.

From 1962 to 1965, its participants implemented a series of substantial reforms, including instructions ending a fifteen-century-long tradition of conducting services, or masses, in Latin. Now both the illiterate poor and the oligarchs of Latin America could attend masses in the vernacular and could understand what the priests were saying.

As Vatican II closed in December 1965, some Latin American Catholics were already wrestling with the implicit message: How can faith be relevant in the modern world? For one young priest in Colombia, the answer was visionary. Camilo Torres, born into a wealthy Bogotá family, concluded that it was the duty of every Christian to resist institutions that perpetuate gross social and economic inequities. Torres declared the need for social revolution, and warned Christians that those who ignored the call to alleviate poverty were committing a mortal sin. Not one to shy away from putting his beliefs into practice, he joined Colombia's nascent guerrilla movement, only to be killed in battle against counterinsurgents. Torres's convictions were made all the more dramatic by his death, and provided an example to emerging liberation theologians.

In the shadow of Torres's witness, at Medellín, Colombia, about one quarter of Latin America's bishops met to discuss the Vatican II reforms in 1968. These bishops tended to represent the activist wing of the Church, and they were sensitive to the plight of the majority poor in their countries. Noting economic inequities and "institutionalized violence" in the region, they accepted the premise that lay activism and social change were necessary. Hardly revolutionaries, they did seem to at least sanction an increased social conscience among priests and nuns, many of whom interpreted the pronouncements at Medellín as a new Magna Carta for the Church in Latin America.

One of the proponents of social activism on the part of Christians was a young Peruvian adviser to the Medellín bishops, Gustavo Gutiérrez. Gutiérrez had been a prolific reader since his youth, when he was bedridden due to a crippling illness. Trained as a theologian, he had been a classmate of Camilo Torres's in seminary; and though he rejected Torres's willingness to embrace violence, he strongly believed that silence in the face of oppression was also wrong. Gutiérrez penned a number of books in the early 1970s that made him one of the most renowned advocates of Christian social activism. He and his cohorts accepted the premises of dependency theory and certainly were aware of the ideas of Karl Marx; but at the core of their thought (or at least, Gutiérrez's) was the Bible. Harking back to the teachings of Jesus Christ, they saw, in their God's nature, a thirst for justice and liberation—a passion reflected in the exodus legend of the Israelites from slavery in Egypt. God, Gutiérrez concluded, had a "preferential option" for the world's poor. He sought their material well-being as well as their spiritual liberation.

Although the label *liberation theology* was soon attached to the writings of Gutiérrez and others (coming from the title of his book *A Theology of Liberation*), current use of it potentially misrepresents the subsequent movement as something other than Christian. Indeed, there was never a single theology of liberation, but rather, multiple ideas from myriad authors—many of whom, like Gutiérrez, emphasized the Bible. Surely the claim of these religious persons to Christianity is just as valid as that of others. If liberation theologians warrant the label of *Marxists*, then Biblical Christians should perhaps be considered communists. For Acts 4:32 states that early believers in Christ "were of one heart and soul; and not one of them claimed that anything belonging to him was his own; but all things were common property to them."

In the early 1970s, many Catholics began to read the books of Gutiérrez and similar thinkers in seminaries around the world. Though only a small minority of the Church embraced liberation ideas, the impact of those ideas on the Latin American Church was profound. Adopting the practices of Brazilian educator Paulo Freire, nuns and priests, many of them foreign-born, began to engage the poor in a process of *concientización*, or consciousness-raising. Rather than dominate the poor in a paternalistic fashion, liberation Christians approached them as equals, shared in their sufferings, and sought to empower them to effect social change. Small groups of peasants organized under the rubric of consciousness-raising and welcomed the aid of liberation Christians in learning to read. These groups, known as Christian Base Communities, had sprouted up throughout Latin America by the mid-1970s, especially in Central America and Brazil. Hundreds of thousands of poor began to read the Bible and believe that Jesus Christ was a God who desired their physical and spiritual well-being. The message of liberation Christianity was, needless to say, fundamentally subversive in societies marked by the concentration of wealth in the hands of a few.

Liberation Christianity played a significant role in fueling the revolutionary upheavals in Nicaragua and Guatemala. Though the U.S. media, and even many academics, described the Sandinistas and Guatemalan guerrilla bands as Marxists or leftists, the reality was much more complex. Nor should the influence of religious ideas surprise us (what would truly have been amazing is if conservative, devoutly Catholic, poorly educated peasants *had* been sitting around reading Karl Marx). In Nicaragua, Christian thinking had especially permeated the barrios of Managua, where masses of poor rallied to the Sandinista cause. Four liberation-oriented priests served in high levels of government, including Ernesto Cardenal, a poet who was the Sandinista Minister of Culture. In Guatemala, the Guerrilla Army of the Poor (EGP) was heavily shaped by liberation Christianity, as was the Committee of Peasant Unity (CUC), a predominantly Indian group that arose in the mid-1970s, out of Catholic Action organizations. Nowhere, however, was liberation Christianity more decisive in fomenting unrest than in El Salvador; and it was here that counterinsurgency evolved into a war on the Christian faith itself.

El Salvador: Revolution Brews in City and Countryside

El Salvador in the mid-1970s was, even by Latin American standards, a nation of stark inequity. A small enclave of light-skinned elites, numbering only a few hundred families, owned and managed a crowded country of some five million people. These elites, who had security-protected, spacious homes in the Escalón neighborhood of San Salvador, held nearly 90 percent of the productive land in the countryside, though they rarely visited their rural estates, many of which were coffee plantations filled with bean-picking peasants during the harvest season. Those coffee beans, like the rich themselves, frequently ended up in the United States; Folgers, a division of the Cincinnati-based Proctor & Gamble Company, commonly used Salvadoran beans. Other exports also tied the powerful families to foreign—largely U.S.—interests. Their sons and daughters attended American universities, and many families owned second or third homes in Florida and Europe.

By the mid-1970s, the top 0.1 percent of Salvadorans had incomes greater than the next 50 percent, and the lower half of the population had next to nothing. Poverty was acute in the countryside—so bad, in fact, that sorghum (used in most places as cattle fodder) became a dietary substitute among the peasantry for beans and corn, which many could no longer afford. Unemployment was severe, and existing work, mostly in agriculture, was seasonal. In short, El Salvador was prime territory for a bloody struggle between the haves and have-nots.

Yet history is replete with evidence of starving people who remain collectively docile. What caused El Salvador to percolate was the influence of liberation theology, which became quite pronounced in much of the countryside through the work of energetic, Bible-wielding priests, lay leaders, and nuns. In the 30,000-member parish of Aguilares, just north of the capital, 700 peasants began attending Base Community Bible studies by the mid-1970s. The local church sported colorful banners about letting "justice roll down like many waters"—until the conservative bishop visited and had the inflammatory words removed. Despite the church hierarchy's opposition, tens of thousands of poor flocked to join the Federation of Christian Peasants of El Salvador (FECCAS), which although it had been outlawed by the government was circulating petitions and holding peaceful but provocative rallies calling for political democracy and land reform.

In the capital, there were similar calls for reform from a more traditional and arguably less threatening sector. A small but active middle class had emerged in San Salvador during the 1960s, made up of businessmen and professionals who sent their children to the nearby national university. As anticipated by modernization theorists, these "middle sectors" supported political change. They wanted free and open elections, and pushed for them by founding and supporting El Salvador's first authentic political party, the PDC, or Christian Democrats. In the mid-1960s the PDC won several local offices, with its most successful politician, José Napoleón Duarte, capturing the mayoralty of San Salvador itself. But the oligarchs had deep-seated reservations about the PDC and the middle class, and instead of building an alliance that could have averted insurrection, they repeatedly opted to use fraud in order to keep their own men in power.

Those men, generally, were not the rich themselves. A tightly run military, subservient to the elite, governed the country at its behest. Generals nominated each other and coordinated fake national elections in order to retain the presidency. Wisely, the United States pressed for some changes in the system (a move consistent with the Alliance for Progress); a younger generation of officers, too, recognized that a dose of reform could stave off serious unrest. For a while, in the early 1970s, some of these reform-minded officers held influential positions in the government, and a balance between change and continuity appeared, at least briefly, to assure the peace. The nature of the American interest in reaching this balance was clear: A number of U.S. corporations had set up shop in El Salvador in order to take advantage of its favorable labor laws and working conditions. There were several light manufacturers in the capital, such as a Phelps-Dodge copper wiring plant, and prosperous agribusinesses, such as Esso and Cargill.

Yet the potential of continued popular passivity, coupled with solid profits, was slowly lost, in part due to the ineptitude of the Salvadoran elite. With their counsel and blessing, hard-line officers edged out the moderates during the mid-1970s, and more patently fake elections in 1972 and 1977 preserved order but alienated portions of the urban middle class. The PDC's Duarte ran for the presidency in 1972 and was denied it by fraud; beaten up by security forces shortly thereafter, he was driven out of the country. His running mate, Guillermo Ungo, remained in El Salvador but watched as the PDC was marginalized and its popular support dwindled. In the mid-1970s, much of the urban populace was leaving the party to join mass democratic bodies known as "popular organizations." Instead of banking on elections, these groups—which included large numbers of university students and labor activists—took to the streets, demonstrating in the tens of thousands and calling for a new government that would support land, wage, and labor reforms.

Demonstrators can shout until they are blue, but as long as they do not take up arms they are only a nuisance to established institutions. A minuscule number of angry university students began to form armed cells and carry out kidnappings; but in the mid-1970s they were still insignificant and on the fringe of El Salvador's political structure. Although the small nation swirled with energy, it did not have to explode. What largely tore it apart were the repeated decisions of the army and elite to shoot peaceful protesters. One of the earlier and more memorable street massacres took place in 1975, when university students marched in opposition to the Miss Universe extravaganza. Rich Salvadorans were delighted to host the worldwide pageant, and spent lavishly on state-sponsored dances, parties, and other galas. Some idealists saw this as shameful, given the poverty in the countryside. When the students gathered, security forces opened fire with machine guns, killing dozens and wounding scores of others. And the beauty pageant was merely the first of multiple bloody affairs. Salvadoran authorities acquired so much expertise at gunning down street demonstrators that the operation almost became a science: Fleets of mechanized street-cleaners stood at the ready; after the bodies were removed, they scrubbed the blood off the pavement, and police officers reopened thoroughfares to traffic within an hour.

After hundreds of Salvadorans had died in downtown massacres, popular organizations gave up on street protests as a tactic (not surprisingly, as the U.S. embassy noted at the time, they increasingly had trouble getting people to show up). They turned instead to forcible takeovers of public buildings, general strikes, and labor unrest, which often nearly shut down the capital. Far worse for vested interests was the fact that the mass of unorganized residents now clearly sympathized with the opposition—after the street slaughters, sentiment was feverishly antigovernment. In response, the oligarchs and their allies created what soon became known as "death squads." From 1979 to 1981, these bands of trained killers, primarily formed from the ranks of the national police and other security forces, ravaged popular sociopolitical organizations. Their standard procedure was to abduct members and take them to a secluded location for torture. After body parts were chopped off and flesh was burned by electricity, cigars, or blowtorches, a bullet to the head ended the life of the activist, and a trip to a trash heap on the outskirts of San Salvador concluded the exercise. El Playón, as the dump was known, featured headless and mangled corpses among its piles of rubbish, with literally hundreds of partial bodies dotting its vulture-covered landscape at any given time.

Mass terror does not always pacify a country. The decimated popular organizations went underground, and their surviving members turned to armed insurrection. The death squads also incited revolt by taking on the institutional protagonist of change: the Church. That liberation theology permeated the Salvadoran Church and prompted its advocacy of reform is undeniable; but instead of selective and thoughtful repression, security forces persecuted the Church wholesale. Assassinations of priests and nuns aroused the indignation not only of devout and naturally conservative peasants but also of influential Catholics abroad. American church leaders tried to convince the Carter administration to distance itself from its client government, but with only limited success.

The head of the Salvadoran Church was Archbishop Oscar Romero. Appointed by a conservative Vatican in 1977, Romero was supposed to have been a voice of moderation. Instead, as he saw his priests die and his flock tremble, he condemned the government and its repression. He wrestled with the age-old theological question about justified use of force. What would the Good Samaritan have done, the Archbishop speculated in an interview with Canadian television, if he had happened upon the thieves *while* they were beating their victim? Romero concluded that Christians must distinguish between proactive violence and self-defense. Like most liberation Christians, he accepted the premise of "just revolution" against an "evil" government, although he stopped short of giving his explicit blessing to the budding guerrilla movement in El Salvador.

Romero was almost joined in his intellectual analysis by the Vatican itself. During the 1970s, the church hierarchy in Italy had been influenced by liberation thinking and other idealistic currents. In July 1978, Albino Luciani, Cardinal of Venice and son of a socialist bricklayer, was unexpectedly placed on the Church's throne in Rome. It was apparent that this buoyant and smiling man, adopting the name John Paul, was not going to be an ordinary pope. He rejected the glamour of the office, abandoning the thousand-year tradition of coronation in favor of a simple ceremony. Although John Paul did not wish to receive Latin America's military leaders into his audience, the Vatican's Secretary of State—whom he apparently planned to fire—had invited them anyway. Three hundred protesters, who had the new Pope's sympathy, were arrested at St. Peter's when Argentina's General Videla arrived. Fortunately for the militaries and the rich, after only 33 days in power, John Paul suddenly and conveniently died. His successor, a conservative Polish cardinal, adopted John Paul's name but little else. John Paul II silenced liberation theologians, appointed high church officials involved in the secretive Opus Dei movement, and catered to the spiritual needs of the rich. When visiting Chile, he stood beside the dictator, Pinochet; and in Mexico, in 1999, he even held a private, special mass for the nation's billionaires. In the late 1970s, however, he could not remove the previously appointed Archbishop Romero from his post; someone else would have to do that.

The Vatican's alliance with earthly powers under John Paul II did translate into a harsh disapproval of Romero, however. When the Archbishop called on El Salvador's rich—whom he judged as the primary perpetrators of violence—to change their ways, he did so alone. When he visited the Vatican, the new Pope let him wait for hours and hours, then chided him for being soft on "communism." Romero tried vainly to explain the nature of events in El Salvador to the Holy Father. He returned to El Salvador despondent, finding no alternatives to the death that was engulfing his Church. He wrote to President Jimmy Carter, arguing that it was immoral for the United States to supply and support the murderous regime. Carter ignored him. Then, with no options left, Romero went even further. Filled with a strange confidence, this often awkward and bookish man cried out one day, in a sermon:

> I would like to make an appeal in a special way to the men of the army.... Brothers, you are part of our people. You kill your own *campesino* brothers and sisters. And before an order to kill that a man may give, the law of God must prevail that says: Thou shalt not kill! No soldier is obliged to obey an order against the law of God.... And in the name of this suffering people whose laments rise to heaven, each day more tumultuous, I beg you, I ask you, I order you in the name of God: Stop the repression![1]

Broadcast nationwide on the Catholic Church's radio station, Romero's appeal was subversive, and posed a danger to the integrity of the army, many of whose rank and file were church-raised peasant boys. A few days later, in March 1980, the archbishop himself was murdered while conducting mass at a small chapel. The next day, army troops visited his childhood village, rounded up its inhabitants, and tortured and executed several dozen of them. Some 100,000 persons turned out for Romero's funeral, and security forces again staged a formidable assault: About two hundred mourners were killed or injured. Inside the basilica, liberation theology priests, including Gustavo Gutiérrez, hastily stuffed the archbishop's casket into the wall while the machine guns outside rattled.

A few days later the United States extended several million dollars in new military aid to El Salvador—a testimony to Washington's commitment to preserve the structures of power; but policymakers also understood that they had a problem on their hands. The Salvadoran regime was making absolutely no effort to pacify its people through conciliatory gestures. Indeed, Romero's death had triggered massive new unrest in the countryside, as thousands of Christians rose up in arms. Washington wanted stability, and remaining true to its Alliance for Progress recipe, it pressed for a modicum of limited reform. Yet there were two problems: First, the oligarchs not only resented American advice but were openly hostile to it. Second, the political space in which compromise was possible had all but disappeared by 1980.

Earlier, in October 1979, a core of junior army officers willing to entertain some reforms had staged a coup with the blessing of the United States. They brought in civilians to manage administrative affairs and provide some much-needed legitimacy, including Guillermo Ungo, and with much fanfare, the formerly exiled and once-popular José Napoleón Duarte. Under pressure from Washington, businessman Mario Andino of the Phelps-Dodge Corporation also joined the government. All of the junta members repeatedly stated that the new regime was different, committed to human rights, and supportive of change.

At about the same time, the United States recalled its ambassador and replaced him with a career diplomat known as far more liberal than most in the State Department. Robert White, once on the scene, pushed the regime toward agrarian reform. A program of land distribution to the poor began—albeit on a very modest scale. This initiative deeply annoyed high-ranking, hard-line military officers as well as the rich, and it might well have hastened the decision to kill Romero. The reformist junior officers and White's embassy were effectively undercut and outmaneuvered behind the scenes. The U.S. bid to pacify the nation by creating a believable political "center" had been too feeble, and had come too late.

Guillermo Ungo, aware of what was going on, warned the power brokers that they must restore military moderates or accept his resignation. Spurned by the oligarchs and hard-liners, he followed through on his threat, tarnishing the reformist image of the coup government. In contrast, the unperceptive and egotistical Duarte hung on—convinced that he could manipulate the antireformists and oligarchs as effectively as they could toy with him. He was wrong. Wholly marginalized, his Christian Democratic party became a shell without popular support, as Duarte himself was perceived as a civilian front man for a terrorist military government.

The disagreement between the United States and its client on how to achieve pacification was a major factor in generating civil war in El Salvador. The people of El Salvador, after Romero's death, liked neither their government nor the United States. Instead, they embraced a new opposition movement, the Democratic Revolutionary Front (FDR), which vowed to establish democracy in the country by what it concluded was the only means possible—armed revolt. The FDR was, in reality, the same as the popular organizations, though they had disappeared from public view because of the repression. It was led, ironically, by an oligarch: Enrique Alvarez, a rich coffee planter who had broken ranks with his class and adopted Romero's gospel of social change. Alvarez was joined by Ungo, who having resigned from the coup government, now cast in his lot with the opposition.

The FDR clearly had a mandate from the people, and after Romero's assassination, it became more and more intransigent—stating that the oligarchs and army were incapable of reform and had to give up power, either peacefully or by force. Alvarez, Ungo, and other leaders fanned out around the hemisphere, taking their case to other nations as they sought diplomatic recognition. The military regime in El Salvador was understandably furious. When Alvarez came back into the country, he and the FDR's leadership were seized and eliminated. Only Ungo, who was in New York at the time, evaded death.

The FDR killings were followed by still more high-profile murders. Two American land reform advisers were gunned down in the San Salvador Sheraton in December 1980, the same month in which soldiers intercepted three American nuns. Accompanied by a lay worker also from the United States, the sisters were abducted at a roadblock and executed. As usual, no serious effort was made to cover up the killings—the point was to scare the masses and rebuke the United States. An enraged Ambassador White visited the scene and watched as the bodies were dragged out of their shallow graves in front of television cameras. "They won't get away with it this time," he muttered. He instructed the embassy staff to launch a full investigation. Enlisted soldiers eventually went to prison for the murders. Upon his release in 1998, one of them confessed that their orders had come from above.

The Period of Massacres

Just a month after the nuns were killed, Ronald Reagan entered the presidency. He quickly fired Ambassador White. The Salvadoran oligarchs and military, so disdainful of U.S. "interference" in their country, welcomed the move. The rich celebrated Reagan's ascent to power with parties in the mansions of Escalón. The new U.S. secretary of state, Alexander Haig, told Congress that the American nuns had been gun-toting extremists—a lie ridiculed by Catholics, who generated enough pressure to bring about the soldiers' eventual trial and conviction. The Reagan administration realized that El Salvador was unstable and that any further attempts at reform or creation of a political center would be futile. This was war, and it was time to get on with it. New packages of military aid poured into the country.

The death squads had done their work in 1977–1980 and had eliminated the popular organizations and the FDR from the capital. By 1981, everyone in San Salvador pretty much stayed at home and avoided any type of action that might even remotely antagonize the government. In the countryside, however, the military wing of the FDR—the Farabundo Martí Front for National Liberation (FMLN), named after a peasant leader in the 1930s who had led a failed revolt—was booming. It controlled whole sections of the country, and increasingly coordinated a diverse, peasant-based guerrilla insurrection. The FMLN was aided by army defectors: A number of peasant soldiers were either heeding Romero's words or reacting against the brutality of their officers. The leader of the rebels, a liberation theology Christian and former university student, Joaquín Villalobos, recognized that the FMLN's best hope was for a quick victory. He therefore undertook a major offensive, although his fighters were poorly equipped and badly trained.

The Salvadoran Army was also primitive and relatively small (consisting of about 13,000 men); but it was a killing machine, with much experience from the street slaughters in the city. With the countryside in revolt, it adopted the same basic tactic, albeit on a grander scale. It staged pincer movements that funneled the rural poor into constricted areas where they could be annihilated. There were several stunning massacres, especially in summer 1980 and early 1981; even years later, we know very little about them. One such operation that is well documented, largely due to field forensics work, was at El Mozote, in northeastern El Salvador. Scholars and others were interested in the massacre at El Mozote because, although it was not the largest, it had received substantial publicity.

In early December 1981, the flagship battalion of the army, called the Atlacatl (named after an Indian who had fought the Spanish in colonial times), helicoptered into a small mountainous district while thousands of other troops cut off avenues of escape. Villalobos and the FMLN high command, realizing that pitched battles were a losing proposition, pulled their fighters out of the zone and warned civilians to flee as well—through broadcasts over their mobile radio station, Venceremos. Thousands of civilians fled, since the army's routine was well known by this time; but others congregated in front of the advancing troops in the village of El Mozote, which had been a hotbed of Protestant missionary activity and consequently enjoyed an unusual reputation for neutrality.

The Atlacatl Battalion arrived in town around dusk and pushed everyone out into the streets, where they made them lie face down in the dirt as they began to interrogate the men. For several hours they allowed villagers to return to their homes, sporadically beating the adults, who tried feverishly to keep their little ones from crying. Then, on orders from their officers (U.S. advisers were not on the scene, but many officers at El Mozote had recently received U.S. counterinsurgency training), the battalion again rounded up the people and separated them. Children were stuffed into a room by themselves, where they cried and cried. Women, housed in separate buildings, heard the screams of their tortured husbands coming from the Catholic Church (predictably, a preferred interrogation site during the war). The process of elimination then proceeded smoothly: Men were taken out in pairs to be hung, shot, or decapitated. The soldiers took their time with the women, raping them in groups on the edge of town, then torturing and executing them. In the process, at least one young girl frightened the warriors. During her rape, she sang about Jesus. A group of soldiers gathered around and cut off her breasts, but even during that common Salvadoran torture, she kept singing. One then stuck the bayonet of his M-16 into her throat. There was still a faint, but amazingly still calm, gurgle of praise to God. Finally, out of fear, the men opened fire with their weapons.

Last, it was the children's turn. An officer started the cleansing in a dramatic way: He took a boy about 2 years old, tossed him up into the air, and caught him on his bayonet. The work was then embraced by the enlistees, who chopped and cut the kids up for an hour. When it was all over, 767 persons had been eliminated in and around El Mozote—a brutal task, but presumably useful for breaking the spirit of the people.

Or was it? As with the death squad operations, there was no serious attempt to hide the slaughter. The point of the big massacres, in fact, was to instill fear in the people and get them to submit. But in the wake of these massive killings, many peasants joined the FMLN. The guerrillas issued largely accurate reports of these operations, and people learned to hate the army and government all the more.

The massacre at El Mozote did another type of damage to the pacification efforts. Two American reporters made their way to the massacre site and revealed the incident to the world. Alma Guillermoprieto of the *Washington Post* had been tipped off by Raymond Bonner of the *New York Times*, and both hiked into the interior with the help of FMLN contacts. Field photographers snapped photos of partially decayed and mutilated corpses. In January 1981, the two major newspapers ran stories about El Mozote, stating emphatically that a massacre had occurred. Although the stories generated little political fallout (only Ted Kennedy and Jerry Studds raised the issue in Congress), the Reagan administration suffered a public relations setback. In the shadow of El Mozote, the strategy of wholesale massacre showed its fundamental flaws: Killings of this size could alienate more peasants than they frightened, and they also aroused media exposure. The military and their supporters therefore began to change their strategy in 1982.

America's Secret War:
Lessons Learned

The civil war in El Salvador is profoundly significant because it became a laboratory for testing modern counterinsurgency techniques. After El Mozote, American military advisers arrived in large numbers and took direct control of the war. Over the next decade, the U.S. military establishment used El Salvador as a model for perfecting the means by which popular-based rural insurrections could be defeated. The lessons of El Salvador assure us that successful revolutions in Latin America are a thing of the past. In this small and impoverished land, American strategists mastered counterinsurgency warfare and produced one of history's most astounding military victories.

To appreciate the meaning of what happened in El Salvador, one must understand its military context. The annals of history are replete with variations on guerrilla-style warfare, but *popular* insurgency—in which the people are overwhelmingly united behind a rebellion—had long proven impossible to suppress. Although isolated and poorly supported guerrillas can be tracked down and defeated, how can an army pacify an entire people, except by killing them? The question perplexed Pentagon planners during the Vietnam war, where, according to CIA analysts in 1965, 95 percent of the populace supported the Viet Cong rebels and opposed the American presence. Strategic hamlets had failed, and political assassinations under the pathbreaking Phoenix program were no more effective. Despite a half million men, technology light years ahead of the opposition, a bombing campaign that dropped more tonnage than that in all of World War II, and a kill ratio of 50 to 1, the United States failed to pacify Vietnam. The war in El Salvador was designed and prosecuted from the vantage point of that difficult experience.

There is no way to defeat a truly popular rebellion except by making it unpopular. In El Salvador, the U.S. military overtly engaged in a political war where a major portion of the battlefield rested in people's minds. Propaganda has been with us, of course, for as long as warfare, but not on this level. The coordination between things military and things political became explicit. Psychological operations, or psy ops, underwent a massive revision and enhancement at the Pentagon in the mid-1980s. A process was perfected whereby simple people could be subtly indoctrinated to view the army as their friend. Psy ops have since become the centerpiece of counterinsurgency campaigns ("low-intensity conflicts," or LICs, in the military's lexicon), for the first time in history.

American Military Group (MilGroup) advisers, numbering on average four hundred at a time (congressional limitations were circumvented by very long rotation cycles), implemented a Pentagon-coordinated war in El Salvador beginning in 1982. They ended the large-scale massacres in favor of selective repression based on sound intelligence. From the start, they stressed the need to politically recapture the "hearts and minds" of a majority of the population—a truly formidable task in the wake of what had transpired. Instead of meeting peasants and killing them, the Salvadoran Army began to greet them and hand out gifts and food. The officer in command at El Mozote, Domingo Monterrosa, was retrained as a PR man. He helicoptered into scores of villages and distributed aid, asking sick children to step forward in order to receive medical care. Enlisted soldiers dressed up in costumes and entertained kids, handing out toys and candy. Backed by the wealth of the United States, the military and government had the resources with which to woo the poor into their ranks—and show them that the FMLN, in contrast, could deliver only struggle and hardship.

A seminal feature of the psychological war was the relegitimization of the Salvadoran government. U.S. aid bought printing presses, political propaganda blared from army trucks, and leaflets fell from helicopters. The most powerful tool of reeducation were the mass media, especially television. In time, oft-repeated ideas in the media began to take hold in the general population. The death squad terror of security forces, for example, was attributed to a clandestine "far right" that Duarte and the Americans, try as they might, could not control. (In fact, there were private death squads tied to the elite; but their links with security forces, especially with the Treasury Police, are certain.) The freewheeling mastermind of the death squads, Roberto D'Aubuisson, rather conveniently was caught in an overseas airport with documents on him that linked him to the assassination of Archbishop Romero.

U.S.-sponsored plans to relegitimize the government were repeatedly hampered by the independent spirit of the Salvadoran elites, who balked at working with Duarte and favored their own political organization, the National Republican Alliance (ARENA). Elections were crucial to convincing the poor that the political process was becoming fair. The problem was, with the popular organizations gone and the FDR unable to participate, voters did not believe that they had genuine electoral choices. Duarte's administration, highly corrupt, was despised (its postal service raided incoming mail from abroad, much of which included small amounts of money sent by Salvadorans working overseas to their families). The elections themselves were manipulative. Voting was made mandatory, and the poor had to show their stamped voting cards at army checkpoints after the election or face arrest for subversion. In the 1984 contest for the Salvadoran presidency, only the influx of campaign money from the CIA saved Duarte from a humiliating defeat. Eventually, when ARENA won power in 1989, the elite celebrated in the streets, chanting "America, eat shit."

Political and psychological efforts to recapture the hearts and minds of El Salvador's people did not, of course, bring an immediate end to the fighting. Under the tutelage of Americans, Salvadoran security forces tirelessly gathered intelligence, hired informants, tortured captured guerrillas, and pinpointed ardent FMLN supporters for elimination. The war was not to be won by all-engulfing public terror but through information and control. The tide turned against the rebels gradually, and by the late 1980s they were reduced to rank terrorism—blocking roads, blowing up power stations, and threatening the hydroelectric system. The army mushroomed to well over 50,000, as the number of full-time guerrillas dwindled. Random machine-gunning from helicopters stopped, and laser-vision-equipped American pilots, operating out of Panama, picked off rebels in the dead of night—a phenomenon that must have mystified the technologically unsophisticated. By November 1989, when Villalobos authorized another "final offensive," he did so more out of desperation than with any hope of victory.

The rebels tried to take the war into the city during this offensive, with fighters even briefly occupying the streets of Escalón, to the horror of the rich. The greatest success of this strategy was to evoke a reaction from the Atlacatl Battalion, which in the middle of the crisis, reverted to its old ways. Soldiers eliminated six Jesuit priests at the Catholic University, and their tracks were not well covered. The sensational murders attracted media attention and raised questions about whether or not conditions in El Salvador, ten years after Oscar Romero's murder, had really changed. Although U.S. senator John McCain tried to blame the FMLN for "provoking" the killings, and U.S. Army Major Mark Buckland (adviser to the Atlacatl) defended the need to remove the "intellectual authors of revolution," the Jesuit slayings undermined the achievements of U.S. psy ops and helped force a negotiated peace settlement that ended the civil war in 1992.

Despite this, the greatest success of psy ops in El Salvador was the U.S. military's ability to prosecute operations without the presence of the nosy investigative news media. When conducting psy ops, the Pentagon actively discourages uncontrolled media coverage of events in the field. As military consultant Carnes Lord, Ph.D., has explained, graphic footage is bad because "images of death and destruction . . . so common in television coverage of war, inevitably encourage the feeling that [war] is futile, immoral, or absurd."[2] As American media coverage of the Central America scene diminished after 1985, public support for U.S. policy in the region rose significantly, as evidenced in polling data.

In the wake of his reports of the massacre at El Mozote, *New York Times* reporter Raymond Bonner was dismissed from his post. He had been roundly attacked by U.S. government officials and conservatives as a liar. The *Wall Street Journal* editorialized on his gullibility, and think tanks like the New York-based Freedom House bemoaned the "liberal" media's portrayal of the Salvadoran regime as repressive. Bonner's removal had a chilling effect on independent-minded correspondents who remained in El Salvador, and they increasingly echoed the official line—that the United States was helping to plant freedom and democracy in the tiny republic.

The U.S. military discouraged media coverage generally, but pressed for favorable reportage whenever possible. It cultivated direct ties with the press, both through on-the-ground relations with correspondents and via contacts with news outlets. In 1988, military analysts wrote, "Relations with the American media constitute a major success for U.S. military policy in El Salvador, . . . [since] more favorable reporting helped take the edge off domestic opposition to U.S. policy."[3] Military planners were coming to realize that the news media could be used to shape public opinion rather than to inform it. In contrast, opposition groups in the United States could not even get some of their paid advertisements about El Salvador aired. One ad, which showed an American writing a check to El Salvador's army as the paper turned to blood, was dismissed by television executives as "too violent."

Media influence and spin control became integral to military strategy after the El Salvador experience, as evidenced, for example, by the decision to target Serb television during the 1999 bombing of Yugoslavia (NATO General Wesley Clark had commanded U.S. forces in Central America during the 1990s). It is also now standard that the military creates its own news outlets and sources, linking them up, whenever possible, with the corporate-owned media. In El Salvador, efforts to silence the FMLN's Radio Venceremos were not always successful; but the creation of the military's own voice, Radio Cuscatlán, did much to impugn Venceremos's reliability and to confuse the general populace.

El Salvador was the great laboratory, but low-intensity conflict and psy ops also were practiced and further refined elsewhere in Latin America during the 1990s. In the southeastern Mexican state of Chiapas, in 1994, seeds of rebellion blew over from Central America and spread among impoverished Mayan Indians. The Chiapas highlands, though part of Mexico, are geographically and culturally wedded to Guatemala, and had experienced a similar influx of subversive Christian ideas. Several hundred of the Maya, calling themselves Zapatistas, after the famous revolutionary hero, rose up in revolt against the corrupt and distant national government. Easily suppressed, they fled to small villages in the jungle, and a counterinsurgency campaign ensued.

A U.S. MilGroup team covertly joined the Mexican Army in June 1994. Many of its members, like Major John Kord and Lieutenant Colonel Alan Hasson Sánchez, had served in El Salvador. Tens of thousands of Mexican soldiers poured into the region, establishing camps, building roads, and dividing the Indian populace by distributing aid ranging from free dental check-ups to haircuts. U.S. funding and training of the Mexican Army also accelerated. Thousands of soldiers followed in the footsteps of their regional commanders, Generals Manuel García Ruíz and Mario Reñán Castillo, in studying with U.S. Special Forces at Fort Bragg, North Carolina. Thousands of others learned counterinsurgency techniques at the U.S. Army's School of the Americas in Georgia. New military hardware—given under the auspices of fighting the drug war—included armored personnel carriers and Apache helicopters. State-of-the-art satellite technology, interfaced with computers, allowed U.S. trainers and Mexican pilots to "fly" over the three-dimensional jungles of Chiapas in preparation for real missions. With such stunning advances in technology, offensive forces have been able to master the terrain better than their primitive indigenous opponents, who still ride on horseback!

Brute force, however, has not won the war in Chiapas. Psy ops, involving a carefully orchestrated effort to divide the Maya against each other, have carried the day. As the Mexican military's October 1994 "Plan of Chiapas Campaign" specified, the goal of the operation is "to cut the relationship that exists between the population and the lawbreakers by secretly organizing certain sectors of the civil population . . . who would be employed in support of our operations." Mexican government-sponsored paramilitaries, composed of Indians willing to kill their brothers, terrorized pro-Zapatista villagers in the late 1990s. Death squads such as these provide a cover for the established order through plausible deniability—that is, when they kill, the government can deny any involvement, and the army then becomes the arbitrator of the peace. By expelling foreign observers and forbidding reporters from sealed operational zones, the Mexican government imposed secrecy on its war in Chiapas (although the use of the Internet by the political opposition has undermined the control of information about the LIC). When paramilitaries massacred forty-five unarmed Zapatista sympathizers in a Catholic Church in December 1997, there was little news coverage of the event. In the United States, no commercial television networks mentioned it, and PBS's *Newshour* insinuated that it was a product of internecine Indian strife, beyond the control of authorities. Killing forty-five Indians at a time, however, was risky. More discreet, small-scale eliminations have been more responsible for driving up the death tally. By 2000, more people had been "ethnically cleansed" in Chiapas than in Kosovo prior to the NATO intervention, yet the American public for the most part has been successfully kept in the dark.

Counterinsurgency efforts at the outset of the twenty-first century continue, especially in Colombia, where guerrilla forces burgeoned during the past two decades, in the absence of a decisive U.S. military presence. In the mid-1980s, a number of Colombian guerrillas disarmed and attempted to integrate into the normal political process, creating the Patriotic Union Party; but a wave of assassinations forced them to return to armed insurrection. Priests and Christian activists have been eliminated at a steady pace in the land of Camilo Torres, as well. The growth of the Revolutionary Armed Forces of Colombia (FARC) in the 1990s finally triggered increased U.S. military aid and more direct involvement under the Clinton administration.

Although LIC and psy ops are not fully implemented in Colombia, a deniable proxy war by paramilitaries has been under way for years. Funded by the government, drug lords, and elites (and indirectly, U.S. aid), paramilitaries regularly invade guerrilla-dominated areas and terrorize the populace. At Mapiripán in July 1997, for example, they decapitated twenty-six civilians assumed to be sympathetic to the FARC, and afterward used their heads as soccer balls. Slayings accelerated in spring 2000, aided in part by the arrival of foreign mercenaries and the Colombian military's growing intelligence-gathering capabilities. Media coverage of the killings is limited, since as a general rule no more than twenty suspected subversives are eliminated at a time. The limited efforts of independent journalists and human rights organizations to identify and prosecute murderers have been successfully evaded. Key witnesses often disappear. In addition, authorities almost always allow the few suspects who are arrested to "escape" afterward from military jails. Several prominent human rights investigators have recently been murdered, as well. Since 1980, at least 55,000 Colombians have died violently, though not all of them for exclusively political reasons.

Most Colombians, including the urban poor behind army lines, at least tacitly support their government. Although there is no reason to believe that the FARC could seize power and maintain it for long, in the short term more bloodshed appears inevitable. The FARC has warned that unbridled paramilitary killing will drive it away from the negotiating table, yet both Colombian and U.S. policymakers seem to favor a military solution. By portraying the rebels as "narco-guerrillas"—when, in fact, all of Colombian society is saturated with drug money—U.S. officials have laid the disinformation groundwork necessary for winning support from Americans for military aid to Colombia. The FARC, with its calls for land reform and wealth redistribution, poses a genuine threat to U.S. economic interests in the region.

Formidable revolutionary movements in Latin America will be rare in this century, largely because of the advent of effective political counterinsurgency techniques. Recent military advances are also stunning—radio transmission interception, for example, has become so sophisticated that insurgents dare not even whisper over walkie-talkies when U.S. reconnaissance aircraft, such as RC-7s, are patrolling the skies—but a complete and lasting victory rests in the political conquest of the human mind. When the FMLN finally laid down its arms in 1992 and turned to politics, it unwittingly consigned itself to defeat, for it entered an arena in which it cannot win. A divided electorate favored the party of the elite in the presidential contest of 1994, despite the impassioned stump speeches by the FMLN's candidate, who cried, "These are the people who killed Archbishop

Romero!" In 1999, the FMLN again succumbed at the polls. And significantly, neither the rich nor the United States have much to fear even if former guerrillas someday win El Salvador's highest office. Joaquín Villalobos, the ex-rebel commander, has become an advocate of pro-business economics, and the FMLN has all but abandoned its revolutionary stance. That it has done so is, in large part, a reflection of the very nature of Latin American politics today.

PART III

Contemporary Latin America

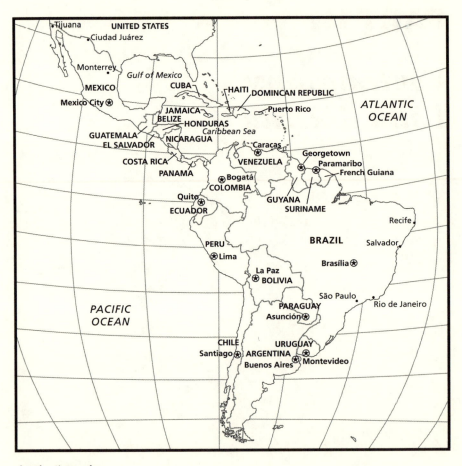

Latin America

8 The Politics of Control

During the war in El Salvador, the U.S. army taught Salvadoran military personnel how to identify "subversives." Among other things, according to the *Combat Intelligence* field manual distributed to soldiers, subversives

1. accuse the government of corruption;
2. ridicule government or military officials;
3. characterize the government and political leaders as U.S. puppets;
4. characterize the Army as an enemy of the people;
5. use slogans against the government, the Army, or the United States;
6. accuse the police or Army of torture.

It is apparent from this list that the United States was not in the business of promoting freedom in El Salvador. In another manual, Salvadoran soldiers were taught that communists "can resort to subverting the government by means of elections" and that subversive activity may include "political meetings" or participation "in political races as candidates for government posts." Obviously, America also was not promoting democracy.

It is not in the interest of the United States to promote freedom or democracy in the Third World. Although in its quest for stability America may on occasion (such as in El Salvador) endorse the trappings of electoral politics or a modicum of economic reform, genuine people's power is anathema—and for good reason. If poor people in poor countries had true political power, they could, if organized, outvote the rich and elect governments committed to real economic change. It can be safely assumed that restructured capitalism in the Third World, accompanied by a redistribution of wealth and by social welfare policies, would profoundly affect trade patterns and could diminish the quality of life for Americans and other First World residents.

Yet if U.S. support for democracy in the Third World is an illusion, even more critical is the myth that Latin America's poor want political democracy. In fact, history suggests that poor people overwhelmingly desire to improve their economic life. Only when democracy seems to provide an avenue for better living conditions do we find mass political mobilization and "democratic revolution." If, collectively, people do not perceive the political process as capable of bringing meaningful economic change, they tend to become detached, apolitical, and disinterested. When this dynamic is at work, elections obviously do not pose a danger to the status quo. At the outset of the twenty-first century, precisely this kind of mass depoliticization is flourishing throughout Latin America. There are cleaner and more frequent elections throughout the hemisphere now than ever before, but the nature of the electoral process has convinced many that politics cannot bring change. The irony, as evidenced in three case studies, is that Latin Americans are arguably more "democratic" but less and less free.

Peru: Limiting Democracy by Consensus

The Peruvian experience over the past few decades demonstrates many of the contradictions concerning what we term "democracy," and clarifies the nature of popular sentiments regarding the interface of economic conditions and political rights. A nation of sharp racial contrasts, with an urbanized white elite still entrenched in power above a rural and poor Indian majority, Peru should pose problems for a conservative and authoritarian government. Yet this is not the case. Late-twentieth-century Peru hardly qualified as a democracy, and for the most part, the majority of its citizens did not seem to mind.

In the age of military dictatorships Peru sailed a slightly different course. Its army took control late, springing a coup in 1968, and implemented a regimen of populist rhetoric and reform under General Juan Velasco, who ruled until 1975. The government nationalized Standard Oil Company's holdings; expropriated haciendas and distributed land to peasants in a quest to break up latifundio; organized workers into cooperatives; and espoused nationalist rhetoric while purchasing Soviet military hardware. It was a very strange military government; it even extended diplomatic recognition to Cuba. The clique of officers at its center were, like Velasco himself, mostly from the rural middle class—part of the explanation for its unusual ideology. But the regime was also clearly intent on undermining the potent intellectual left in Peru, as college campuses during the 1960s spawned multiple communist parties and inflamed revolutionary passions. It was authoritarian and reformist from the top down, one reason why the

United States tolerated it (albeit with reduced aid packages and much public criticism). Washington welcomed a shift within the military in 1975, when a new clique of officers seized power and began what they termed the "second phase" of governance, with a decidedly more conservative turn. In time, they weeded out the "leftists" within army ranks and clamped down on political dissent, finally bringing to Peru the trappings of a more conventional military government.

The late 1970s were not healthy for the Peruvian economy, as foreign investors remained cool and inflation deepened in the wake of oil price hikes. The generals decided to return to the barracks, yielding to civilian rule under Fernando Belaunde in 1980. Belaunde, who campaigned on the slogan "a million new jobs," began to reverse the state-led growth model, only to watch the economy further deteriorate. He and his advisers, representing an urban political class resentful of the military's "misrule," cut the army budget and all but eliminated its intelligence-gathering apparatus, unwittingly doing so on the eve of a dramatic revolution.

The Sendero Luminoso, or Shining Path, was an obscure Maoist faction that had broken away from the conventional Peruvian communists in 1969 under the charismatic leadership of Abimael Guzmán, a philosopher and intellectual with an uncanny ability to coin poetic and simple revolutionary phrases. Unlike in Central America, where the Church served as a conduit for revolutionary struggle, in Peru the educational system was at its heart. Guzmán and his ideas prospered on university campuses during the late 1970s, and a small but determined cadre of followers coalesced just as the economy soured under Belaunde. Second-tier state universities provided fertile grounds for recruitment, as lower-middle-class students facing dim futures turned to the movement with religious zeal. The regional University of San Cristóbal Huamanga, in the city of Ayacucho, was the foremost nest of the Senderos. From there the group launched an armed rebellion in spring 1980.

In the Ayacucho province, southeast of Lima, college youths quickly transmitted their faith in the cause to family members and secondary school students. Sendero promised its adherents a bright future—its line was that Ayacucho would be a new nation within five years—and because they confronted a bleak reality, many chose to believe this promise. Young males relished the power displayed by college youths brandishing weapons and spouting revolutionary slogans. At first, Sendero's promises seemed certain. Corrupt local police forces were swept away with relative ease, and the conservative rural peasantry at least tolerated Sendero leadership, in part because of their moral rigidity and mostly local origins. Sendero intolerance for cattle rustlers, for example, won over several village ranchers.

But Sendero Luminoso did not connect with Peru's Indian masses. Its ideas, based on Chinese communism and Guzmán's dictates, were too foreign. At first, with its authoritarian hierarchy, peasants could accept it as a new kind of paternal lord, or *patrón*. Even from the start, however, this bridge between the revolutionaries and the populace was tenuous. In Ayacucho the Senderos put young cadres in charge of villages and zones, displacing Indian elders and violating time-honored traditions. Guzmán, who urged his followers to "hammer the countryside" with revolutionary zeal, sanctioned capital punishment in order to instill a strict moral and social order—again, a process beyond the control of the community and disruptive to Indian social norms.

At first unwilling to sanction a firm military response—due to friction between civilian and military authorities, rather than out of compassion—the Belaunde administration gave Sendero enough space to initially prosper. Guzmán's prophecy that the countryside would choke off the cities appeared all the more plausible, prompting more Peruvians to join the revolutionary bandwagon. Electricity blackouts and increasingly hysterical mass media reportage fed fears in Lima and elsewhere, and many city dwellers and the conservative Peruvian Catholic Church tolerated Belaunde's eventual curtailment of civil liberties and his new security measures. Elements in the army and police formed death squads with the help of foreign counterinsurgency experts. Torture became a standard practice in interrogations.

In Ayacucho in 1983–1984, the army was given a free hand. It swept through the heart of Sendero country with massive and indiscriminate terror, killing thousands. Multiple massacres of villages showed the peasantry that their new *patrón* could not protect them. Indeed, Guzmán's cadres retreated in advance of the army, leaving the provincial populace wholly at its mercy. The Peruvian marines, comprised of racist mestizos from Lima and elsewhere, slaughtered Indians with machine-gun-laden helicopters. Undercover units, dressed up in various guerrilla guises, decimated the university populace and triggered interfactional revenge in the process. The Senderos, for their part, were not far behind in the use of terror. Their countersweeps in the late 1980s were aimed at instilling a fear in the Indians greater than that generated by the military. The masses would have to select between the proverbial lesser of two evils.

In time, the Indians of Peru chose to stand with the army. The bloodletting in 1983–1984 had convinced many to abandon the cause of revolution, and when the Senderos began to respond in kind, they did so just as the army wisely changed tactics. As had happened in El Salvador, new counterinsurgency methods shifted the Peruvian soldiery from random to selective terror. Using local informants, security forces identified and eliminated subversives and their collaborators. Wholesale massacres by the army ceased, and Sendero terror could not dissuade a now-cooperative peasantry. The poor, discarding dreams of change and merely longing for peace, understood that their odds were best with the powers of the state. Peasant defense patrols called *rondas* formed under army tutelage and curtailed movement in a manner similar to those in Guatemala. In one Ayacucho district, peasants stoned a dozen Senderos to death, decapitated their bodies, and then carted the remains off to the local army garrison for approval and a possible reward.

A frustrated Sendero command increasingly shifted its operations northeastward, into the coca-producing valleys of the Peruvian Amazon. An alliance with drug lords reinvigorated the movement near the end of the decade, but a similar process of military co-optation began in the early 1990s. Army officers, convincing drug barons that they meant them no harm, undercut the Sendero alliance. By the mid-1990s the Peruvian military was in bed with the drug cartels, and Sendero was dismembered. The sensational 1992 capture of Abimael Guzmán in a Lima hideout sucked the life out of the waning revolutionary crusade. A humiliated but defiant Guzmán, in prison stripes, briefly stood caged before the press, before disappearing into an incommunicado hell. Only a separate urban front—the more traditional, Cuban-inspired Tupac Amarú Revolutionary Movement (MRTA)—continued to pose a serious security threat.

In the midst of the heaviest repression, Peruvians elected a left-leaning populist, Alan García, as president. His chaotic administration (1985–1990) was another factor in the equation that eventually ushered Peru into a depoliticized, nondemocratic reality. García, a socialist, attempted to resume the state-led economic model and in the process deeply antagonized both domestic and foreign capital. Rich Peruvians moved to Miami or New York, and many U.S. corporations pulled out of the country, accelerating capital flight. García hoped to rectify the situation by nationalizing the banks in 1988 (inspired by Mexico's example of a few years earlier), but was met with such stiff opposition that he was forced to abandon his plans. His efforts to curtail human rights abuses, meanwhile, also came to naught. At the outset of his term he briefly succeeded in slowing the killings, and his government even prosecuted a few of the security network's torturers. The army responded to García's moralism by slowing down its campaign against Sendero Luminoso. Hence, as García's stormy term came to an end, Peruvians faced a collapsing economy and a reviving guerrilla movement.

Looking for a new alternative, voters rejected traditional party-based politicians in favor of dark horse Alberto Fujimori, the son of Japanese immigrants. The elite-owned press had long lampooned García's administration for its corruption (García had bribed the army high command extensively in order to stave off a threatened coup, and he was also implicated in other scandals); and Fujimori campaigned against the Lima political establishment. His upset win in 1990 was followed by another surprise: After receiving a Democracy Award during a summit of Latin American leaders in

1991, he abolished the legislature and began to rule by emergency decree. This so-called *autogolpe* was accepted by a majority of Peruvians, who embraced the media-touted conviction that only stern measures could save the nation from going over the brink. Fujimori also abandoned statist economics and initiated "Fujishock" policies designed to stifle hyperinflation, which had reached 700 percent in 1990. Business capital began to return, and Wall Street firms pumped funds into the revitalized emerging market.

Fujimori gave the military a free hand in eliminating subversion. Although conclusive documentation remains unavailable, evidence indicates heavy U.S. involvement in the counterinsurgency campaign drawn up by the National Intelligence Service (SIN) in 1991. Vladimiro Montesinos, in control of SIN operations, had previously been dismissed from the military government for spying on behalf of the United States. A web of state-of-the-art surveillance techniques was used to track and disrupt the Sendero leadership. Fujimori's suspension of civil liberties eliminated the role of the judiciary. Subversives were tried by secret panels of military judges, and had no access to their accusers or to the investigatory evidence. Human rights groups in Peru refused to provide legal aid to Senderos or MRTA, assuring captured rebels of the harshest possible sentences (usually preceded by information-gathering torture sessions). Sendero Luminoso's back was broken within a year.

Despite the admittedly massive human rights violations that took place under Fujimori's administration, Peruvians overwhelmingly backed him and sanctioned the end of democracy in their country. The president enjoyed cordial relations with a military establishment that, in reality, held the reins of power. The rich liked him, and the middle classes—a tad resentful due to their loss of political rights—were at the very least ambivalent. But Fujimori's strongest support came from the poor, who welcomed an end to inflation and accepted the fairly silly idea that he was "just like them." Indeed, Fujimori's greatest accomplishment in the 1990s was his brilliant and pioneering use of television. Using public relations consultants and staging picture-perfect photo ops for a supportive media, he portrayed himself as a simple man of the people. Hopping into Andean villages on a helicopter given to him by the CEO of American Airlines, El Chino, as he was called, frequently dressed in native garb and joined in Indian feasts and dances. His "Fujimobile," inspired by the Pope's touring vehicle, was a tractor. Media imagery reached a new plateau in Peru, teaching illiterate peasants to love a leader who, in reality, probably had little compassion for them.

Although polling data showed periodic drops in his popularity, Fujimori was able to easily win reelection when he partially restored the electoral process in 1995. When MRTA rebels seized the Japanese embassy and took hostages the following year, he again used the fight against subversion to boost his ratings. The fourteen Tupac Amarú guerrillas had hoped to revive their movement with the sensational raid, which nearly nabbed Fujimori himself (posing as waiters, they had infiltrated the embassy on the eve of a gala celebration). Foolishly, the rebel leader, Néstor Cerpa Cartolini, engaged in prolonged negotiations and released most of his hostages instead of beginning to execute them. This allowed agents from the U.S. Federal Bureau of Investigation and Peruvian special forces to perfect plans for a counterattack. Since the embassy had been equipped with sensitive eavesdropping devices in case of this very type of emergency, they were able to monitor rebel movements and detect daily patterns.

Cerpa and his men at first offered to release their hostages in exchange for the freedom of four hundred imprisoned comrades. By April 1997, they had dropped their demands and were asking for the release of a mere twenty, probably realizing that—amazingly—they were receiving almost no sympathy from Peru's docile Indian majority. An Oklahoma-based evangelical Christian ministry aired radio messages based on Romans 13, reminding the poor that their government was "from God." Television portrayed the rebels as thugs, and public sentiment even began to favor a military solution. In April, commandos stormed the compound when most of the guerrillas were playing soccer in the courtyard. They killed them all, and celebrated their brilliant victory by chopping off the guerrillas' heads and serenading Fujimori with a rousing rendition of the national anthem. The president's popularity again soared, even though Peru's free market economy had not improved the living standards of the poor.

Although criticism of Fujimori resurfaced as the twentieth century came to a close, his popularity demonstrated, perhaps more effectively than ever before in Latin America, that appropriate rhetoric and media imagery can generate solid support for a regime that is highly militarized and undemocratic. Recent polls show that Peruvians regard human rights organizations as fronts for subversion—a mantra repeated by the news media for years and now fully ingrained in popular thought. During the 2000 electoral campaign, television coverage of Fujimori dominated the airwaves, but after a decade in office many Peruvians—even some senior military and security officials—felt that his time was nearly up. Another candidate, Alejandro Toledo, garnered enough support so as to nearly upset Fujimori in the first round of balloting and force a run-off. A former World Bank economist, Toledo was certain to continue Fujimori's economic policies and posed no threat to elite or U.S. interests. Elections and the presidency provide democratic trappings for a regime that is still dominated by a cadre of security officials behind the scenes.

Haiti: From Dictatorship to Disinterest

Haiti is another important example of the evolution of democracy without freedom in Latin America. Although the Caribbean nation is distinctive—in race, language, culture, and the severity of its poverty—its recent turmoil demonstrates the near-universal desire of Latin America's poor to seek democracy only as a means of improving the conditions of their lives. Democracy for democracy's sake holds little appeal: If it fails to deliver food and jobs, the masses will begin to care little about it. Given its size and proximity to the United States, Haiti also has been sharply influenced by U.S. policies. Washington's desire for stability has transcended the end of the Cold War, and the fundamentals of its policies have persisted under both Republican and Democratic administrations.

The culture of Haiti's uneducated and superstitious masses has contributed to the country's political history. In 1957 the dictatorship of François ("Papa Doc") Duvalier began. Duvalier's personal cult rested in part on the medical doctor's strange use of voodoo, including the widely held belief that he was an incarnation of Baron Samedi—the high priest of death who reputedly turns his enemies into zombies. For those who were not completely persuaded, Papa Doc had another means by which to convince them (or to turn them into corpses): the Tontons Macoute. Named after a bogeyman common to Haitian children's stories, the Macoutes terrorized the rural poor and exercised arbitrary judicial and economic authority. Alongside the Haitian army, which they outnumbered, the Macoutes fended off a succession of guerrilla movements, many of which had the backing of Haitian expatriates in the United States and operated near Haiti's border with the Dominican Republic.

Before he died in 1971, Papa Doc ceded his power to his less astute son Jean-Claude ("Baby Doc"). One of Baby Doc's most serious gaffes was his marriage to the daughter of a rich mulatto. The elder Duvalier had wooed the masses not only by embracing the popular religion of voodoo but by cultivating a racial ideology termed *noirisme*, which glorified things African and disparaged the culture and status of the light-skinned elite—though their economic power remained intact. By marrying Michele, Baby Doc undid one of the most important knots that tied his regime to the impoverished majority. Popular resentment against him festered. By the mid-1980s, as demonstrations and general strikes unfolded (fueled, in part, by a Haitian brand of liberation Christianity), Baby Doc held onto power only through the terror of the Tontons Macoute. Late one night in February 1986, he loaded Michele and his family into his BMW, drove to the airport, and boarded a U.S. Air Force plane, heading into self-exile in France. Jubilant crowds destroyed Papa Doc's elaborate tomb in Port-au-Prince's main cemetery the next morning, symbolically celebrating their freedom from the Death Doctor's grip.

For several days after Baby Doc's departure, Haitians engaged in what they termed the *dechoukaj*, or uprooting, of the hated dictatorship (not surprisingly, an agrarian society often adopts farming terms into its political lexicon). Public rage engulfed the Macoutes, many of whom were captured and burned or stoned to death by furious mobs. Nearly all of the surviving Macoutes went underground, and a concomitant power vacuum could only be filled by the army. The U.S. embassy and Baby Doc had made arrangements for a provisional government under General Henri Namphy, a highly political officer who soon aspired to establish his own dictatorship. The urban poor, however, would have nothing of it. In April they marched on Fort Dimanche, which had been used as a prison under the Duvalier regime and symbolized its tyranny. Soldiers opened fire, shooting dozens and sending the crowd fleeing, but not before radio coverage of the demonstration revealed the leadership of a charismatic Roman Catholic priest, Jean Bertrand Aristide.

Popularly known as "Titid" (Haitian patois for *petit Aristide*) because of his small stature, Aristide soon became the foremost leader of opposition to the Namphy regime. Raised in a family of modest means in the countryside, he had received a basic education from his mother and later had won scholarships for study abroad—mastering theology and several languages by his early adulthood. A convinced convert to liberation theology since the 1970s, Aristide returned to Haiti and opposed the Duvalier dictatorship with sermons from his pulpit. With Namphy in power, he began to enjoy a national following, as Catholic radio broadcast his messages and the illiterate slum dwellers in Port-au-Prince responded to his leadership, staging new rallies and general strikes in order to topple the military regime.

The challenge for Namphy, and the United States, was to legitimize the government in the eyes of the Haitian people. The obvious avenue, elections, posed dangers—perhaps an Aristide would run, or a genuine opponent of the economic and political power structure would win. Civil unrest swelled in the capital during the hot summer of 1987, despite the army's policy of shooting unarmed demonstrators. After months of turmoil, Namphy finally agreed to schedule elections. The major candidates that emerged included three that were unpalatable to those who controlled Haiti: Louis Déjoie, Gerard Gourgue, and Sylvio Claude. Déjoie was the son of the man cheated out of the 1957 election by Papa Doc, and therefore had automatic anti-Duvalierist credentials. Gourgue, a schoolteacher and human rights activist who had briefly served as the front man for the Namphy regime before realizing that it was nothing more than "Duvalierism without Duvalier," enjoyed considerable popular support. Protestant Pastor Sylvio Claude had been highly critical of the dictatorship and was once imprisoned by Baby Doc. In contrast to these three, the mulatto elite and the United States backed former World Bank economist Marc Bazin (dubbed "Mr. Clean" by the masses, because of his white business suits). Bazin had served in Baby Doc's government, and despite having the best-financed campaign (in a nation without televisions), he had no chance of winning the votes of a highly informed and engaged electorate.

Facing the prospect of authentic democracy, Namphy's government used the army to sabotage the election through a series of massacres. The general then canceled the vote, and the United States, having supplied the troops with ammunition, symbolically cut off military aid and expressed its disgust over the failure of Haitians to embrace "democracy." In January 1988, new elections, this time tightly controlled and rigged, brought a compliant history professor into office. Leslie Manigat won by a landslide as perceptive Haitians stayed away from the polls. Mocked as the fattest president in Caribbean history, he wore the long presidential sash, though Namphy and his army retained genuine power.

Haiti again seemed under control. Street demonstrations subsided, low-level state terror quietly resumed, and a spirit of political fatalism began to engulf the land. Then, in September 1988, authorities made the questionable decision to eliminate Aristide by unleashing the reinvigorated Tontons Macoute on his congregation. Knife-wielding Macoutes, apparently high on cocaine, charged into his parish during a Sunday morning service and killed many, chopping up one pregnant woman as she knelt in a corner screaming. The first salvos of machine gun fire splattered the altar, but amazingly, failed to hit the startled Aristide, who was standing at the pulpit. Quick-thinking aides pulled Titid to safety and hid him in a nearby office. Police, who had sealed off the neighborhood, stood by as Macoutes searched in vain for the priest, hunted down survivors, and set fire to the sanctuary.

The sensational attack triggered renewed unrest, this time in the army ranks. *Ti soldats*, or ordinary soldiers, offended by the killing of Christians during worship, disobeyed their officers. New waves of civil unrest erupted in Port-au-Prince. With the blessing of the United States, Namphy stepped down in favor of a second Duvalierist general, Prosper Avril. Avril, try as he might, could not pacify either the army or the country. A volcano of popular discontent again racked Haiti—a surge so strong that the people called it *Lavalas*, the Flood. At the eye of the storm stood none other than Aristide, who by now enjoyed the mystique of a survivor of multiple assassination attempts, though his mental health had begun to crumble under the strain. Not even the CIA-funded, macabre display of tortured pro-democracy leaders on television, during Halloween 1989, could cow the masses back into submission. Avril was forced out of office and was flown into exile, like his predecessors, by courtesy of the United States. An attempt by the army to use a civilian judge, Ertha Pascal Trouillot, as a front, again failed to appease the people. Massive demonstrations finally led to authentic elections. A demoralized army and its elite allies watched a triumphant Aristide sweep to victory in December 1990, in Haiti's first-ever clean vote. Winning 67 percent to Marc Bazin's 16 percent, Aristide assumed office on February 7, 1991, exactly five years after Baby Doc had left the country. Haiti had become a democracy.

Aristide's presidency threatened the fundamentals of economic power in Haiti, despite the fact that he respected private property. Even after his inauguration, instead of throwing a dinner for the diplomatic corps, he entertained five thousand street children as his "personal guests." New laws increasing the minimum wage to about US$.35 an hour were ignored by American corporations, but the spirit of governance had changed. Aristide cut the size of the government bureaucracy and began to efficiently manage Teleco, the state-owned phone company, which had long been milked of its profits by Duvalierists. Confident and loved by the vast majority of his people, he stood up to the United States, claiming in a September 23 speech before the United Nations that Americans themselves were at the center of the world's drug trade.

The very next week, following his return to Haiti, Aristide was overthrown by a military coup. The Haitian army, firmly under the control of General Raúl Cedras, unleashed a bloodbath of unprecedented proportions, as machine-gun-equipped soldiers mowed down masses of would-be protesters (probably about a thousand persons died in Port-au-Prince alone within two days, although reliable statistics are difficult to come by). Sylvio Claude and other popular leaders were assassinated. Aristide, brought before Cedras in handcuffs, was saved only by the intervention of foreign embassies and was flown out of the country. His followers were hunted down by a new paramilitary force, the Front for the Advancement and Progress of Haiti (FRAPH), led by Emmanuel ("Toto") Constant. Later nominated for the Nobel peace prize by an American academic, Constant was a valuable asset to the CIA, which appears to have funded many of FRAPH's operations.

Three years of renewed military rule finally broke the spirit of the Haitian people. It also wore down Aristide. Unable to stomach the knowledge that his friends and allies were being eliminated, Aristide cut a deal with the United States. He agreed to return to Haiti, abide by the dictates of U.S.-supported international financial institutions (see Chapter 9 for more about this), hold new elections, and step down from the presidency. This agreement, attractive to the United States in part because Haitian boat people were overwhelming the coast of Florida, assured an end to Aristide's disruptive economic practices and ideas and promised to restore stability.

A highly public spectacle followed, with famous Americans visiting Port-au-Prince in order to "threaten" the coup leaders with military action if they refused to step down. The army officers went into comfortable exile (the United States rented Cedras's homes for $15,000 a month after he left, helping him in retirement; another coup leader, Colonel Carl Dorelien, strangely won 3.2 million dollars in the Florida lottery in 1997). Constant fled to the United States, where he was protected from extradition to Haiti to stand trial for human rights abuses (one of his earlier torture victims, then living in New York, nonetheless tried to sue him). U.S. troops, leading the occupation forces, quickly snatched away FRAPH's documents and shipped them into storage for "reasons of national security." When an American junior officer upon arriving in Haiti tried to keep his pro-Aristide contacts from being abducted and tortured, he was court-martialed for "conduct unbecoming an officer" and discharged from the U.S. army.

Although Aristide's return was greeted with euphoria by the poor, the flirtation with democracy had run its course. Once it was apparent that the new government was unable to carry out meaningful economic reforms, the populace stopped voting and grew disinterested. The presence of Aristide and his successor, René Preval, actually pacified Haiti, since people did not resent them. Yet at the close of the twentieth century, it was the wealthy mulattos who were busily organizing new political parties in preparation for the elections game. The majority of Haitians ignored the process, with voter turnouts sinking to levels below those in the United States. In the first fully U.S.-endorsed and -arranged elections, in April 1997, only 5 percent of Haitians voted. The possibility of Aristide's returning to power in December 2000 elections appeared to evoke greater enthusiasm among the populace.

Mexico: From One Party to Multiparty "Democracy"

The second most populous Latin American nation and the one of greatest importance to the United States, Mexico has a distinctive political culture that enabled it to avoid military takeover in the postwar era. Its large, multifaceted, and sophisticated society was governed for more than seventy years by the Party of the Institutionalized Revolution (PRI), founded by Plutarco Calles in 1929. Although it underwent two name changes and some restructuring in its early years, the PRI effectively became the electoral wing of the state by 1940, when it cheated the opposition out of victory and brought into the presidency a moderate successor to Lázaro Cárdenas, the socialist who had distributed land and seized foreign oil companies. During its reign in the middle of the twentieth century, the PRI won every major election, usually by a landslide.

This is not to imply, however, that the PRI completely lacked popular legitimacy. In the 1990s, several news wire services routinely referred to Mexico as an *authoritarian democracy*—a seeming oxymoron that actually makes sense. From the 1940s to the 1960s, Mexicans experienced the so-called "Peace of the PRI," a period when the party ruled with a degree of consensus and the state exercised relatively little political repression. Control of the nation's purse strings, and strong bonds between government and capital, made it possible for the PRI to repeatedly buy off the opposition. The party wisely made room for new leaders, absorbing them into its ranks with carrots instead of driving them away with sticks. The organizer of slum dwellers on the outskirts of Mexico City might agitate for sewage lines and city services, but he could also count on a new government job and pension if he delivered votes and support to the PRI. As long as the economy expanded, the PRI could co-opt its opponents.

Even under the Peace of the PRI, the government had its limits, without which everyone would have clamored for political prizes, overloading the system. Low-level state violence was common in the predominantly Indian regions of southern Mexico, where periodic opposition movements and land reform campaigns were suppressed. Organized labor, too, consistently felt the arm of authority, especially when independent unions attempted unauthorized strikes. A walkout by railroad workers in 1959 resulted in widespread violence. The army broke up labor rallies, beat up workers, and arrested strike leaders, many of whom were subsequently sent to prison under a new antisubversion law.

The government faced its greatest political crisis in 1968, in the capital. Its riot police overreacted to a simple fracas between high school students, inadvertently unleashing middle-class resentment of the lack of political rights. The timing could not have been worse: Mexico City was scheduled to host the Olympic Games at the end of the summer. The president at the time, Gustavo Díaz Ordaz, ordered troops into the streets to bring the populace into line. More police brutality followed, and demonstrations led by university students exploded in size. As hundreds of thousands of Mexicans took to the streets, Díaz Ordaz warned the nation on television that too much unrest would not be tolerated. When the protests began to subside, the army executed a crushing blow. On October 2, at an ancient Indian plaza called Tlatelolco, it surrounded a small rally of a few thousand antigovernment diehards. A massacre ensued, leaving several hundred protesters dead. Critical documents of these events remain secret; but the massacre was almost certainly premeditated and authorized by the highest levels of the Mexican government.

After the events at Tlatelolco, the legitimacy of the PRI was increasingly questioned. Disillusioned college students formed guerrilla bands in the early 1970s, which were hunted down and eliminated by security forces in a small-scale dirty war. In the 1970 presidential vote, millions of Mexicans submitted blank ballots in silent protest. The real roots of the growing political crisis, however, were economic. An inflationary spiral and slow job creation undermined popular support and the ability of the government to buy off its opponents. When the economy went bust in the early 1980s, support burgeoned for the opposition.

On the eve of the 1988 elections, as had been the case for more than a half century, the Mexican president handpicked the PRI's candidate. What was unusual in 1988, after several years of economic depression, was that the PRI's candidate, Carlos Salinas de Gortari, faced an enormously popular opposition figure in Cuauhtémoc Cárdenas. Cárdenas had an outstanding political pedigree: He was the son of Lázaro, the nationalistic president of the 1930s, who had named him after the last Aztec emperor. About the only thing going for the PRI was Cárdenas's dreadful public-speaking style, and that was not enough. On election night, with Cárdenas racing ahead in the ballot count, the nation's computerized tabulation system strangely went off line. When repaired, it showed that Salinas had eked out an unexpected victory.

The 1988 race and Salinas's administration marked the end of the one-party system's popular legitimacy in Mexico. Although Salinas possessed a Harvard Ph.D. and received accolades from U.S. officials, including Bill Clinton, he eventually left office in disgrace and retired to Ireland, taking with him a dubiously acquired personal fortune estimated at US$5 billion. His brother Raúl was convicted in 1994 of having arranged the murder of a PRI official (their former brother-in-law), José Francisco Ruiz Massieu. During Salinas's administration, the Mexican elite began to commit fratricide, surrounded by a web of intrigue that apparently was tied to drug money.

Under Salinas, Mexicans mobilized at the grass roots as they never had before. Political and quasipolitical organizations flourished, from peasant groups and women's rights organizations to new labor and human rights committees. At the national level, political ferment expressed itself in the rise of two new political parties. Cárdenas, emerging from the 1988 election debacle, championed the cause of the Party of the Democratic Revolution (PRD), with its loci of power in Mexico City and the poor, southern states. The National Action Party (PAN), founded decades earlier by devout Catholic businessmen and long viewed as a "loyal opposition" to the

PRI, acquired new popularity and independence. It held particular appeal in the tier of northern states along the U.S. border.

The powerful and centralized Mexican government under Salinas, realizing opposition politics were becoming unavoidable, created space for the PAN and repressed the PRD. Several local offices, and eventually, governorships, fell into the hands of the party ideologically closest to elite interests. The PRD, in truth, had far more popular legitimacy during the early 1990s, not only because of the 1988 election but also because it held out possibilities of real social and economic change. Hundreds of PRD activists died violent deaths in the 1990s at the hands of police, especially in rural areas. Independent Mexican news sources also lost several dozen journalists. The major Mexican newspapers and television network, owned by PRI supporters, emphasized the PAN at the expense of the PRD.

As the 1994 presidential contest approached, the PRI's chances for a clean election victory improved. Mexican economic fortunes seemed to rebound under Salinas, though the boom was artificial and temporary, being tied mainly to an influx of speculative investment dollars and a frenzy of activity surrounding the ratification of the North American Free Trade Agreement (NAFTA; see Chapter 9). Its designated candidate, Luis Donaldo Colosio, launched a drab campaign that failed to catch fire. His untimely assassination in March (possibly the result of a drug-related conspiracy, though conclusive evidence is lacking) evoked a sympathy vote for his campaign manager-turned-candidate, Ernesto Zedillo.

Zedillo and the PRI won the election handily, and with very little fraud. The economic upswing and Colosio's death set the stage for a PRI comeback; but the victory was primarily won through the twin powers of money and media. The ruling party outspent its combined opponents by a margin of 100 to 1. Fearful of Cárdenas, Mexico's billionaires voted for the PRI with their pocketbooks. Roberto Hernández, the nation's banking magnate, arranged a dinner party where he encouraged each guest to contribute US$25 million to the PRI's war chest. Thus, in a single night, the party raised $750 million (due to a public scandal over the dinner, though, the donations were made under the table).

One of the men at the dinner, who ended up giving $70 million to the PRI, was Emilio Azcarraga, the richest man in Latin America at the time. Azcarraga owned Televisa, the only major television network in Mexico in 1994. Televisa's newscasts were critical in shaping the election's outcome. Network managers and PRI officials had conferred about techniques for influencing public opinion. One tactic was a nightly news emphasis on world hot spots like Bosnia, where reporters stressed the horrors of civil war and disintegration of once orderly societies. Subsequent polls showed a rise in concern among Mexicans about the risks of political change.

When it came to domestic election coverage, the strategies of the network were more direct. Zedillo and the PRI received five times more coverage than either of the major opponents, and camera angles and speech excerpts magnified Zedillo's stature and diminished those of Cárdenas and the PAN's candidate, Diego Fernández de Cevallos. When polls showed the PAN gaining on the PRI in the last week before the vote, with Cárdenas running far behind, Televisa switched its emphasis in order to pump the PRD and divide the opposition tallies. Even more shrewd than Televisa's disproportionate emphasis on Zedillo, however, was its overemphasis of minor candidates that no one knew. It routinely provided more news coverage to previously unknown figures than to Cárdenas or Fernández de Cevallos. In particular, the Labor Party, an obscure organization that barely registered on the political landscape, came out of nowhere in 1994 to run an expensive and divisive campaign. The Mexican government, it turns out, funded the Labor Party as a way of further clouding the election, and—by having it adopt positions identical to those of the PRD—stealing opposition votes.

Lastly, the official party was aided by Cárdenas's failure to utilize polling data and public relations managers capable of staging posh photo ops and catchy sound bites. Cárdenas's campaign rhetoric emphasized human rights in Chiapas and democracy—themes that were of little interest to most Mexicans. In fact, surveys showed that democracy ranked twenty-fourth in importance to voters, behind pressing concerns like pollution and health care. Professional polling also showed that Mexicans believed television was an impartial and reliable source of news. The PRI crushed the PRD in 1994; and by the close of the century, it was again the most popular political party.

The same media-infused tactics were employed in the 2000 elections, during which Cárdenas's campaign was even more effectively marginalized. Having shed its Catholic eccentricism, the PAN became a truly pro-business party completely acceptable to the nation's rich (several of its longtime, religiously motivated leaders had withdrawn from the party during the 1990s). The PAN's colorful candidate, Vicente Fox, was a Coca-Cola company executive-turned-politician who offered Mexicans policy prescriptions almost identical to those of the PRI. Vested interests, both within Mexico and the United States, thus had nothing to fear during the elections: The two major "opposing" parties, in fact, were ideologically identical.

The Rise of *Mediacracy*

In 1994, Pentagon strategists worried that democracy in Mexico would undermine U.S. interests. "Relations with Mexico's government have been extraordinarily positive," one analyst argued at a Latin American Strategy Development Workshop that September, "but a democratic opening in Mexico could test that special relationship by bringing into office a government willing to challenge the U.S. on economic and nationalistic grounds." That danger, however, has passed. Even with a deep downturn in the economy in 1995, Mexicans still looked to the PRI (and perhaps, their televisions) for direction. When Bill Clinton visited party leaders at Roberto Hernández's ranch in 1999, there was little doubt that he was conferring with Mexico's long-term power brokers.

The nature of electoral politics in Latin America is reassuring to those who fear that democracy could mean renewed nationalism and economic policies inimical to the rich or to the United States. As evident with Fujimori in Peru and Zedillo in Mexico, public opinion can be manipulated through careful analysis of polling data and the work of skilled media consultants. Independent journalism in Latin America is limited (in part due to the fact that murders of unofficial journalists have increased sharply in recent years). Until people collectively begin to question the source of their news, the prognosis for preventing real political change is good. An interesting observation, in fact, is that the one Latin American nation too destitute to have televisions in its slums (Haiti) has been the most politically explosive.

Ironically, Latin Americans now have more elections but arguably less freedom. Throughout much of the region, grassroots organizing peaked in the 1980s, when economic conditions soured and people believed that changes in government could bring improvement. In Brazil and elsewhere, popular groups helped restore civilian rule by bringing an end to military regimes. These myriad networks, however, have declined in recent years. If democracy involves grassroots organizing, then the trend today is decidedly antidemocratic. We have entered, instead, an era of *media*cracy.

Electoral politics are increasingly media-dominated and detached from grassroots political action. Links between local activism and political parties are limited, and as a result, Latin Americans often ignore the electoral process altogether. Voter turnout has declined in recent years. In Chile's second-largest city in 1997, one contest was even won by "none of the above." Popular disinterest has fueled a bizarre pattern of media and campaign sensationalism. One political talk show tried to boost ratings in Chile by having candidates play Ping-Pong while answering journalists' questions. Throughout the region, colorful "anticandidates" without political credentials have been elected—including musicians, dancers, sports figures, and television stars.

Clearly, a deeper scientific analysis of political dynamics is needed in order to understand the dynamics of popular disinterest in politics. But the phenomenon appears at least partly due to the shrinking ideological spec-

trum among parties and politicians. On seminal economic and social issues, major candidates in political races often agree. A presidential contest
in Honduras between two wealthy ranchers, for example, had such a lack
of policy substance that it ultimately revolved around questions of who was
the more sexually virile. The lack of meaningful choices has apparently
turned voters off. Most socialist and opposition parties in Latin America
have shifted decidedly in favor of pro-capitalist economic policies. One
reason for this is the fact that middle-class citizens dominate the small segment of society that remains politically active. Another is that candidates—
those with sufficient money, intelligence, and political acumen to run—
overwhelmingly come from the upper classes. For example, in Chile's
elections in 2000, it did not matter greatly to vested interests whether
"rightist" Joaquín Lavín or "socialist" Ricardo Lagos won—both candidates stood for basically the same things. Although Lagos eked out a victory, his government continued to pursue pro-business policies favorable
both to wealthy Chileans and to U.S. corporations.

What Latin America is experiencing politically has been called "simulated democracy" by Chilean sociologist Tomás Moulian. The appearance
of choice is pushed by mass media owned and controlled by corporations
and the rich, freezing out all genuine opposition. Opponents must either
conform ideologically or be ignored by the press. If ignored, they become
trapped in a self-defeating circle: The press does not cover them because
"they can't win," and they can't win because the press does not cover them.
Like that observable in Russia and elsewhere, Latin American "democracy" is media-defined and -manufactured. This process of manipulation,
often facilitated by American consulting firms, is tremendously advantageous for the United States, since it undercuts the possibility of real choice
or economic change.

The new political dynamics, however, are not foolproof. When there
have been legitimate ideological differences, the electorate has sometimes
come to life. In Venezuela a charismatic ex-army paratrooper who once
tried to overthrow the government, Hugo Chavez, lambasted both of the
major political parties and ran on an opposition platform in 1998. In the
closing weeks of the campaign, realizing that the masses were awakening
to Chavez's efforts, the two "rival" political parties joined together and
promoted a single candidate (telling proof of simulated democracy). Despite their money and a major media blitz, Chavez pulled off a stunning
upset. Running a populist campaign in which he criticized capitalism and
praised Fidel Castro, the nationalist sent shivers through financial markets
and alarmed both the White House and Wall Street. After his election the
new president resolved to rewrite Venezuela's constitution. Pro-Chavez
delegates for the Constitutional Assembly won 96 percent of the races. In
the face of this overwhelming popular mandate, traditional politicians

vowed to fight to "save democracy"—a twist of wording that shows just how divorced mainstream electoral politics can become from the popular will.

In December 1999, 70 percent of Venezuelans approved a long and cumbersome constitution instituting a wide variety of political and economic rights. Many poor, believing that Chavez can deliver better living conditions, revere the man. Significantly, too, the constitution—recognizing the nature of the elite-owned media—calls for "truth" in news coverage; but methods for monitoring media reliability have been watered down due to fears of censorship. Chavez has shown himself to be an astute learner, combating the media's negativity by airing his own broadcasts. On a two-hour Sunday radio talk show called *Hello, President!,* he spontaneously fields callers' questions. In spring 2000, facing new constitutionally mandated elections, he routinely bumped prime-time TV shows off the air in order to give long-winded speeches. Despite corporate-owned media's charges of corruption and defections among his closest political allies, Chavez, at least temporarily, retained the support of his nation's politically awakened poor.

Recent developments in Venezuela are, in all probability, an aberration. They suggest, however, that even in the politics of control the unexpected might occur. Yet a final reason why opposition parties have shunned major economic alternatives is that, in reality, those alternatives no longer exist. After his election, Chavez watched as Caracas's stock market plummeted and rich Venezuelans pulled their money out of the country (and in some cases, themselves and their families). In 1999 the young president sought to reassure investors, toning down his nationalist rhetoric and making a quick visit to Washington. As an optimistic analyst noted in the *Wall Street Journal,* about the only thing Chavez could really hope to do is run his government's limited social services more efficiently. Structural economic change in Latin America has made political decisions less and less significant.

9 Big Money: Debt and Wealth Extraction

Political and economic dynamics in Latin America have undergone profound changes in the past twenty years. If the elites and U.S. corporations, among others, desire political stability in the region, then the rise of more "democratic" governments has, perhaps, been a blessing. In the face of growing economic frustration, the majority poor are arguably less likely to oppose governments that they perceive as legitimate (even victories by so-called opposition parties, during the next few years, might be best for vested economic interests). A political and economic fatalism may even sweep the land, as Latin Americans realize that over the past generation, their nations have been divested of economic sovereignty.

The Debt Crisis

Debt has been critical in allowing vested interests in the United States and other First World countries to gain macroeconomic control of Latin America. A sequence of events unfolding in the past thirty years facilitated this takeover, which is now central to preserving the comforts and prosperity that Americans enjoy. But why did Latin America borrow so much money in the first place, and how did these big but still manageable financial transactions mutate into a giant dragnet that has ensnared the region? Although rich Latin Americans have certainly been willing to sacrifice nationalism in exchange for the prospect of making money by cooperating with the First World, the loss of economic sovereignty is not merely the story of global elite collusion.

Latin America entered the postwar era with relatively little public and private debt. Widespread defaults on outstanding bonds and loans during the Great Depression soured big investors on the region, as did the economic nationalism of the populists. During the early 1940s, First World banks were completely absorbed by the exigencies of World War II; and after the war, they focused heavily on the financial requisites for rebuilding western Europe. It was not until the early 1950s that Latin Americans again began to seek large amounts of credit from First World lenders. They did so in the context of "developmentalism," with a view toward improving infrastructures, such as highways and communications systems, as well as undertaking new projects, such as mammoth dams for hydroelectric power. Many of the loans in the late 1950s and early 1960s came from quasigovernmental entities, such as the World Bank and the newer Inter-American Development Bank. The premise of the Alliance for Progress—that development would undercut the forces of radicalism and instability—weighed heavily in the motives of these public policy-influenced institutions.

It was actually not until after 1970 that Latin America borrowed heavily from private First World banks. But once the borrowing began, it soon mushroomed out of control. The region entered the decade with low public and private debt; it left it with nearly US$250 billion in debt. Mexico started the 1970s with about $3 billion in borrowed capital, both public and private. By 1981, Mexicans owed the First World $75 billion.

Why did Latin Americans borrow so much money? There is no single answer to this question. Credit, however, was readily available, and on generous terms. For decades, borrowers in Latin America had been required to provide specific information about their spending plans in applying for loans. But in the 1970s big banks lent freely, with almost no strings attached. Even Bolivia, an impoverished and politically unstable country with just about the worst credit rating in the world, received massive infusions of cash from Citibank and other corporate lenders.

The pivotal question, then, is actually the reverse: Why did First World banks so generously extend credit to poor countries, and to a lesser extent, to their domestic industries? Again, the answer is complex. But in short, after the rebuilding of Europe, U.S. banks in particular were flush with highly liquid capital. In order to make money, obviously, banks need to lend. In the years following World War II, the U.S. government—leery of what had happened during the Great Depression (when there was a run on the banks and the financial system came close to collapse)—continued to tightly regulate banks and the money supply. Insurance deposits, limitations on loans and interest rates, and other features of government oversight, although arguably ensuring the safety of the banking system, stifled profits. By the late 1960s, policymakers began to listen to bankers' complaints. Although the U.S. government was unwilling to deregulate the domestic banking industry, it did sanction the industry's expansion into poorly regulated overseas markets. In 1960 only eight U.S. banks had branches overseas. By 1980 the number had reached 140. The internationalization of finance capital began in earnest during the 1970s.

In the late 1970s, big banks engaged in a frenzy of lending. As the U.S. government under Jimmy Carter printed too many dollars in order to cover ballooning federal deficits, inflation reached unprecedented heights. The steady decline in the value of the dollar meant that banks earned less and less from the servicing payments of their debtors. Borrowing was, in short, cheap. Banks wanted to extend even more new loans, in order to make more money; and Latin Americans gauged that continued dollar inflation was a hedge against unmanageable debt.

Other factors also were involved in the so-called "dance of the millions." Many of the borrowers in Latin America were military men in charge of governments. They were free of almost all public accountability, and massive borrowing provided tremendous opportunities for graft. Hundreds of millions of dollars ended up in private offshore accounts in Switzerland or the Cayman Islands. Generals and their cronies, as well as many natural political allies from among the ranks of the elite, robbed their people blind. Also, there was a contagion effect to borrowing and lending: Smaller lenders reasoned that if General Hugo Banzer (the dictator of Bolivia) and his regime warranted big loans from Citibank, then he certainly was a safe bet for more loans from lesser banks. From the borrower's perspective, when short-term obligations were coming due, why not simply pay them with new and even bigger loans? The cycle of lending and borrowing ballooned outward, until 1982, when it popped.

The beginning of Ronald Reagan's presidency in 1981 signaled a sharp change in U.S. fiscal policies (in contrast to its relative continuity with the previous administration's military and foreign policies). The U.S. treasury department and Reagan's economic advisers quit printing money and tightened monetary controls in order to rein in rampant inflation. A slowdown in the overheated U.S. economy ensued, but the changes worked well for the United States: Inflation was brought under control and a new anti-inflationary regimen was begun, largely under the auspices of the Federal Reserve. For indebted Latin America and the Third World, in contrast, the sharp reversal out of an inflationary cycle into fiscal caution was the worst possible change. It made dollar debt (when adjusted for now-low inflation) larger than ever, at the very time that rises in oil and other commodity prices slowed and export earnings plummeted. Within a very short time after Washington's fiscal policy change, several Latin American nations were on the verge of bankruptcy.

In August 1982, Mexico's government stunned the financial world by announcing that it could no longer service its foreign debt. Bankers in New York at first responded callously, telling Mexican officials that it was their problem. But the magnitude of the potential default alarmed Wall Street and clearly threatened the stability of banks in the United States and beyond. The Reagan administration stepped in, as did the International Monetary Fund (IMF)—a "development" institution that had been marginalized during the private lending boom in the 1970s and that was now prepared to play the ostensible role of an intermediary between troubled borrowers and upset lenders.

In late 1982 and 1983, the United States, IMF, big banks, and Latin American finance ministers negotiated new conditions on the region's mammoth dollar-denominated debt. Shrewdly and significantly, U.S. officials insisted that debtors come to the negotiating table one at a time. In this way, creditors largely avoided the possibility of a nascent debtors' cartel, through which Latin Americans could have, theoretically, used their collective clout to negotiate better terms of repayment. The IMF, too, served American interests with aplomb. Based in Washington, D.C. and financed and controlled by the rich governments of the First World, the organ pressured Latin Americans to sign agreements that involved IMF economic oversight of their domestic economies. By the end of 1983, almost every major debtor nation had agreed to rather draconian terms of debt repayment. Banks stood to make bounties, as renegotiated interest rates on loans and service commissions soared. The First World's so-called lending institutions began to extract money from Latin America.

Latin American elites in government, and to a lesser extent in the private sector (the two economic domains have never been neatly separated), did not completely surrender during talks with New York and Washington. Despite comforting economic reports from banks projecting a rebound in world growth and an expectation that debts would evaporate by the end of the decade, some governments openly complained about the stiff conditions. The civilian administration of Raúl Alfonsín in Argentina especially balked, and Ecuadorians even went so far as to organize a low-level form of debtors' conference. In 1984 the United States announced that Mexico would be receiving a more favorable repayment schedule and extensions, in part because of its exceptional cooperation and aggressive implementation of IMF-counseled domestic policies. This big, visible carrot prompted other nations to line up and seek similar relief. Argentina and other troublemakers were isolated until they, in turn, signed onto some modestly better conditions.

This process of gently loosening severe restrictions, while dividing Latin Americans from each other, was repeated again in 1985. Fidel Castro caused the United States a mild headache when he spoke publicly about the nature of debt and servicing payments. Castro said that the debts owed to the First World would never be paid off, and that the United States should cancel them and underwrite the losses by cutting its enormous military budget. His argument for a demilitarized world was, of course, a call for a new kind global equality. If implemented, it would have profoundly altered power relations between the First and Third Worlds, irreparably damaging America's ability to extract global wealth. Castro's complaints coincided with the election of socialist Alan García in Peru. García had campaigned on the debt issue and announced limits on debt payments in his inauguration speech in Lima. Washington was worried.

Shortly thereafter, at a meeting of IMF and World Bank officials in Korea, Treasury Secretary James Baker announced that the United States would increasingly emphasize economic growth over rigid austerity as a means of debt repayment. He then traveled to Brazil and discussed trying out the new approach on one lucky country. Several Latin American governments catered to Washington in subsequent months, seeking to reap the benefits of the new policy approach—which was never fully implemented. It was clear by 1986 that Latin American debtor states could be masterfully divided; but it was also evident that a new, forceful hand was needed in order to assure their collective compliance with the fiscal policies favored by leaders in the First World.

The Rise of International Financial Institutions and SAPs

During the debt renegotiations of the 1980s, the IMF moved swiftly from its position on the periphery of the world's financial order to its very center. In 1987, when the Fund received a new director, French economist Michel Camdessus, it was poised to in effect become a gigantic, global collection agency. Many bad loans from private banks were transferred to the IMF, which itself began to raise capital (primarily from First World governments) and actively lent new money to Latin America as part of a sophisticated debt management program.

The IMF cooperates in these efforts with a sibling, the World Bank, also headquartered in Washington. Both have become prominent in the past two decades, but have existed since the end of World War II. In 1944, as the great conflict wound to a close, Allied financial ministers and consultants gathered at a small New Hampshire village named Bretton Woods. Motivated by the specter of renewed global depression at the end of the war, they discussed broad economic strategies. Since they attributed much of the prewar slowdown to misguided trade policies, especially protectionism, they created several international bodies, including the IMF and World Bank, with the intent of undermining isolationist tendencies. Delegates from the United States helped steer the conference away from the more internationalist schemes of British economist John Maynard Keynes, who envisioned a worldwide reserve currency and central bank, and a standard of exchange founded on something besides the U.S. dollar. These newly formed international financial institutions (IFIs) helped rebuild Europe in the late 1940s, then declined in importance. The World Bank rebounded during the early 1970s, with an accelerated Third World developmentalist agenda.

Although ostensibly "international," the IMF and World Bank are very much under the control of rich nations. A diffusion of field offices has given the appearance of a decentralized structure and global plurality; but influence and voting power overwhelmingly rest with lenders. If poor countries were given equal managerial power, both institutions would undoubtedly function differently—probably to the detriment of First World residents. Different lenders have different amounts of clout, commensurate with their financial contributions. Thus, although the United States directly controls only 18 percent of the IMF's board, it holds the largest share of power and can easily win cooperation from compliant west Europeans. There is a macroeconomic consensus between Europe and the United States on what the IFIs should do. Traditionally, the IMF has been headed by a European, and the World Bank, by an American (its current head, James Wolfensohn, is an Australian-born U.S. citizen).

Despite mild differences in goals and rhetoric—both claim to be assisting the world's poor—at the close of the twentieth century the tasks of the IMF and the World Bank were similar. Since 1988, when they created a joint structural adjustment facility to coordinate their plans for the Third World, the two entities have worked closely together. Though the IMF has upstaged the Bank and enjoyed a more public profile, both IFIs macro-manage economic affairs and facilitate wealth extraction from the Third World. Although since 1983 they have taken several hundred billion dollars more out of the Third World (in debt servicing payments) than what they have put into it (in new loans), the primary avenue of extracting wealth is not through debt management but through the macro-management of poor nations' economies in ways that benefit First World investors. This task is continuing under the leadership of Camdessus's successor at the IMF, Horst Koehler.

These developments are not the product of any shadowy First World conspiracy. On the contrary, both IFIs have long argued that their fundamental policies are designed to benefit poorer nations and set them on the road to development (though rational observation of subsequent economic trends belies this rhetoric). The ideas proffered by the IFIs are based on *neoliberal economics*—a contemporary revival of classic economic theory as articulated by Adam Smith, David Ricardo, and other eighteenth- and nineteenth-century thinkers who expressed faith in the "invisible hand" of the marketplace. The architects of neoliberal policies are often referred to as *technocrats*. Generally young, bilingual, educated at U.S. or European universities, and ambitious, technocrats accumulate massive bodies of economic data and scrutinize global trends, expecting to usher in worldwide prosperity or at least steady growth.

There is no orchestrated plan behind global economic management—no secret council of plotting brains meeting clandestinely somewhere. It would also be erroneous to deeply question the transcendent faith in neoliberal economics evident at the IFIs and among technocrats. The only truly weird phenomenon here is that this faith continues. Since neoliberal economics has taken hold in Latin America and elsewhere, wealth has increasingly concentrated upward. Today 57 percent of the world's population tries to survive on only 6 percent of the world's income. The poor are getting poorer; the rich are gaining ground. Latin America's debt, at an all-time high, is now over $700 billion. Neoliberalism is a boon for Americans and has begun to deliver a golden era of new wealth, power, and comfort for the United States.

Although they operate without an overarching design at the global level, IFIs do very directly dictate macroeconomic policies to Third World countries and have effectively divested them of anything resembling macroeconomic choice. IFIs asserted control in Latin America in the mid-1980s, when the reinvigorated IMF began to implement and closely monitor structural adjustment programs, or SAPs. SAPs were required of nations seeking debt relief; refusal to submit to a SAP meant the withdrawal of IFI support, credit problems, and an inevitable sequence of investor nervousness and capital flight. Some governments have agreed to these terms only reluctantly and with much protest; but none have risked economic meltdown by a full-scale refusal to cooperate.

The first step in establishing a SAP is to draw up a "letter of intent" (the IFIs have developed their own lexicon). This agreement, signed by the host government with the IMF, has traditionally been sealed and unavailable to the public or press. It outlines the duties and expectations of the country in order for it to receive disbursements, or new bridge loans and funds facilitating continued financing of its debt. The IMF then places what it calls a Residential Representative (ResRep) in the country. The presence of the ResRep assures First World investors that the IMF is on the scene, monitoring compliance and giving its approval of favorable economic housekeeping. (Conversely, if investors see that the ResRep is feuding with local authorities—or worse, packing his bags—they know to pull their money out.) Finally, the IMF and World Bank issue new loans in small doses, or what they call "tranches." This mode of gradual financial relief is designed to assure compliance with SAP terms, since less-than-submissive governments might be tempted otherwise to sign a letter of intent, secure a large loan, and then renege on the SAPs' harsher provisions, or hold out against First World dictates.

The SAPs themselves involve what the IMF benignly terms "reforms." These macroeconomic changes are, indeed, reforms from the First World perspective. In aggregate, they seek to undo the tenets of economic nationalism. They rest on the premise—although there is a legitimate question about to what degree some IFI advocates really believe this premise—that a renewed preference for the worldwide marketplace in Latin America will revive the region and bring it economic prosperity. Certainly there is absolutely no doubt that SAPs have been highly beneficial to the United States. Since the mid-1980s, American finance capital has rediscovered Latin America. Corporations have gained access to new raw materials, acquired subsidiaries, absorbed competitors, and gained some of the cheapest labor in the world. The sustained economic growth in the United States owes a debt to the widespread neoliberal revolution that has taken place south of the border.

As previously discussed (in Chapter 4), economic nationalism involved asserting government control over raw material resources, creating import substitution industries, and fostering a domestic market for light consumer goods. Hence, most of Latin America entered the 1980s with high tariff walls, light industrial sectors dominated by domestic capital, and middle-class consumers who bought often shoddy merchandise from quasimonopolistic, government-pampered local businesses. Most also had employment-heavy public sectors, largely funded by still-profitable nationalized utilities and mineral industries. Mexico and Brazil, for example, each had several million persons on government payrolls. Economic nationalism may have created some jobs and even a very modest social service safety net for the underemployed masses, but no one can argue that it was either orderly or efficient.

Under IMF tutelage, SAPs overhaul Latin American economies and open them up to foreign influence and capital. This process, advantageous to the First World, could not be beneficial to the majority of Latin Americans under any circumstances. The region's massive underclass does not fit neatly into a capitalist economic equation. Lacking education and ill-equipped to contribute to economic productivity, the poor have only unskilled labor to offer—in local markets saturated with an oversupply of unskilled labor. Economic nationalism had routed a small portion of the region's productive capital downward, into the dead end of social services and low-end employment opportunities, instead of investing it in an entrepreneurial environment where it could concentrate. As tariff walls came down, domestic industries floundered among waves of cheap, higher-quality imports. Unemployment soared. Middle-class consumers enjoyed better products in the short term; but once competition diminished, costs for imported goods, depending on currency valuations, often rose.

Simultaneously, the IMF has insisted on *privatization*, or the sale of government-owned raw material industries and utilities. Economic nationalists had taken direct control of copper and tin mines, oil fields and refineries, railroads, telephone systems, and the like. Almost all of these government-run entities were monopolistic, top-heavy, operating with outdated equipment, and overstaffed. If an end to protectionism threatened to antagonize the rich—by spelling doom for myriad domestic import substitution industries that they owned—the manner in which public sectors were sold delighted them. Privatization has been an avenue for elite aggrandizement. Generally, government entities have been sold well below market value, often to a combination of domestic elites and foreign corporations. Many have been sold as partial, temporary, or full monopolies, assuring tremendous profitability through guaranteed high fees for products and services and the simultaneous slashing of labor and wage costs.

Privatization has been like an enormous carrot, tantalizing Latin America's rich and wooing them into new alliances with foreign capital. Because they have been given a piece of the action, elites in many countries have embraced or at least tolerated a range of IMF-inspired reforms. Resistance to SAPs, predictably, has come from below. Nongovernmental organizations have tried to mobilize the poor, and marches and even anti-IMF riots have ensued, on occasion, in Argentina, Venezuela, and elsewhere. Options for resistance, however, are limited, given the nature of Latin American democracy and the relative inability of the majority poor to control or even directly influence their governments.

Beyond reducing tariffs and privatizing public possessions, SAPs involve taking control of Latin American fiscal and budgetary policies. During the 1980s, when credit vanished and debts soared, military governments ran hefty deficits and printed money. Hyperinflation soon ravaged much of the region, adding to the sense of economic chaos and frustrating anyone with even a modicum of non-dollar-denominated savings, from the working poor to the middle class. Under these conditions the IMF counseled "shock therapy," which involved an anti-inflationary package of tight monetary policies, high interest rates, and reduced public sector spending. Many governments also altered their currencies: Mexico, for example, lopped three zeros off its peso, declaring it the *nuevo peso;* and Brazil abandoned its currency altogether, creating a new denomination called the *real.* While these policies cast most countries into recession, they did put an end to the dangerous inflationary cycle, as money regained its value.

Controlling inflation has not, of course, alleviated debt, nor have privatization schemes. In 1987, when SAPs began to take hold, all of Latin America owed $410 billion to the First World. During the 1990s, as waves of privatization and new IMF initiatives swept the region, debt totals actually rose (even when adjusted for dollar inflation). The sale of public properties temporarily filled government coffers; but even big auctions yielded only a few billion dollars—a fraction of what is needed to even service the debt. And property can only be privatized once. The subsequent loss of revenue from profitable government-owned operations is almost surely counter-productive for Latin American nations over the long term.

The IFIs pushed for further belt-tightening, or austerity, during the 1990s. Governments were required to cut expenditures, increase revenues, and rein in budget deficits. Tax reform is, of course, a way to increase revenue; but the IFIs have been less domineering when it comes to deciding how countries should raise taxes. Since rich Latin Americans wield great political influence in the region, the trend in the 1990s was to drop income tax rates and sharply increase sales taxes. Unlike the United States, most Latin American countries now spend only a small portion of their resources on the military, and under austerity programs even these budgets have been reduced (though U.S. military aid and security assistance often fill the gap). Cuts, however, have come primarily in social services, giving rise to what some have termed the phenomenon of the "disappearing state." In Haiti, for example, the World Bank pressed for less spending on such things as infant mortality reduction programs. It also told the Haitian government that "education . . . is a cost" that "is necessary but should be minimized" so that more money could go into debt payments to the United States.

Such recipes hurt the world's majority poor, but they benefit Americans. The belief that Latin America can export its way back into prosperity has not been proven true by experience, but it has resulted in a dramatic increase of affordable goods—from toys to T-shirts—pouring into America. In the final years of the twentieth century, the United States was the only country in the world importing more than it exported. Free trade is assumed to be efficient because of the concept of comparative advantage, where one nation produces unique goods for another. Hence, Latin Americans have been encouraged to develop a whole range of new export commodities that Americans can enjoy, such as—in the area of agriculture—tropical nuts and exotic fruits. In turn, the United States continues to supply much of the world's grain. The IFIs have been integral to encouraging this emphasis on Third World exports.

Structural adjustment has been subjected to a moral critique from an exceedingly small but vocal collection of nongovernmental organizations in the First World. British-based Oxfam and other humanitarian operations, noting the erosion of living standards among the poor, have raised objections to what the IMF and World Bank are doing. In the mid-1990s, a network of human rights and religious groups orchestrated a campaign called "Fifty Years Is Enough," calling for the reform or abolition of the major IFIs. A Christian-inspired, mostly European-coordinated "Jubilee 2000" campaign followed on its heels. Based on the Biblical yet categorically anticapitalist notion of forgiving the poor their debts periodically (an ancient Jewish tradition recorded in the book of Deuteronomy), the mostly Christian advocates of "Jubilee" have urged debt relief and First World generosity. Proponents fasted on the steps of the IMF's Washington, D.C. headquarters on New Year's Day 2000, to usher in the new millennium. Their calls have been embraced by religious leaders, such as South Africa's Bishop Desmond Tutu, and echoed by the Pope—a majority of whose billion-person-plus flock resides in poorer countries. Critics have also had a field day with IFI extravagance. Staffers at the IMF and World Bank are largely exempt from income taxes, and make good salaries. Almost all board meetings and conferences take place in comfortable First World settings, with few Third World participants. A single conference once cost the IMF $15 million, with trappings that even members described as luxurious.

Criticism has prompted the IMF and World Bank to alter their public image and spout a more acceptable rhetoric that highlights their reputed concern for the poor. Public statements now include appropriate phrasing, and the World Bank's Web site opens with talk of its mission to fight poverty. With much fanfare, both IFIs announced modest programs of limited debt forgiveness at the close of the 1990s. In June 1999, at a G-8 summit in Germany, Bill Clinton and European leaders approved a more ambitious $100 billion debt relief initiative. The related Heavily Indebted Poor Countries (HIPC) plan, touted in the press as an expression of First World concern and generosity, in fact links debt relief with deeper austerity and more sweeping structural adjustment. The whole notion of easing debt has been employed as a means of actually tightening links to the IFIs. There has been no meaningful move toward complete debt forgiveness—which would likely slow the macroeconomic processes so favorable to the affluent nations of the West. And although critics continue to protest, neither IFI is even remotely endangered. Political leaders support them, as do most academics—some of whom enjoy lucrative IFI contracts and research funds. The IMF even catered a free party for scholars at the 1996 meeting of the Latin American Studies Association, in Washington, D.C.

Latin American nations have implemented SAPs unevenly; and by the beginning of the twenty-first century, a few countries still had not been brought completely to heel. The most visible holdouts have been Ecuador and Venezuela. In the mid-1990s, Ecuadorians elected Abdalá Bucaram, who had campaigned against the IMF; after the elections, he reversed his position and submitted to its orders. Massive street demonstrations ousted his government, and subsequent politicians refused to completely surrender the small nation's economic sovereignty. Ecuador was condemned in financial circles, and direct foreign investment dried up. The country defaulted on part of its debt in October 1999, obligating the government of Jamil Mahuad to accept IMF intervention and cooperate. Restless Indian masses would again have nothing of it, however, and in February 2000, with the acquiescence of some army troops, their renewed civil unrest forced Mahuad to resign. With its economy shrinking and its currency, the sucre, in free fall (from 6,000 to 25,000 to the dollar within 18 months), the new government was again obligated to barter with the IMF. Despite the will of the people, it agreed to a SAP that includes severe austerity measures. But Ecuador will continue to be a volatile place until its people weary of protesting, the media change public opinion, or disciplined security forces employ repression to break the cycles of protest.

In Venezuela, the election of Hugo Chavez appeared to signal a political defeat for the IFIs; the nationalistic Chavez had long openly criticized IMF recipes for his country. However, once in office, he toned down his remarks, even visiting Wall Street to ring the closing bell. He proceeded with debt payments and limited privatization schemes, though he was also clearly groping for economic alternatives—even touring the Far East in hopes of finding new investors. Between 1998 and 1999, foreign investment in Venezuela dropped by 40 percent, as U.S. corporations cooled toward Chavez. Worse still for the upstart government, in December 1999 rains flooded Venezuela's coastline, killing more than 30,000 citizens. Emergency relief from the First World in the wake of the disaster was limited. In 2000, about all that was keeping Venezuela's economy churning were unusually steep crude oil prices, which Chavez used to fund his job-providing state bureaucracy and various social programs for the poor.

Latin Americans themselves largely recognize the role of the IMF and understand SAPs (even while many Americans, though far better educated, are less familiar with the system). There are divisions, however, over what course the region should take, or what other options exist for furthering domestic economic development. Corporate- and elite-owned media downplay the influence of IFIs and stress the importance of faith in the marketplace. When the region's economy began to slow in 1999, Peruvian novelist-turned-politician Mario Vargas Llosa argued that *more* privatization and free trade were what Latin America needed in order to turn things around. Many, especially among the rich, would agree with him. The poor are not uniformly hostile to neoliberalism; but concrete changes, such as hikes in mass transit fares or cuts in food subsidies, tend to deeply arouse them. Uneducated, they often do not know what to think. When the Brazilian economy faltered in early 1999, one impoverished Brazilian sincerely complained on a radio talk show that the culprit was France—because they beat Brazil in the finals of the World Cup. Such confusion among the masses helps undercut anti-IFI sentiments and keep potentially inimical popular movements at bay.

The Clinton Administration and Crises in the 1990s

An important step in deepening the links between First World prosperity and Third World economic change came with the 1992 election of Bill Clinton, a committed IFI supporter and free-marketeer. Americans have generally regarded Ronald Reagan as the president who made neoliberal economics politically fashionable; but Clinton pursued and fulfilled a whole host of new pro-business trade and investment policies. Reagan's administration, in fact, in many ways followed bureaucratic traditionalism. It underwrote U.S. economic growth through national debt, continuing a pattern of deficit spending begun by Jimmy Carter. In contrast, Clinton tirelessly pushed forward the globalization of the U.S. economy.

Whereas Reagan's critical economic appointees were political, Clinton broke new terrain by abandoning notions of government neutrality in favor of openly pro-business investment specialists. One particularly important first-term cabinet official was Commerce Secretary Ron Brown, who earlier in his career had worked as a lobbyist for the Duvalier dictatorship. Brown maintained close ties with corporate executives, took an active hand in promoting overseas investment opportunities, and pressed for Third World globalization—until his U.S. Air Force plane crashed into a mountainside in Bosnia. Building on Brown's work, Robert Rubin assumed leadership in the U.S. treasury department in 1995. Rubin's appointment also broke with political tradition; he had worked for twenty-six years on Wall Street and was a partner in a large investment firm, Goldman-Sachs. As Rubin's influence rose with Clinton's blessing, the administration lost its one globalization critic (and Rubin nemesis), Labor Secretary Robert Reich.

Bill Clinton was uniquely positioned to globalize the U.S. economy because he was a Democrat, was perceived by many as liberal, and possessed the political acumen with which to contain the inevitable discontent of the so-called "left wing" of the American body politic. His lip service and public posturing largely appeased a whole range of factions and personalities that willingly believed he was giving them the most they could ever hope to get. Such manipulation produced memorable political moments: Jesse Jackson rallying crowds in the face of Clinton's impeachment; Marxist academic Cornel West eulogizing Ron Brown; and the AFL-CIO's John Sweeney endorsing Clinton's trade policies on the eve of the World Trade Organization's November 1999 meeting in Seattle. A similar co-optation of supposed dissident forces occurred in Britain with the election of the Labour Party's Tony Blair; and in Germany, with the ascent of Social Democrat Gerhard Schroeder. It is doubtful that Reagan, George Bush, Margaret Thatcher, or Helmut Kohl could have implemented globalization policies with such ease and public complacency.

Clinton's administration, not Bush's, produced the North American Free Trade Agreement (NAFTA) and accelerated a whole range of efforts to globalize world trade and investment—to the benefit of the United States. Canada and the United States had integrated their already tight economies with a pact in 1988. The idea of bringing Mexico into the trading bloc, however, was novel because of the nation's poverty and extremely low wages. NAFTA negotiations under the Bush administration had produced a treaty with political liabilities. Clinton, aware of these shortcomings, had his trade representatives iron out two ancillary agreements on labor protection and the environment. Having thus appeased some of the critics within his own party, he lobbied feverishly to win others, and through much wheeling and dealing he muscled the treaty past Congress with warm Republican support. The president's "Fast-track" authority, which prohibited Congress from altering the agreement negotiated by the administration, aided in this task.

NAFTA's labor and environmental provisions have since been ignored. Since they depend upon enforcement by the signatory nations, Mexico's laxity over industrial waste as well as its ambivalence regarding union busting has allowed corporations to continue standard practices unabated. Workers in the U.S.-owned Clarostat plant in Juárez, for example, assemble electrical switches with phenol and epoxy resin, chemicals that cause skin irritation. When some workers tried to form a union, they were fired. Blacklists shared among U.S. corporations assured that they would not find other work. The Mexican government has arrested and imprisoned independent labor organizers on trumped-up charges of tax evasion and various criminal offenses. With regard to environmental protection, a 1997 study found that nearly 98 percent of the companies operating in Mexico were noncompliant with the agreement. Industrial toxic wastes have polluted Tijuana's public water supply, and hazardous pollution levels plague residents throughout industrialized Mexico. In the wake of the 1997 findings, the Mexican government announced a new program designed to encourage companies to do a better job of policing themselves.

NAFTA was opposed by segments of organized labor in the United States, which recognized that corporations would move industrial jobs in pursuit of cheap labor. Although post-NAFTA studies vary widely in their conclusions, the best evidence is that, in fact, this has occurred (the few contradictory studies tend to be biased; the oft-quoted UCLA findings, for example, were funded by the Commerce Department and drawn up by a former pro-NAFTA lobbyist). Median wages for members of the United Auto Workers in the United States in 1999 were $22.50 per hour, compared to well under $2 per hour in Mexico—quite an incentive to move. Tens of thousands of industrial jobs have shifted southward, but although NAFTA made this exodus easier, the bleeding of America's low-skill, high-pay industrial jobs was already under way. The argument made by NAFTA supporters—that Mexican demand for U.S. goods would create an even larger number of jobs—was always fanciful. With an economy smaller than that of the state of Ohio, and with most of its workforce making subsistence wages, Mexico was never in a position to significantly increase its demand for U.S. goods.

This is not to say that NAFTA has been disadvantageous for the United States. On the contrary, access to close-proximity cheap labor has been a boon for corporations, consumers in search of affordable goods, and investors in the stock market. Since NAFTA's implementation in 1994, Mexican agricultural exports to America have risen by 60 percent. Truckloads of tomatoes, oranges, strawberries, and other produce roll past hungry Mexicans (a half million die annually of malnutrition-related diseases) on their way to the border. And the treaty has certainly assisted the drug trade: Its "line release" provisions—which allow trucking companies to receive fast, inspection-free border crossings—have helped make Mexico the major conduit for illegal narcotics. By 2000, most of the illegal drugs flowing into the United States came by way of Mexico.

When Ernesto Zedillo ran for the Mexican presidency in 1994, he campaigned on the slogan "NAFTA prosperity is here!" It was an important element in the PRI's election victory, as 85 percent of Mexicans, believing their media and government, favored the agreement. In the aftermath of NAFTA, however, Mexico—for reasons largely unrelated to the treaty—collapsed into a brief depression. Just three weeks after assuming office, in mid-December 1994, the new president was forced to devalue the Mexican currency by floating it against the dollar.

The basics of currency exchange are easy to understand and vital to grasping broader macroeconomic trends. Third World nations, with their own money, have traditionally pegged their currencies to the dollar. The Mexican peso, for example, was once set at 12.5 to the dollar, meaning that each peso was worth $.08. For a number of reasons, from domestic inflation to trade imbalances, a currency can weaken or become overvalued. When this occurs, imports from the United States are unduly cheap (since those pesos, for example, are no longer really worth eight cents but continue to buy eight cents' worth of U.S. goods). Exports, in contrast, become expensive, hurting domestic businesses. By intervening in the currency market, the central bank of a nation can defend its currency from devaluation (by buying it with stockpiled dollars). Eventually, however, if a currency continues to weaken, the fixed rate is removed and the currency floats—or finds its true value with respect to the dollar in currency exchange markets.

During the 1980s and 1990s, the IMF tended to oppose devaluations—an antimarket position. The rationale was that devaluations should be avoided in order to control the greater menace of inflation. Indeed, a devaluation almost always sparks a rise in prices, as imported goods become costlier, the currency is perceived as less valuable, and wages rise in compensation for a decline in purchasing power. The circumstances facing Mexico in late 1994, however, left its government no other choice.

On the night of December 19, rich Mexicans began to sell their pesos for dollars. In an astounding example of ineptitude, high-paid Wall Street investment analysts failed to detect the move. The next day the Zedillo government floated the nuevo peso, which immediately lost 15 percent of its value. Within weeks, the value of Mexico's currency had dropped by 50 percent against the dollar. Caught off guard, American investors holding stocks in nuevo peso-denominated Mexican companies lost a small fortune. The Mexican government lost its shirt. Zedillo's predecessor, Carlos Salinas, had refused to float the peso before leaving office, and underwrote the overvalued currency in mid-1994 by issuing $30 billion worth of short-term, dollar-denominated treasury bonds *(tesobonos)*. After the devaluation—with the nuevo peso down and its foreign currency reserves gone—the Mexican government could not pay for these bonds.

Since most of the *tesobonos* were held by Americans, Clinton stepped in. A less business-friendly administration might have let the chips fall where they may; but Rubin and others, with their links to Wall Street, insisted on saving U.S. investors (Rubin almost certainly had personal exposure to the crisis, since Goldman-Sachs had traded heavily in Mexican bonds, and as a member of the firm's limited partnership, he might have been financially liable to angry investors). Avoiding congressional approval by using discretionary funds, the president routed billions of dollars to Mexico, to bail out American investors (most of the funds went to redeem *tesobonos*).

The bailout did not help Mexicans. In November 1995, Zedillo stood on the White House lawn and handed Clinton a symbolic oversized check. Laudatory comments about the amazing Mexican "economic recovery" followed, as evidenced by the early repayment. What Clinton and the news media failed to mention was that Mexico had borrowed money from other sources (mostly the German Bundesbank) and at higher interest rates in order to stage the show. The bailout was all about saving high-risk investments, and seemingly committed the U.S. government to the role of guarantor for worldwide investment schemes—in the eyes of some, a very dangerous precedent.

By late 1995, the Mexican economy was in tatters. The devaluation triggered inflation, which peaked at more than 50 percent; 28,000 businesses went bankrupt; real wages declined by 27 percent; the GDP shrank by nearly 6 percent; and a million Mexicans lost their jobs. Most alarming of all, the banking system was nearly insolvent. A $65 billion government bailout saved the fortunes of men like Banamex billionaire owner Roberto

Hernández. Fortunately for the rich, a depoliticized Mexican populace largely went along for the ride. Zedillo blamed everything on Salinas, and took credit for the modest recovery that began in 1996. The president was portrayed in the media as a man of the people, and polls showed that nearly a fifth of Mexicans blamed the Indian rebels in Chiapas for their financial problems (more than anything, perhaps, a testimony to the wildly popular radio commentator Luis Pazos, who railed against the Zapatistas as socialists who wanted to turn back the clock). Although real wages in the mid-1990s had dipped to 1961 levels, the economic chaos in Mexico did not even approximate the beginnings of political destabilization or popular revolution.

Still, the Mexican collapse was foreboding, in part because the nation had been the golden boy of IMF-dictated policies in the 1980s, abiding by SAPs and austerity programs with as much vigor as any other country in the world. Both the Salinas and Zedillo administrations were dominated by pro-IMF technocrats, including José Angel Gurría, Zedillo's post-devaluation Minister of Finance. Yet even in 1997, when Mexico's GDP surged by 6 percent and exports accelerated, real wages remained stagnant. The rest of Latin America had flattened in terms of wages and poverty levels in the 1990s (though GDP, computed in a variety of ways, rose sharply in many countries as exports soared). After the deep economic declines of the 1980s, stability had seemingly provided support for the argument that conditions were improving. Mexico's stumble suggested that conditions could also get worse.

The boom-and-bust cycle in Mexico in the early 1990s was but a spark in comparison to the worldwide fire that broke out a couple of years later. With significant consequences for Latin America, a July 1997 devaluation in Thailand triggered a panic that threatened the stability of the world's financial order. The robust economies of southeast Asia's "tigers" had experienced high growth for decades. Hence, it was all the more astounding when the collapse of the Thai currency, the baht, spread to neighboring countries and was followed by a bust in the overvalued Asian real estate market. Early in the crisis, the IMF's Michel Camdessus called the turmoil "a blessing in disguise," because it would open up the region to investors and accelerate neoliberalism. When Indonesia's large economy began to wobble, however, the seriousness of the downturn became evident to all.

IMF attempts to restart Asian economic engines in early 1998 failed. The Indonesian economy slid into a depression, triggering unrest in a nation of nearly 200 million. Korea, long a model of postwar prosperity, watched its currency wither and its corporate giants fall. Japan, with the second-largest economy in the world, began to show signs of strain; and in midsummer the feeble Russian economy tanked and the bankrupt government defaulted on Western loans. All along the way, IMF recipes and bailouts seemed worthless. Frustrated investors lost confidence in the IFI and began to criticize it. To be sure, the IMF undermined its own credibility by issuing bizarre and rosy economic forecasts. For example, it projected a 7 percent growth rate in Asia just as the region's economies began to shrink, and new Russian growth just three months before the country's economic collapse. The world's economic order seemed poised on the brink of cataclysm.

In fall 1998, worldwide economic panic was reversed through government intervention. West European central banks, along with the U.S. Federal Reserve, cut interest rates. Japan's government undertook a massive bailout of its banking system, along with tax cuts to spur consumer spending. A new series of IMF loans presumably shored up the next economic domino, Brazil. Around the world, investors regained their confidence; money managers shifted portfolios out of safe havens (namely, U.S. bonds); and the bull market resumed its vigorous romp, at least on Wall Street.

The financial panics of the mid-1990s did much to stop the momentum of the Clinton administration's globalization efforts. Congress refused to grant Clinton Fast Track authority for a hemispheric trade agreement, and efforts in that direction slowed. The General Agreement on Tariffs and Trade (GATT) had produced a new international body, the World Trade Organization (WTO), in 1995, which was confronted by open public hostility at the end of the decade (see Chapter 10). The WTO began, in turn, to draft (under the guiding hand of the U.S. treasury department) a multilateral agreement on investments (MAI). The MAI would have effectively globalized investment policies, strengthening the hand of corporations and in effect codifying the tenets of neoliberalism. Under the MAI, for example, Third World nations would be forbidden from nationalizing property and could be sued by corporations for damages incurred by "strife" or "public disorder." In late 1998, the Socialist government of France abandoned the MAI negotiations and roundly rejected the draft treaty. Robert Rubin resigned his treasury department post a few months later, returning to Wall Street for a lucrative position at Citigroup. His departure was yet another signal that Clinton's pro-business reforms had largely run their course.

In the final quarter of the twentieth century, Latin America came under the macroeconomic control of First World interests, with the acquiescence of most of its elites. Nationalism as a force in the world has dramatically declined (except in the United States). Rich Latin Americans own homes in North America and commute back and forth on a globe made small by air travel, satellite dishes, and the Internet. Their children attend U.S. colleges and speak English (many of the region's political leaders are American-educated). Middle-class Latin Americans line up almost daily at U.S. embassies, aspiring to move to the land of plenty, at least temporarily. Money has usurped ideology in international relations; few Latin Americans care about their international standing, but nearly all worry about making money or just surviving. Even in January 2000, when Panamanians took control of the symbol of U.S. dominance in the region, the Panama canal, many did so with a sense of foreboding. Departing American soldiers meant lost jobs and less economic security, and it remains to be seen whether new tourist schemes and industries will compensate. For Latin America's poor, who must remain in the region all their lives, the prognosis is not good. Profound changes in the economic and political landscapes over the past two decades have led them into an impasse of unrelenting crisis.

10 Latin America in Perpetual Crisis

Latin America has entered an era of crisis without an end in sight. It is not the kind of crisis that shatters institutional structures and thereby creates space for a new beginning. On the contrary, the ultimate crisis for the region is that it is locked into economic and political processes from which, at least for the foreseeable future, there is no escape. The international economic order that has emerged in the past quarter century makes scholarly theories of modernization and dependency obsolete. Having lost (or in the case of the elite, ceded) macroeconomic control to international financial institutions, the region is beholden to the will of rich nations and corporate power brokers. Effective counterinsurgency methods have removed the revolutionary option; politically, Latin Americans must learn to be content with *media*cracy.

The region is neither modernizing nor dependent. It is now in a symbiotic relationship with the First World, primarily the United States. Rather than a theory of centuries-old economic exploitation, we must begin to think in terms of a relatively youthful and recently established system. Building blocks for the system appeared in the late nineteenth century, and its foundation was laid in the shadows of World War II; but the walls of economic and political control have risen only since the 1970s. Critical globalization policies under the Clinton administration topped the project off, just before the dawn of the twenty-first century.

New Economic Realities and Their Social Effects

In the first decades of this century we can expect to see Latin American nations endure economic cycles of monetary devaluation and recession, which will help feed continued prosperity in the United States. These trends are inevitable because of the nature of neoliberal policies and the shift of wealth to the richer parts of the globe. The Mexican peso crisis of 1994 and the world economic scare of 1997–1998 demarcated the beginning of this phase. Eventually, the fixed currencies of other countries in the region will float; and at some point, the U.S. dollar or a hemisphere-wide monetary unit will likely replace the Latin American national currencies (Ecuador's adoption of the U.S. dollar as its currency in 2000 is a sign of accelerating momentum in this direction).

The first post-crisis devaluation came in Brazil, in January 1999, after worldwide government intervention had saved the world's stock markets. Fernando Henrique Cardoso, the academic who helped father dependency theory in the 1960s, had won the Brazilian presidency after introducing a plan for a new currency (the *real*) in the early 1990s to combat hyperinflation. The Brazilian real held its value due to the tight fiscal policies of the IMF-tutored Brazilian government. Cardoso's political clout rose, and he twice trounced the political opposition in presidential elections (in 1994, and again in 1998), winning the support of the elites and military—which was ironic, given his past as a "Marxist academic."

Speculators on foreign currency markets hedged against the real in 1998, assuming that Brazil would be the next emerging market to falter in the world crisis, after Russia. The currency was, in fact, grossly overvalued; but in the face of elections, and with the tacit support of the IMF, Cardoso lifted interest rates and bled currency reserves to prop up the real. In a final bid to avoid full-scale devaluation, his government broadened the currency's trading band, allowing it to lose only part of its value. Slipping to 1.25 to the dollar from a near equal rate of exchange, the real had considerably weakened, triggering the beginnings of capital flight. Released from constraints in mid-January, it slid to as low as 2.2 to the dollar (largely because of the ineptitude of Brazilian officials) before settling at a market-determined rate of around 1.7.

The fallout from this particular currency devaluation was significantly less damaging than that from earlier devaluations elsewhere in the world. Investment houses and banks reacted calmly to the move, and the financial press soon heralded a post-devaluation "recovery" (a dubious claim, for most Brazilians—10 million in the northeast were starving). Unlike previous fiscal jolts, the real's demise not only failed to trigger panic in financial circles but it was comparatively well-received. For several months afterward, the Brazilian stock market soared. The First World's investment community had discovered that Third World currency devaluations were no reason for worry, and foreign capital remained invested in Brazilian equities.

In fact, foreign currency devaluations—long assumed to be negative by investors—have advantages for corporations and First World consumers. A Third World currency devaluation effectively bumps the issuer nation down a notch on the global financial chain; it cheapens exports and forces increased worker productivity, at the same time augmenting debt and international fiscal control. Cardoso's 1998 campaign promises of "governing for the poor" through new social programs were quickly dashed by the Brazilian crisis. Among the plans that could not be implemented was a campaign to help landless peasants acquire property. The crisis even forced a reluctant opposition eventually to support deeper austerity measures. Stanley Fischer, the Deputy Managing Director of the IMF, oversaw these macroeconomic policies, assuring Brazilian compliance with IFI dictates. Like the Mexican peso, the real began to float freely on currency markets. It will steadily lose value over time, instead of passing through regular boom and bust cycles.

Brazil's depreciation placed pressure on other Latin American currencies, making further devaluations unavoidable. Most vulnerable has been the Argentine peso which, under the Carlos Menem government, was fixed at a 1-to-1 ratio and backed by an equal amount of dollar reserves. Because Argentina exports one-third of its goods to Brazil, a competitive devaluation must follow the fall of the real sooner or later. Menem attempted to persuade Argentinians to adopt the U.S. dollar as their national currency. Federal Reserve Chairman Alan Greenspan accepted the idea in principle, making clear, however, that the U.S. government would not be responsible for backing Argentina's banks. Nationalists balked, and the nation slid into an unavoidable recession as interest rates rose in order to buttress the peso—at least until the October 1999 presidential elections. Menem's Peronist party suffered at the polls, with an opposition coalition emerging victorious under professional politician Fernando de la Rua.

In many ways de la Rua's election is fortuitous for business interests, because his "left-of-center" administration will eventually have to devalue the currency and absorb the blame. The poor, many of whom supported de la Rua, may be more willing to swallow the distasteful IFI medicine because it is administered by his hand. At his December inauguration the president announced new IMF-prescribed austerity measures and taxes. When government workers rallied to demand payment of wages in arrears a few days later, security forces opened fire and killed a couple of them. The economic crisis in Argentina does threaten the MERCOSUR (Southern Cone Common Market) trade agreement among Argentina, Brazil, Uruguay, and Paraguay, and may well trigger new forms of protectionism. Plagued by unemployment and high interest rates, Argentina entered the twenty-first century pondering a dark future—literally dark, sometimes, as power outages have left whole swaths of the spacious nation without electricity.

Yet compared with economies elsewhere in the region, Argentina's economy is strong. Other countries have broadened their currency trading bands in recent years and watched their money shrivel. U.S. dollars, which are like gold to the middle class, are stashed away by all who can afford to accumulate them. Devaluation-resisting nations in northern South America plunged into deep recession in 1999. Both Colombia, which eventually floated its currency, and Venezuela saw their economies shrink by several percentage points; and the Andean region fared no better. When Ecuador defaulted on its $6 billion "Brady bond" debt in October, the default necessitated new austerity measures and taxes, and the nation's overseas collateral is now subject to seizure. (Brady bonds, backed in part by U.S. securities through the treasury department, had been designed as a means of keeping near-insolvent countries afloat.)

Currency weakness helps keep Latin America poor, mocking the prophecies of modernization theorists, who have long promised prosperity just around the bend. But far more significant than the region's poverty is the fact that most major economic indicators are moving downward. Macroeconomic trends are easy to discern: After a contraction during the 1980s, the region's economies flattened—as foreigners played in stock markets and privatization spurred investment and temporarily alleviated the debt crisis. From 1981 to 1989, the per capita income of Latin Americans dropped by 10 percent. In the 1990s, modest economic growth returned to some areas, but the nature of this growth was uneven. Export-oriented IMF policies caused GDP data to rise sharply, even as real wages stagnated or declined. Peru, for example, registered astounding GDP figures from 1993 to 1995, as real wages moved in the other direction. GDP data can be highly misleading, since statistical methodology varies and sometimes still fails to account for the critical factor of foreign ownership. If Americans buy clothing from a U.S.-owned subsidiary in Nation X, and most of the profits ultimately remit to the parent company's American stockholders, should the value of the exported clothing be computed as part of Nation X's GDP?

A second macroeconomic trend in Latin America and around the world in the past twenty-five years is wealth concentration. The rich in Latin America have been getting richer at the expense of the poor, compounding hardships for the majority and fueling material ambitions (and especially during the 1990s, new consumerism) among the small but comfortable urban middle class. All sectors of society are now largely disinterested in politics and ideas of social change. The middle class, especially its youth, is fixated on status and money. At a police checkpoint in the suburbs of Santiago de Chile, officers intending to crack down on drivers using cell phones found that a large number of the assumed phones were actually wooden blocks—used by middle-class residents to feign affluence.

Latin America is now one of the most overtly capitalist regions in the world, and rich and poor residents alike are bombarded by aggressive corporate advertising ploys. Recently, Pringle's potato chips hired scores of advertising agency employees to dance around in colorful leotards in downtown Santiago, tossing small cans of potato chips in the air to passersby. At a festival in Puntarenas, Costa Rica, corporations did not just sponsor musical entertainment, they provided it! Scantily clad women danced around a giant popcorn mascot, leading the crowd of several thousand in cheers for "Act Two." Next, it was time for Siempre (Always) tampons. Music blared and bodies swung as a master of ceremonies attempted to arouse cheers for "feminine protection."

Socioeconomic tension between the middle class and the poor has sharpened in recent years. Much of the middle class does have disposable income: Three hundred thousand Argentinians were able to afford a series of concerts by the Rolling Stones and Bob Dylan in the mid-1990s, and the consumerism they embrace characterizes a lifestyle that is arguably more American than Latin. Middle-class kids are learning English, mastering the Internet (ten million Latin Americans were on line by summer 2000), and enjoying occasional vacations to Florida and Disney World. They are growing socially and culturally distant from the semiliterate, tradition-bound, rural masses. Middle-class nationalism is increasingly limited to cheering for their nation during the World Cup.

The poor, in contrast, evince confusion and despair. The rise of electoral democracy has by no means made them better informed. Messages conveyed by elite-owned news media have undercut the ability of masses to organize, and growing economic dislocation has left barrios and villages filled with people who are focused on their own physical survival. Grassroots political mobilization is in decline. Spontaneous explosions of discontent have erupted in the past few years, in several small nation-states—Paraguay, Guyana, and Ecuador—but meaningful collective action in Latin America is becoming rare.

The poor are not a monolithic mass; they are divided. Working poor, including those in the informal economy of barter and services on the streets, often despise those who are completely down and out. They distrust and shun them, and willingly concur with the upper classes and media, that the "dregs" of society are problematic and should be kept in line. The culture of intolerance that has surfaced especially over the past generation explains any number of sensational acts in recent years. In Barranquilla, Colombia, for example, the Free University's medical school was ensnared in a scandal when reports surfaced that its security guards had lured dozens of homeless people into its halls at night and then beat them to death with baseball bats. Tossed into a vat of formaldehyde, their bodies were dissected in the anatomy laboratory and their vital organs sold on the black market for use in the First World.

The underclass of poor in Latin America—those with virtually no possessions and no visible means of survival—includes 30 million street children, popularly known as *abandonados*. The offspring of indigent families or unwed mothers who cannot support them, these are primarily adolescent males with little or no education, who drift into an animal-like existence on the streets. Banding together in gangs for survival, they lead short and violent lives—as captured in the award-winning Brazilian film *Pixote* and reflected in Colombian sociologist Alonso Salazar's book *Born to Die in Medellín*. Often high on glues long outlawed in the United States but marketed by corporations overseas, they resort to petty theft in order to survive.

Abandonados have been a primary target of "social cleansing"—mass murders carried out by privately funded security forces in the name of public order. In Brazil, these *justiceiros* (justice-givers) mete out to street kids what the majority of the public thinks they deserve. In one sensational case, nearly twenty teen males were rounded up, beaten motionless with clubs, assembled onto a gasoline-soaked pile, and burned alive. The few attempts undertaken to control such vigilantism—such as those by São Paulo State Governor André Montoro in the late 1980s—have been met with public hostility (Montoro was voted out of office). Social cleansing peaked in 1988–1991, when about 12,000 persons were eliminated throughout South America (5,600 in Brazil alone); since then it has declined. Human "trash" is now regularly purged by increasingly efficient police forces.

Hemisfears: The Making of Law-and-Order Societies

Latin Americans fear the breakdown of order in society. Even the poor, who are the primary victims of violence, easily recognize that there is something worse than living in abject poverty—namely, poverty combined with theft and violence. One of the seminal features of the postmilitary *media*cracies has been a stern emphasis on the dangers of crime and disorder. Local and national television newscasts throughout the region cover criminal acts with great, often graphic, detail. The need for thorough law enforcement, and strict penalties for the guilty, are among the most common themes publicly addressed by politicians. This focus on law and order has seemingly inoculated the region with a kind of collective fear. It has also been used for distinctly political purposes; an implicit message in the discourse is that dissent or popular agitation for change might well bring anarchy.

Human rights abuses by police and security forces in Latin America are at an all-time high, surpassing in number those committed by the region's earlier military regimes. Although the rhetoric of human rights has increased, practices have moved in the other direction. For example, several times more people have been tortured and killed by police in Brazil in the 1990s than during the entire twenty-five years of Brazilian military rule. Police violence is perpetrated overwhelmingly against the poor, who have almost no legal or political recourse in the face of beatings and abuse. Middle-class support for strict law enforcement is widespread, despite the excesses. Even more amazingly, the majority of the poor have also tended to sanction the impunity of police; only a small fraction of slum dwellers have experienced torture or police abuse firsthand. In most cases, torture and/or extrajudicial murder is applied to thieves and legitimate criminals.

Public ambivalence about state terror rose sharply in the late 1980s and 1990s, as a crime spree swept parts of the economically troubled region. In Argentina, voters have supported known torturers and military leaders since the era of the dirty war. Aldo Rico, who led antidemocratic coup attempts against the Raúl Alfonsín government, established a political party that captured more than 10 percent of the vote in the nation's largest province. General Domingo Bussi, who oversaw dirty war operations in northwestern Argentina, was apparently denied election to a state governorship in 1991 only through fraud.

Police in the large cities of Latin America now almost routinely use electroshock torture on prisoners, generally for interrogation purposes. Attempts by a minuscule number of human rights advocates to uncover police abuse and convict the perpetrators have often faced hostile public reaction. In Buenos Aires, for example, the case of police officer Luis Patti generated pro-police rallies when investigators tried to convict him of torturing inmates with electric shocks. Sympathetic medical doctors came forward with the hypothesis that the prisoners may have been torturing themselves; and polls showed the public favoring Patti's use of electricity in order to make suspected criminals talk and "dance" (the military euphemism for shock torture, which makes the victim's body gyrate). Patti soon became a national celebrity in Argentina and even appeared on a number of television talk shows. In one appearance, he did the tango, later joking that both he and his prisoners had danced. Eduardo Duhalde, the governor of Buenos Aires province at the time, praised Patti as exemplary, and President Menem appointed him to oversee a major police investigation.

Elsewhere in Latin America, social cleansing by the police has reached staggering proportions. In Brazil, the police have gained such broad public support for this practice that they enjoy de facto impunity from human rights prosecution. Torture and elimination of the criminal poor by authorities, especially by the national-level military police, has displaced the vigilantism of the *justiceiros*. Hundreds die in custody each year just in Brazil's two major cities, Rio de Janeiro and São Paulo (in the former, there were 942 eliminations between 1993 and 1996). The pace of police killings is accelerating. In all of Brazil, between 1997 and 1999, there were 2,500 confirmed murders by the authorities; and unknown killings might well number in the thousands. In Jamaica, the police perpetrated nearly a quarter of the island's murders in the 1980s and 1990s. Some of the victims were innocent of any wrongdoing and had merely been in the wrong place at the wrong time; almost all were poor. The long-standing Latin tradition of outlawing the death penalty is made moot by actual police practice; nonetheless, some nations, such as Trinidad and Tobago, are formally reinstating the death penalty. Public interest in investigating and curtailing police brutality is almost nonexistent.

Prisons in Latin America house tens of thousands of poor who confessed under torture to crimes they never committed. The roughly one-half million inmates in the region's jails are not usually tortured or routinely beaten, but most suffer a hellish existence nevertheless. Prisons are badly overcrowded, dilapidated, and filled with filth and squalor. Few inmates have mats or beds; most are lucky if they have enough room, in crowded communal cells, to stretch out on the concrete floor. Insects torment them, and seasonal changes bring constant discomfort—summer heat in one congested Brazilian prison is so severe that the lucky inmates are those who can tie themselves to window bars in order to stay near fresh air. Although torture is rare, violence is common. Most jails only separate men from women, not petty criminals from hardened offenders. With an average ratio of one guard to about two hundred prisoners, there is no effective authority or control. Gangs terrorize the weak: Extortion and prisoner-on-prisoner violence are rampant.

The general populace in Latin America, including the poor, are disinterested in prison conditions. Support for strict punishment of criminal elements has become so strong, in fact, that it is now one of the best ways for politicians to win elections; almost no one advocates more humane treatment. In Mexico, in July 1999, one gubernatorial candidate who had been trailing in the polls surged to victory after running TV spots with the slogan "Human rights are for humans, not for criminals." In Aguilares, El Salvador, once a hotbed of liberation theology, citizens recently held a general strike in order to agitate for more police and crime prevention. As a consequence of media-fueled fears, new measures facilitating social control are restricting civil rights. In Peru, a whole range of criminal activities, including robbery, have been categorized as "aggravated terrorism," meaning that suspects can be held incommunicado and interrogated for two weeks. Peru pioneered military courts and secret trials in its early-1990s dirty war against Sendero guerrillas, but the precedent of an underground judiciary has since spread through the region. Colombia, with strong public approval (as well as that of the U.S. government), has begun its own secret trials, denying defendants traditional constitutional rights, such as the knowledge of their accusers' identities, and access to witnesses.

There is a political dimension to the emergence of law-and-order societies in Latin America, though it appears to be lost on the majority poor. By curtailing basic civil rights, authorities enhance their ability to suppress political dissent. In some ways, with the decline of grassroots organizations and collective visions of a different economic reality, the snatching of purses and the picking of pockets become political acts. Similarly, the power to curtail those acts helps maintain political order. Hence, as poor Latin Americans vote into office the most strident "law and order" candidates, they undercut their own position.

Sometimes the political uses of crime are transparent. One of the conditions attached to the 1997 victory of the political opposition in Mexico City elections was that the new mayor, Cuauhtémoc Cárdenas, would not be allowed to appoint his own police chief. For the next two years, crime surged in the metropolis—the spree being at least partly attributable to the police themselves, who engaged in criminal acts and also failed to hunt down perpetrators. Against this backdrop the dominant PRI party and President Ernesto Zedillo gained greatly in public opinion, especially among the middle class, by portraying themselves as crusaders for law and order. In summer 1999, when popular television personality Paco Stanley was gunned down, pro-PRI television stations featured around-the-clock coverage of weeping celebrities and ordinary citizens, many calling on Mayor Cárdenas to resign (the righteous indignation suddenly ended when it was discovered that Stanley used cocaine and was involved with a drug cartel—after which TV stations resumed normal programming).

The obsession with crime and punishment has useful political dimensions for those in power but otherwise contributes little to the stability of the region. The line between political and social killings has blurred. Scores of journalists, labor organizers, and human rights advocates disappear regularly in Latin America—swept away, often quietly, in the midst of other, less overtly political violence. U.S. involvement in political repression is difficult to trace because of the secretive nature of security establishments; but American links to Latin American police forces have increased dramatically in recent years and are growing even stronger through the international expansion of several intelligence services, such as the FBI. The highly politicized security forces of Latin America, such as Mexico's Federal Judicial Police, have long maintained close ties with their U.S. intelligence counterparts. But today even many of the region's civil police (e.g., local forces in the volatile regions of southern Mexico) receive

U.S. training. High-profile training programs such as those with the national police forces in Haiti and El Salvador have definitely created more professional civil patrols that engage in less torture than their predecessors. This is not to say, however, that Americans do not use torture. On the contrary, highly classified military and intelligence personnel engage in (and more often, observe) torture, and hundreds of ex-military Americans assist Latin American security forces and paramilitaries in the secretive underside of counterinsurgency.

America plays an important role in facilitating torture in the Third World generally. The United States is the primary supplier of torture equipment. Rule 5999B of the Commerce Department's Commodity Control List stipulates that "specially designed implements of torture" require validated licenses for export; but since 1984 these documents have been kept from the public. Data garnered under the Freedom of Information Act for a 26-month period in the 1990s, however, revealed that $27 million of torture-related equipment left the United States—a considerable amount, even though the more sophisticated electrotorture tools are often outlandishly expensive. Control devices that work well for torture are manufactured by a range of U.S. companies, including Austin, Texas's Nova Technologies and Cleveland, Ohio's Stuntech Corporation.

Electricity has been the preferred method of torture in Latin America since the heyday of the military regimes. Old methods, such as the use of hand-cranked generators, have been replaced by cattle prods, tasers, and stun guns. The stun belt, used by some police departments in the United States for prisoner control, also has found its way into Third World torture chambers. Delivering an eight-second shock of 50,000 volts, it can cast a victim into mind-piercing agony at the touch of a button. For an ignorant peasant, the sudden, gut-wrenching pain and terror created by this remote-controlled device must be beyond comprehension.

Americans are creative and skillful torturers. Several have written instructional manuals on torture, complete with ISBN numbers, that are circulated in Latin America and other parts of the Third World. Most torturers operate quietly and avoid public exposure. As U.S. Marine Corps torturer Patrick McDonald explained in his book *Make 'Em Talk*, when facing any type of investigation "*deny everything*, admit nothing—and make counteraccusations."[1] Another American, whose torture handbook has been used in Colombia and Central America, explained methods of castration:

> You can draw out a castration, beginning by piercing the organs with pins and/or burning them with flame. Move on to skinning, carefully removing the skin from his penis and/or stripping away the scrotal skin leaving the testes attached but fully exposed. Instead of hacking the testes off, impale one on a knife point and slowly slice it open. Or slice away small chunks of penis

and/or testicle proceeding slowly, cauterizing each newly cut surface with a hot iron to prevent the loss of too much blood. In this way you can draw out a simple castration to last for hours, though you'll probably spend quite a bit of time reviving him, too.[2]

American torturers work secretively, but it is possible that the general public would not be upset with what they are doing. Torture, in fact, seems to arouse as much curiosity among First World residents as it does moral outrage. When the human rights group Amnesty International released a video of graphic assassinations a few years ago, the public reaction was not what it expected. Instead of disturbing European and American viewers, it became a much-coveted object of titillation, prompting the organization to stop distribution. In the early 1990s, Peruvian torturers successfully marketed photographs of torture sessions to First World tourists by way of taxi drivers. "Snuff tapes," or videos of real torture sessions, have a fed a small, still largely clandestine business in rich countries. In one tape, made in Colombia by paramilitaries, anonymous torturers dressed in wrestling masks flog a naked woman into a bloody pulp, then bring the film to a climax by severing one of her arms with a chain saw. Eventually, public interest in viewing torture may allow the snuff business to move above ground in the United States.

American Prospects and Dangers

The consequences of Latin America's decline into crisis, for the United States, are overwhelmingly positive—at least economically. Indeed, rather than entering an age of economic decline, as had long been predicted, the American eagle is in ascent. The next fifty years will likely mark the high tide of U.S. wealth and power, delivering to its quarter of a billion residents (less than 5 percent of the global population) the very best that the world's resources can offer. Macroeconomic control of the Third World, a process begun in the 1980s and brought to fruition under Bill Clinton, is the ticket to an ever improving standard of living for all Americans.

Much of the minuscule political opposition in the United States (the so-called "left") has argued that U.S. policies in Latin America and the Third World hurt Americans and undercut their prosperity: Bernie Sanders, an independent socialist member of Congress, has charged that the IMF is bad for America; Ralph Nader contends that First World living standards are in decline; and Gore Vidal has prophesied the "decline and fall of the American Empire." Their presumptions and predictions are badly misguided.

U.S. policies toward the Third World have revived the domestic economy and introduced an age of rising and sustainable standards of living, because they have fundamentally shaped a new economic order in which

Americans live at the direct expense of the world's poor. This is quite different from what has historically been the case. Myths aside, much of America's own history has been colored with poverty. The "good old days" were not that good, and many of our forefathers, even into the late nineteenth century, lived comparatively difficult lives. Wealth slowly embraced America in the context of the two world wars (the Great Depression notwithstanding), as Europe destroyed itself and the United States became the West's primary creditor nation. Victorious and physically unscathed, in 1945 the United States began to dominate the world, holding 75 percent of its gold and possessing much of its industrial muscle (for many years, Pittsburgh produced more steel than the entire Soviet Union).

Postwar prosperity lasted into the 1960s, when rebuilt central Europe and Japan finally began to reach and exceed their prewar industrial outputs. Renewed competition, coupled with a subsequent energy crisis, weakened the dollar and shook the U.S. economy. From the 1970s into the 1990s, consumerism and comfort were sustained primarily by debt in the form of enormous government deficit spending. Now, on a grand scale, things have again changed: America has a new economy built on Third World labor and extracted wealth. And this economy, unlike its debt-driven predecessor, is a model that can be continued indefinitely. With sustainable growth, America's future is exceedingly bright.

If not all Americans see a bright future today, the reason is not a lack of national wealth but its unequal distribution. Money and resources have been flowing in from around the world, but the economic pie, though expanding, has been poorly divided. The four hundred richest Americans,* including 270 billionaires, have a net worth of more than $1 trillion, whereas 35 million Americans entered the twenty-first century with incomes below the official poverty line (roughly, $13,000 for a three-member family). The media-owning Cox family, though not even in the top ten among America's rich, still has more wealth than the entire nation of Guatemala, with $19 billion. The wealthiest 5 percent of the American populace increased its proportion of net U.S. wealth from 16.6 percent in 1973 to 21.2 percent in 1994. The 20 percent with incomes at the low end, in contrast, lost ground (declining from 4.2 to 3.5 percent in the same years). For the lower half of the U.S. populace, real family incomes flattened out through the early 1990s, after more than a decade of modest decline.

The boom years at the close of the twentieth century, however, broke this pattern of stagnation, with wealth still drifting upward but with so much pouring in that even lower classes are benefiting and making gains. Macroeconomic indicators reflect this: In the mid-1990s, real wages began to rise

---

* The word *American* in this sentence refers to persons residing primarily in the United States. Many of America's richest persons voided their U.S. citizenship in the 1990s as a means of evading taxes.

again and the middle class stopped shrinking. Real household incomes also climbed, with the median surpassing $39,000 by early 2000, and home ownership increased (reversing the earlier trend), as low and steady interest rates fueled a housing boom. As America moves deeper into the twenty-first century, it will find itself awash in newfound wealth, and the prospects of all of its citizens should improve. The already very small political opposition will either have to reassess its message, or more likely, slide into oblivion.

The primary reason why America's economic good times are sustainable is the near-endless supply of slave-like Third World labor. Workers throughout the 80 percent of the globe that is impoverished are desperate to eat and will toil for next to nothing. Although chattel slavery as a legal mechanism no longer exists in our world, tens of thousands of children are literally chained and beaten in small workhouses throughout southern Asia. Apart from a few large agricultural operations in the Caribbean and northeastern Brazil, slave-like conditions are rarer in Latin America. The poor, however, are so desperate that they will work *like* slaves; physical beatings probably would not increase worker productivity. Hunger and the (false) hope of a better tomorrow are sufficient incentives.

In most sweatshops—for example, those in Honduras, which now employ over 100,000—conditions are intolerable by First World standards, but bearable to the poor. Most of the workers—primarily women, but about 15 percent children under age 15—work fourteen-hour shifts and are allowed two quick visits to the bathroom. Some supervisors yell obscenities, and male bosses invariably require sexual favors, but physical abuse is uncommon. Textile plants in Central America and elsewhere are constructed in so-called "Free Enterprise" or "Export Processing" zones, where taxes are waived, full profit remittance to the United States assured, and labor unions forbidden. With dirt-cheap workers and low overhead, corporations are able to make sterling profits. Eddie Bauer-brand shirts produced in El Salvador, for example, cost the company only $.19 each yet sell in the United States for more than $12. The Walt Disney Company, which contracted its various children's clothing manufacturing operations out to sweatshops located in Haiti during the 1990s, was able to reduce worker wages even further, to less than $.30 an hour, meaning that pajamas selling at Wal-Mart for $10.97 were made for but a few cents—almost pure profit! Not surprisingly, the globalization of the U.S. economy has brought soaring corporate profits, and the U.S. stock market nearly tripled in value between 1994 and 2000. U.S. consumers are big winners, too. Nearly half of America's households are now vested in the stock market, and retail inflation for consumer items has been almost nonexistent in recent years.

The pursuit of cheap labor by U.S. corporations has been both a formal and an informal process: IFIs promote policies in keeping with the creation of discount labor economies, and the invisible hand of the marketplace does the rest. As businessmen seek out the lowest possible labor costs, they effectively trigger a kind of "bidding war" among the world's poorer countries. That war has thus far been won by China, which has set the standard for cheap labor through the strength of its authoritarian communist government, assuring investors strike-free workers at wages of less than $2 a day. Under the Clinton administration, China regularly received Most Favored Nation trading status. For highly mobile industries with limited capital equipment, the Chinese bid is highly attractive. Latin American nations, with low-skill wages still hovering around $1 an hour, have difficulty competing with China.

Formal mechanisms that preserve the low wage marketplace include the powerful World Trade Organization (WTO), created in 1995 to enforce the GATT and headquartered in Geneva, Switzerland. At a WTO ministerial meeting in 1996, member nations including the United States voted to bar labor rights from the organization's agenda. Obviously, standardized labor rights are inimical to U.S. interests, since exploitation of cheap Third World labor could come under attack. Conversely, when the WTO finally banned child labor at its 1999 meeting in Seattle, it did so only on paper, with much fanfare but no meaningful mechanisms of enforcement.

The WTO exercises tremendous power over trade decisions, with which signatory nations (nearly every country in the world) must comply. In its decisions the WTO promotes access to the cheapest possible Third World wages and products. The most famous WTO case involving Latin America, thus far, has been that of bananas. The European Union, looking out for small landholding farmers and motivated by a tinge of postcolonial guilt, had instituted preferential quotas for Caribbean fruit over the cheap produce grown on corporate-owned banana plantations in Central America. At the behest of Chiquita Brands, the Clinton administration (a recipient of Chiquita campaign contributions) sued before the WTO and won a ruling that struck down west European preferences—a devastating blow to a number of small island economies, though beneficial to America.

Ralph Nader's Public Citizen organization, as well as others, have argued that WTO decisions like the banana ruling are detrimental to the United States (and that this particular ruling will destabilize the Caribbean). Such contentions assume much, and ignore the undeniable benefits of keeping Third World wages in the basement. The vast majority of the WTO's early decisions have helped First World residents, positioning them to further exploit poor nations and enhance already established patterns of wealth concentration. WTO measures to uniformly define and protect intellectual rights, including corporate patents, scientific knowledge, and artistic copyrights (under its so-called TRIPS provisions), are also thoroughly to the advantage of the First World. This is no surprise: The WTO is, after all, an entity beholden to moneyed interests and created by powerful political forces.

Yet critiques of the WTO by dissident First World elements are not completely unfounded. They are founded, first, on the conviction that exploitation of the poor by the wealthy is morally wrong; moral convictions, alas, are not facts, and to this belief the rational scholar cannot respond. Second, critics argue that in standardizing trade-related practices, international organizations like the WTO threaten, at some levels, the labor and environmental protections that make the American way of life safe and comfortable. With the support of oil companies, for example, Brazil and Venezuela brought suit before the WTO to strike down provisions of the U.S. Clean Air Act that prohibit certain gasoline contaminants. These contaminants, filtered out only at expensive, state-of-the-art refineries, cause respiratory irritation and can damage lungs. The WTO ruled in favor of the plaintiffs, forcing the U.S. Environmental Protection Agency to weaken its controls. Kinks like this aroused perceptive Clinton administration officials, as well as other influential policymakers, long before the WTO's Seattle meeting in November 1999. It was hoped by some that cooperative, peaceful protests by administration allies like big labor could help facilitate needed adjustments within the WTO. In this context, corporate-owned media outlets publicized both the ministerial summit and the prospect of some large protests.

From the perspective of the WTO and the Clinton administration, however, several things in Seattle went awry. First, much of the opposition assumed a moral stance that called for the abolition of the WTO instead of its limited modification. Second, the forcefulness of the protests was far greater than anyone had anticipated. Using carefully planned nonviolent tactics, rings of citizens locked arms and effectively shut down the WTO convocation by physically preventing its delegates from entering the auditorium. Third, Seattle's police, perplexed and frustrated, unleashed a wave of violence that turned the heart of the port city into the likes of a war zone. Unable to move the nonviolent protesters, police opened fire with tear gas and rubber bullets. Close-range discharges injured targets and bystanders alike, enraging many and triggering anger and violent unrest. Seattle's mayor, disregarding the U.S. Constitution, issued a decree forbidding public assembly within a fifty-block radius and authorized the police and National Guard to make hundreds of arrests (even a few shoppers and a politician on his way to the WTO were picked up).

Despite the resulting inflammation of emotions surrounding the WTO event, the political fallout from the Seattle debacle was more favorable for the WTO and the U.S. government than one might have expected. Unlike the protesters, most Americans had not a clue what the WTO was about, much less about the nuances of its agenda or the effects of its policies. Television footage of angry protesters breaking windows enraged the great "silent majority," and condemnation followed, filling radio talk shows and letters to newspapers across the land (most Americans have a strong disdain for protest, even though their nation was conceived through disobedient acts like the Boston Tea Party). The corporate-owned media weighed in: *Newsweek* assured its readers that the anti-WTO activities were rooted in ignorance and "bad for workers everywhere." Television networks focused on a minority of fanatical demonstrators: "Who were those *violent* protesters in Seattle?" asked a CBS *60 Minutes* telecast. "Anarchists," came the answer, bent on "revolution against the United States!" Most importantly, neither the print nor the broadcast media told the general public much about the WTO, leaving Americans in the dark. When 1300 protesters were arrested at anti-IFI demonstrations in Washington, D.C., in April 2000, corporate-owned media again portrayed them as ill-informed. "They don't even know what they're protesting," charged Rush Limbaugh, a radio commentator often attuned to popular political sentiments.

The small portion of the American populace that is morally critical of world institutions and attempts to change government policies poses a genuine threat to vested interests and the general prosperity of the nation. Unlike the opposition, which resorts to the self-serving and flawed argument that globalization is not in the U.S. interest, the moral "left" will probably not be blown away by future circumstances. It is and has been, however, exceedingly small. Realistically speaking, perhaps less than .001 percent of Americans accept the validity of a moral critique of U.S. economic policy in the Third World and attempt to do something about it. In the 1980s, these individuals would have opposed aid to the Contras. Some have embraced other Third World causes, such as support for the anti-apartheid movement in South Africa.

Since the 1991 Gulf War, such grassroots opposition has sharply declined. Older activists, many of whom were first politicized by events in the 1960s, have died or have given up, and younger Americans are mostly disinterested. With regard to Latin America, however, a small movement flourished even in the late 1990s: Louisiana-born Catholic priest Roy Bourgeois spearheaded a campaign to close the U.S. Army's School of the Americas at Fort Benning, Georgia. The school, which trains Latin American military personnel in counterinsurgency techniques, is just one of nearly two dozen direct security-related programs. Singled out by activists, it has come under public pressure, and it was forced to acknowledge, in September 1996, that it has been involved in training and working with torturers.

Bourgeois and his organization, the School of the Americas Watch, have only been able to force cosmetic changes in the program, and it remains to be seen whether or not they can shut it down. New "human rights instruction" and a pending name change have more than appeased a supportive

Congress. President Clinton also stood by the School of the Americas against its moral critics. But most important of all has been the inability of activists to access the news media. Despite enormous acts of nonviolent civil disobedience each November (on the anniversary of the 1989 Jesuit slayings in El Salvador), Bourgeois's campaign remains hidden from the general public. In 1997, when he and about six hundred persons were arrested for trespassing (one of the largest acts of civil disobedience in the history of the South), not a single major commercial network television newscast even mentioned the event; 2,100 trespassers in 1998, and 4,400 in 1999, also were completely ignored. Media silence, like low-intensity conflict, is the best line of defense for mitigating grassroots involvement in important political decisions.

In Latin America people like Bourgeois and his followers are quietly eliminated. Why are they tolerated in the United States? Certainly there is evidence to suggest that intelligence and security agencies closely monitor their behavior. Nor is there any apparent lack of will on the part of the U.S. government to eradicate subversives; after all, the United States is deeply involved in doing exactly that in the Third World. The primary reason why dissent is tolerated within America is that it is rare and isolated, and thus irrelevant. There is no reason to pursue an otherwise risky policy of direct repression when the political opposition is so weak that it can accomplish next to nothing. The Fort Benning protests, in fact, border almost on a ritual of disobedience, where compliant protesters willingly board buses and cooperate with the police. They have actually been helpful to the economy of Columbus, Georgia. And even in the government's worst-case scenario—should Congress respond to public pressure and cut funding—countless other, more clandestine operations would fill the void. Political opposition in the United States is ignored because, for all practical purposes, it does not exist.

But if domestic dissent poses such a modest threat to the American way of life, there is another danger that looms far larger: unbridled immigration. Tens of millions of impoverished Latin Americans would undoubtedly flood into the United States if our borders were open and they were allowed to do so; and the consequences would be cataclysmic. But immigration, of course, is strictly monitored, and the U.S. government grants visas almost exclusively to the well-to-do. The high seas insulate much of the country from the unwanted, though poor Haitians, Cubans, and other Caribbean people risk their lives in rickety crafts almost daily to reach U.S. shores. The greatest influxes of unauthorized immigrants are those consisting of Mexicans and Central Americans who enter the United States along its massive border with Mexico and conceal themselves in nearby transnational urban centers and loosely guarded stretches of open desert.

U.S. regulation of migration has fluctuated, historically, with the needs and economic fortunes of Americans. During the prosperous 1920s, relatively few worried about the rising number of "illegals"; but the hard times of the Great Depression fueled an anti-immigrant fervor that led to Mexicans' being rounded up wholesale and shipped south by train. During World War II, an acute shortage of agricultural workers justified the Bracero Program—a joint U.S.-Mexican governmental initiative authorizing migration that was extended in the postwar boom years until 1964. Most illegals stayed in the United States only during harvest season, preferring to periodically return to families and friends back home. The advantage of their labor was obvious: California citrus growers, among others, found in Mexicans a hardy and largely docile workforce, willing to labor for low wages and under conditions unacceptable to most U.S. citizens.

In the 1970s, as Mexico's postwar economic expansion slowed and development along the border lured Mexicans northward, illegal entry into the United States soared. Border Patrol apprehensions, which had numbered only 55,000 in 1965, reached 680,000 a decade later. Efforts to control the influx sputtered, and public anger festered in the early 1980s, as America again entered a brief recession. The Immigration Reform and Control Act of 1986, popularly known as Simpson-Rodino (after its congressional coauthors), attempted to remedy the situation by granting amnesty to long-term residents, requiring documentation of others, and punishing U.S. employers of illegals with fines. A black market in fake legal immigration documents, known as "green cards," ensued, and government enforcement of penalties—erratic under Reagan and Bush—was nearly nonexistent under the pro-business rule of Clinton. Simpson-Rodino had failed.

Californians, inundated by new migrants as Mexico's economic woes persisted, passed a statewide ballot initiative known as Proposition 187 in 1994. This measure, which cut off all but essential services to noncitizens, even enjoyed the support of a large segment of Mexican American voters. Tied up in the courts for years, and openly ignored by major school districts and many medical service providers, Prop 187 had mixed and largely ineffectual results. It was premised on the notion that illegals are a burden to the welfare state—a debatable assumption, since noncitizens are rarely able to access benefits. And it hardly made America any less attractive; even without broad social services, life for most newcomers is markedly better in *El Norte* (The North).

Under the Clinton administration, steps were taken to curtail and control migration by tightening security along the border. Contrary to much popular wisdom, the border *can* be secured; technological advances in radar, sensors, and night vision equipment make even long-distance monitoring feasible. Major border enhancements came under a $3.1 billion buildup dubbed "Operation Gatekeeper," with new walls erected in urban areas and sophisticated tracking equipment for rural swaths, including infrared cameras and seismic sensors that detect movement. In order to discourage desert crossings, the United States aired television ads in Mexico that showed bodies withering under the hot desert sun. With bipartisan congressional support, Gatekeeper was augmented through the Immigration Reform Law of 1996, which among other provisions, doubled the number of border patrol agents.

Efforts to close the border have been only partially successful, however. The formidable walls and obstacles in border cities have redirected crossings into the remote backlands of Texas and Arizona. The increased difficulty of migrating has spawned an enormous people-smuggling business by "coyotes"—young Mexican guides who usher groups across the border in exchange for money. Because illegal immigrants pay the equivalent of several hundred dollars to cross, they now tend to stay in the United States much longer. Few know anything about their guides, and as illegals they are vulnerable to exploitation and violence at the hands of the coyotes. Although apprehensions continue in large numbers, U.S. Border Patrol agents are rarely able to catch or prosecute coyotes.

The fundamental weakness of border control is this: Immigrants do not fear *la Migra*, as the Border Patrol is called. If they are captured, they are simply returned to the other side of the line, which they can try to cross again. Multiple arrests are not uncommon; one agent caught the same group of young women at the same border point four times in a single day! Although Amnesty International and other human rights groups have investigated and publicly condemned instances of physical beatings and other abuse of illegals by U.S. authorities, such occurrences are not widespread or systematic. Any penalties imposed on illegals, including jail time, tend to be better than the conditions normally experienced by the poor and do not serve as deterrents. Until some form of collective fear is instilled in would-be immigrants, the border will never be effectively closed.

As evidenced by continuing high levels of illegal immigration, Americans lead special lives. What other group of people, in all of history, has enjoyed comparable pleasures and comforts? Egyptian pharaohs and Roman emperors at the zenith of their civilizations hardly experienced the level of ease and convenience now found even in middle-class American homes! Today, much of our way of life is founded on fun. Disney, not U.S. Steel, is on the Dow Jones index, and even golf has become a billion-dollar pastime. There's a stadium-building frenzy as cities vie for sports teams; and theme parks woo visitors by the tens of millions each summer. American kids and adults alike enjoy countless hours of play through strikingly creative video games. Other pursuits, such as pornography and gambling (both of which have flourished since the early 1980s), now constitute significant domestic "industries" generating hundreds of millions of dollars of sales. The United States, thanks in part to trends and conditions in Latin America, has become history's first postindustrial leisure society.

Epilogue:
A Strange World

That the rich of this world live at the expense of the poor should not surprise us. Yet for some readers, the role of the United States in undercutting democracy, facilitating human rights abuses, and altering economic structures so as to assure its disproportionate share of the world's resources may come as a shock. Americans seem to be inoculated with notions of their own moral goodness, believing that they promote noble ideas to a morally debased world that sees them as the Free and the Brave. In truth, one should not expect the rich, in a world of haves and have-nots, to be imparting benefits and wisdom to the poor. *That* would be a very strange world indeed!

Rich people do not become rich, nor maintain their power, by looking out for the oppressed. While the U.S. media highlight expressions of American generosity—from disaster relief to so-called debt "forgiveness"—the vast majority of such benefaction occurs within the context of an inequitable economic system and with the overarching goal of maintaining that system. This is the generosity of a master who feeds his slave—what Brazilian educator Paulo Freire called the "false generosity" of the rich. It is true that Bill Gates—whose net worth is more than the entire GDP of Central America—gave $100 million to immunization programs in 1999. But his wealth, like that of America's, is now largely gleaned from the sweat of the poor. Some wealthy individuals, having played the money-making game, sometimes return a great deal of their wealth back to the poor—of course, keeping enough so as to avoid poverty themselves. Whether such giving constitutes authentic benevolence, however, is a matter for moralists to debate. In terms of foreign aid as a percentage of GDP, the United States ranks below Ireland and twenty other First World countries (and even this fact misrepresents reality, since USAID is exceedingly political in the nature of its distributions).

If equality were the goal of globalization, governments would standardize wages instead of trade. The world would quickly become a different place, if Mexican assembly plants and Caribbean sweatshops paid U.S.-level wages. Wealth would shift from the First World to the Third, and consumerism would balance out geographically as Latin American workers acquired disposable income. That's why, despite its new leadership, the AFL-CIO still does little in the way of transborder organizing. Although John Sweeney and his supporters have put a halt to organized labor's practice of dividing Third World workers by funding parallel, pro-U.S. unions, they are still fighting a defensive battle—trying to keep high-paying blue-collar jobs in the United States, in the face of cheap overseas labor that, as nationalists, they do not attempt to defend.

But if the United States looks out for itself, how is it that so many, even in academe, communicate a different reality? If the process of research in the social sciences is rational, how can so many U.S. scholars contend that America is, in fact, an agent of economic fairness and egalitarian democracy? There is considerable division in academic circles about the nature of U.S. economic and political goals. The two disciplines most related to these pillars of inquiry, economics and political science, are split (especially economics, where a majority evidence faith in global capitalism, and a small but vocal minority view it as dubious and unstable). Part of the reason for academe's overall faith in America's basic "goodness" is simply the fact that within the United States there is a great deal of economic and political justice. Although wealth is certainly skewed, America's poor have resources that their Third World counterparts can only dream about—from state welfare benefits and affirmative action to government civil rights protections and legal recourse. As scholars grow up and live in the United States, observing and enjoying the fruits of our socially sensitive society, it becomes easy to assume that such sensitivity exists on a global level.

But beyond this, the most important reality in academe is a lack of access to a full range of sources. In reality, academics studying the world are like intellectual boxers with an arm tied behind their backs. We can punch holes through the wall of human ignorance, but only selectively, and without a clear view of what's on the other side. Even in an economic regimen in which U.S. corporations are central, intimate knowledge of the corporate decisionmaking process is exceedingly rare. Only a tiny fraction of business archives are ever opened to scholars—most of them, only decades after the fact (often when a firm goes out of business). And although we have ready access to diplomatic and political documents, the massive military and intelligence bureaucracies of the United States and of Third World countries are nearly a complete information vacuum (even the CIA's *budget* was a state secret until it was forced open by a lawsuit in 1997). The much-touted recent release of documents relating to U.S. involvement in the 1973 Chilean military coup, for example, still overwhelmingly originated in the State Department (95 percent), with only a pittance coming from the CIA (2 percent)—a minuscule fraction of its massive holdings. And a reluctant Clinton administration only released these documents because it was obligated to do so by Spain's judicial system under the Mutual Legal Assistance Treaty. Most damning of all is the consistent failure of academics to acknowledge these severe limitations. We seem to write books and teach as though we have a complete view of the world, when in fact our vantage point is terribly restricted.

Moreover, academics—even those who study the Third World—tend to spend most of their time within the comfort zones of the world, limiting their travels overseas to the environs of urban wealth, pleasant hotels, and air-conditioned conference rooms. Given the nature of academic inquiry, we do not necessarily experience direct contact with the poor or the violent. Historians, who perhaps (as I would argue) have the most impressive research methodologies, typically follow by a generation or so the events that they study. It has become common in recent years to project Third World "agency" (the ability to influence and change things) into contemporary times through so-called subaltern and cultural studies that wrongly assume a stagnant structural foundation. In this way, historians are actually helping perpetuate the illusion that Latin America still has meaningful political and economic choices.

Whether among historians, political scientists, economists, or sociologists, a great deal of information used in scholarship is derived from public sources, including the media and newspapers. Are the news media in the United States biased? Many claim that they are; others insist that we have a free and trustworthy press. Certainly the spin provided by the media on world economic trends is often creative. Articles in one issue of the *Wall Street Journal*, for example, argued that a currency devaluation was actually good for Brazil—because Americans would be able to vacation cheaply there—and that Americans have borne a heavy "burden" by "absorbing products" from the Third World.[1] Still, the answer to the question of bias is not rationally determined by anecdotes.

We can expect that the press, to the degree that it is funded and owned by business, has an inherent bias. Common sense tells us this. Our press may be free from direct government control, but it is hardly free of bias! Corporate owners are not going to welcome criticism of their operations by organs that they own or fund via advertising. Although there are no formal mechanisms of censorship in America, media outlets are responsive to the expectations of their owners and advertisers, and less attuned to the ideas of political malcontents. Where statistical data have been gathered, the bias is obvious. In its NAFTA coverage before the critical congressional vote, for example, the *New York Times*—considered one of America's most liberal news outlets—quoted sources that supported the treaty 70 percent of the time, and cited opponents less than half as often.

Bias is also clearly evident when we test corporate news sources for double standards. The classic study using this methodology, Noam Chomsky and Edward Herman's *Manufacturing Consent: The Political Economy of the Mass Media* (1988), looked primarily at the media's portrayal of communist Cambodian human rights violations in comparison with those of capitalist

Indonesia. But other, similar studies could be undertaken on any given topic. In the media's coverage of Latin America, leaders who are not sufficiently pro-business almost always have some stigma attached to them: For example, Jean Bertrand Aristide's mental health, in the 1990s, was routinely questioned, although there was no medical proof of his instability. Almost every major piece on the rise of Venezuela's Hugo Chavez in 1998–1999 charged that he was dangerously dictatorial; yet Peru's Alberto Fujimori, whose regime had generated far more concrete evidence of authoritarianism, was only sparingly mentioned in the same vein.

Part of the responsibility for this double standard rests with news editors. Reporters in the field tend to file stories that differ considerably from those that end up in print. Their reports go through a chain of supervisors, who sit in offices in the United States and often have little understanding or experience of conditions elsewhere. Correspondents are mindful that their stories must please their editors. They also know that risks abound when they antagonize official sources. As one reporter observed, while covering the U.S. occupation of Haiti in 1994–1995, authors of negative stories were subsequently refused access to official memos and press conferences. There are plenty of reasons to be compliant.

In the mid-1980s the media consolidated their foreign operations, and today relatively few U.S. correspondents actually live in Latin America. The vast majority fly in and out for major, anticipated political events, such as elections and presidential inaugurations. As a result, U.S. news outlets depend heavily on their Latin American counterparts and government sources. Obviously, this reliance greatly handicaps their ability to provide accurate news. The official press in Latin America is, as we have observed, significantly compromised. Scores of independent journalists have been murdered by security forces, especially in Argentina, Colombia, and Mexico. Television interviews of major political figures are often staged. For example, when Peru's security chief Vladimiro Montesinos granted an "interview" to Peruvian television in May 1999, he gave the journalist a list of questions that he was permitted to ask.

The *assumption* that official sources are accurate is standard in news coverage. Sometimes accounts are corrected after the fact, but this is the exception—as the saying goes, old news is no news. In June 1995, Mexican police dragged a number of unarmed peasants from the back of a truck in the Indian village of Aguas Bancas and executed them, killing about two dozen. The facts surrounding this political massacre are certain, in part because a police videocam tape was later leaked to human rights groups. Yet the *New York Times*, relying on Mexican government sources, reported the following day that "at least fourteen people were killed this morning in a *clash* between the police and local peasants." Citing a Mexican spokesperson, it referred to a "gunfight" that erupted after "a peasant attacked a police commander." In conclusion, the newspaper observed, "All the dead appeared to be members of a left-wing peasant group" (*left-wing* suggesting, of course, that they were antidemocratic).[2] The same assumption of veracity is not evident, however, when business-owned news outlets discuss reports of business-related violations ("*Allegations*" exist, the *Newshour* on PBS once explained, "that some Nike shoes were made in Asia in sweatshop conditions").

Although usually resting their stories on a modicum of truth, on occasion the corporate media get it completely wrong and spew forth nonsense: 1999 was an economically devastating year for Brazilians, in the wake of the currency devaluation. Yet that fact did not prevent ABC News from reporting that Brazil's economy was "booming", in its coverage of Year 2000 millennial celebrations. "People are optimistic," the correspondent assured Americans from Rio de Janeiro (in contrast, a follow-up report from Cuba accurately reflected the bleak reality facing that island nation).

In the United States, although the government does not own or dictate to the news media, much of the political content carried by the media comes from official briefings and press releases. The White House press corps, for example, works closely with the president's staff; even in the United States, the supposedly informal press conference is largely a staged event. Each morning at the White House (or on the road, if the president is traveling), the press secretary briefs reporters on the day's agenda in a casual session called the "gaggle." At formal press conferences, where the cameras are rolling, the same secretary fields questions that he can largely anticipate. Reporters for the major networks and newspapers enjoy reserved seating in the front rows, whereas alternative media sources, such as Pacifica Radio, are often denied entry when the president or someone else important is slated to speak. A camaraderie between newsmakers and newstakers develops, since the same reporters who travel with the president are the ones filling the chairs at press conferences, whether in the United States or abroad.

Despite the size and significance of the news media, relatively few reporters gather information directly from overseas; those in the United States rely heavily on official sources; and lead stories are disseminated from a surprisingly small number of centralized media outlets. There is not the plethora of news-gathering organizations that America's hundreds of large newspapers suggest. Wire services and flagship dailies determine the national and international news stories offered in regional and local print, radio, and television markets. Each day, for example, the *New York Times*'s lead articles go out over the wire service and are picked up by editors around the country. The process of deciding what's news is in the hands of relatively few.

This dynamic is linked to the phenomenon of media concentration. With the advent of deregulation and improved satellite technology, giant transnational media empires have emerged. News is no longer disseminated solely on a national level: Time Warner and Disney, the world's two largest media firms, now reap a third of their profits outside the United States. Along with other giants, including Viacom, NewsCorp (owned by Australian Rupert Murdoch), and Bertelsmann (a German firm), corporate media are integrating—buying up cable providers, book publishers, music labels, and film studios. In 2000, Time Warner merged with America-On-Line, the world's largest Internet service provider. Media conglomerates such as these help limit the diversity of news stories and sources available to First World residents.

If America's media are not truly independent, what would a genuinely free press look like? Noncommercial, citizen-managed and -supported media have sometimes emerged when a new technology has taken hold. In the 1920s, for example, the vast majority of U.S. radio stations were citizen-owned—until the Federal Communications Commission, created in 1927, began to license them and shift the industry into the hands of corporations. In a similar fashion, the Internet has disseminated a modicum of information beyond that provided by the corporate news media.

But even though we can rationally observe evidence of bias in a business-owned press, it does not follow that Americans dislike the news they get, or would care to hear anything substantially different. Polling data show a fairly robust faith both in television and in the news. If anything, critics often complain of a "liberal" bias (which, on domestic social issues, might well exist). And during the highly regulated coverage of the Persian Gulf conflict in 1991, polls consistently demonstrated that a majority of Americans favored *more* government control and censorship of news reporting, not less.

The business-owned media are in large part responsible for Americans' views of themselves and the world. A less biased system of distributing significant information would profoundly alter those views. But no matter how one perceives the nature of the information Americans' get, there is little excuse for rational scholars to fail to acknowledge the news media's inherent bias. Presumably, unlike the sentiments of a casual observer, academe is based on a calm quest for factual truth. Yet many political scientists consider newspapers valid primary source material, failing to take into account the nature of their bias.

Because so many academics rely heavily on the news media (without a comparable access to critical, direct sources), many scholarly books and articles reflect the media's biases and assumptions. It is not that these assumptions and ideas are always incorrect. The problem is, rather, that they provide only a limited glimpse of reality—a glimpse, as it were, through a pinhole. Others must step forward and punch bigger holes in the wall, from different angles, in order to reveal more of what is behind it.

Notes

Chapter 1

1. Helen M. Bailey and Abraham Nasatir, *Latin America: The Development of Its Civilization*, 2d ed. (Englewood Cliffs, N.J.: Prentice-Hall, 1968), p. 525.

Chapter 2

1. As quoted in John Cummins, *The Voyage of Christopher Columbus* (New York: St. Martin's, 1991), p. 94.

Chapter 3

1. As quoted in Robert E. Conrad, ed., *Children of God's Fire: A Documentary History of Black Slavery in Brazil* (Princeton: Princeton University Press, 1983), p. 27.
2. As quoted in Irving A. Leonard, *Baroque Times in Old Mexico: Seventeenth-Century Persons, Places, and Practices* (Ann Arbor: University of Michigan Press, 1959; reissued 1990), p. 189.

Chapter 7

1. As quoted in James R. Brockman, *The Word Remains: A Life of Oscar Romero* (Maryknoll, N.Y.: Orbis Books, 1989), p. 217.
2. Carnes Lord, "The Psychological Dimension in National Strategy," in *Political Warfare and Psychological Operations: Rethinking the U.S. Approach*, eds. Frank Barnett and Carnes Lord (Washington, D.C.: National Defense University Press, 1989), p. 25.
3. A. J. Bacevich, James D. Hallums, Richard H. White, and Thomas F. Young, *American Military Policy in Small Wars: The Case of El Salvador* (Washington, D.C.: Institute of Foreign Policy Analysis, 1988), pp. 32–33.

Chapter 10

1. Patrick McDonald, *Make 'Em Talk: Principles of Military Interrogation* (Boulder: Paladin Press, 1993), p. 57. The italics are McDonald's.

2. Richard W. Krousher, *Physical Interrogation Techniques* (Port Townsend, Wash.: Loompanics Unlimited, 1985), p. 85.

Epilogue

1. Matt Moffett, "Devaluation May Prove a Boon for Brazil," and Michael M. Phillips and Dagmar Aalund, "U.S. Differs With Europe and Japan on Cause of World Economic Problems," both in the *Wall Street Journal*, February 22, 1999.

2. "Fourteen Killed in the South," *New York Times*, June 29, 1995. (The italics are mine.)

Suggestions for Further Reading

Chapter 1   Introduction: Why Is Latin America Poor?

Vicky Randall and Robin Theobald, *Political Change and Underdevelopment: A Critical Introduction to Third World Politics*, 2d ed. (Durham, N.C.: Duke University Press, 1998). Overview of theories of development, especially their political dimensions, in the context of Third World studies.

Colin Leys, *The Rise and Fall of Development Theory* (Bloomington: Indiana University Press, 1996). Collection of essays by a British political scientist and Africanist who is highly critical both of modernization theory and of American academics.

Robert Packenham, *The Dependency Movement: Scholarship and Politics in Development Studies* (Cambridge: Harvard University Press, 1992). A well-written introduction to the polemical world of scholarly debate; the book itself is also a polemic. Some sections will be difficult for beginners.

Chapter 2   A People of Conquest

Jacqueline Phillips Lathrop, *Ancient Mexico: Cultural Traditions in the Land of the Feathered Serpent*, 6th ed. (Dubuque, Iowa: Kendall/Hunt, 1998). A short, readable text with excellent illustrations, that overviews ancient Indian cultures from preclassical through postclassical stages.

Inga Clendinnen, *Ambivalent Conquests: Maya and Spaniard in Yucatán, 1517–1570* (Cambridge: Cambridge University Press, 1987). Different worldviews prevented the Maya and Spaniards from understanding each other. Pre-Contact ritual is explored through the lens of an inquisition carried out by the Franciscans in 1562, shortly after the Conquest.

Hugh Thomas, *Conquest: Montezuma, Cortés, and the Fall of Old Mexico* (New York: Simon & Schuster, 1995). In an epic style reminiscent of William Prescott, Thomas narrates the Spanish arrival and defeat of the Aztecs.

Chapter 3   The Colonial Centuries

Robert E. Conrad, ed., *Children of God's Fire: A Documentary History of Black Slavery in Brazil*, 2d ed. (University Park: Pennsylvania State University Press,

1994). The brutality of slavery—in Africa, through the middle passage, and on the Brazilian plantation—is captured through carefully edited primary documents.

Louisa Schell Hoberman and Susan Migden Socolow, eds., *The Countryside in Colonial Latin America* (Albuquerque: University of New Mexico Press, 1996). Colonial Latin America was primarily rural and agrarian. This collection of essays, written for college students, looks at the lifestyles and significance of different social and ethnic groups.

John E. Kicza, ed., *The Indian in Latin American History: Resistance, Resilience, and Acculturation* (Wilmington, Del.: Scholarly Resources, 1993). A collection of scholarly articles, mostly reprints, that examine the history of Indian interaction and resistance, primarily in the colonial era.

Chapter 4   Progress and Populism

John Mason Hart, *The Coming and Process of the Mexican Revolution*, 2d ed. (Berkeley: University of California Press, 1997). Hart offers a background to the Revolution (ca. 1876–1910), then focuses on the military phase from 1910–1917. He stays cognizant of the United States and its attempts to influence the course of events in Mexico throughout.

Thomas O'Brien, *The Century of U.S. Capitalism in Latin America* (Albuquerque: University of New Mexico Press, 1999). This short book traces American business and investment over the past century, with a sensitivity to regional variations. It provides a good overview of populist and nationalist resistance to U.S. economic influence in the middle decades of the twentieth century.

Steven Topik and Allen Wells, eds., *The Second Conquest of Latin America: Coffee, Henequen, and Oil During the Export Boom, 1850–1930* (Austin: University of Texas, 1998). Historical essays focusing on specific commodities demonstrate that a reopening of Latin American economies, beginning in the late nineteenth century, profoundly altered the region.

Chapter 5   Nationalism and the Military Response

Louis Pérez, *Cuba and the United States: Ties of Singular Intimacy*, 2d ed. (Athens: University of Georgia Press, 1997). An overview of U.S.-Cuban relations from the late nineteenth century by a leading scholar.

James McGuire, *Peronism Without Perón: Unions, Parties, and Democracy in Argentina* (Stanford: Stanford University Press, 1997). Perón's legacies included a strong labor movement and weak political institutions, a volatile mix that helped fuel subsequent domestic conflict. This scholarly account surveys that conflict from Perón to Menem.

Matilde Mellikovsky, *Circle of Love over Death: Testimonies of the Mothers of the Plaza de Mayo* (Willimantic, Conn.: Curbstone Press, 1997). The latest collection of oral histories of the famous Mothers, gathered by a supporter. They provide insight into the political and psychological dimensions of human rights advocacy.

Tina Rosenberg, *Children of Cain: Violence and the Violent in Latin America* (New York: William Morrow, 1991). The author socialized with elites and those directly involved in repression, both in South and Central America, in her quest to understand their mentality.

Chapter 6   Revolution in Central America

Jeffrey Paige, *Coffee and Power: Revolution and the Rise of Democracy in Central America* (Cambridge: Cambridge University Press, 1997). A socioeconomic analysis of the entire region, based in part on interviews, that finds some business-oriented elites favoring political change and new-style democracy over feudalistic repression.

Martha Honey, *Hostile Acts: U.S. Policy in Costa Rica in the 1980s* (Gainesville: University Press of Florida, 1994). Thorough account of CIA and Contra operations in Costa Rica by an investigative journalist, who also addresses U.S. economic penetration of the small country. At times poorly organized, the book also too often insinuates that Costa Ricans opposed U.S. policies when, in fact, the populace remained overwhelmingly disinterested.

Robert M. Carmack, *Harvest of Violence: The Maya Indians and the Guatemalan Crisis* (Norman: University of Oklahoma Press, 1988). Among a range of essays are several by anthropologists with direct contacts on the ground. These reveal some of the nuances of localized acts of violence and divisions among Indian communities in the heyday of the repression.

Chapter 7   Christianity and Counterinsurgency

Mark Danner, *The Massacre at El Mozote* (New York: Vintage Books, 1994). Though not without its historical flaws, this reconstruction of a major massacre in El Salvador in 1981 captures the brutality of the military's policy, and the efficiency of U.S. officials in covering it up.

William Stanley, *The Protection Racket State: Elite Politics, Military Extortion, and Civil War in El Salvador* (Philadelphia: Temple University Press, 1996). Drawn from sensitive U.S. government documents and interviews in El Salvador, this book reconstructs the systematic elimination of the civil opposition after 1977, paying particular attention to rifts within the military and police forces that comprised the infamous "death squads."

Javier Giraldo, *Colombia: The Genocidal Democracy* (Monroe, Maine: Common Courage Press, 1996). A short book that provides an outline of the nature of state terror in Colombia into the mid-1990s. Written by an activist.

Chapter 8   The Politics of Control

Steve J. Stern, ed., *Shining and Other Paths: War and Society in Peru, 1980–1995* (Durham, N.C.: Duke University Press, 1998). A useful collection of essays, including several that focus on the critical province of Ayacucho and make clear that the Sendero insurrection was in decline before the dirty war accelerated under the Fujimori regime.

Amy Wilentz, *The Rainy Season: Haiti Since Duvalier* (New York: Touchstone, 1990). A stunning account of the popular uprisings that toppled Duvalierism, told by a young journalist who witnessed the dramatic process firsthand. Wilentz also shares her understanding of Haitian society, religion, and the idealistic leader of the poor, Jean Bertrand Aristide.

Andres Oppenheimer, *Bordering on Chaos: Guerrillas, Stockbrokers, Politicians, and Mexico's Road to Prosperity* (Boston: Little, Brown and Company, 1996). A mainstream journalist with connections, Oppenheimer stays candid and objective through much of this chronology of jarring recent developments in Mexico's body politic. His study of the 1994 election includes incisive media analysis.

Alex Depuy, *Haiti in the New World Order: The Limits of Democratic Revolution* (Boulder: Westview, 1997). Examines the rise, removal, and return of Aristide, and the severe limits placed on him and his supporters by international politics and finance.

Chapter 9   Big Money: Debt and Wealth Extraction

Robert Devlin, *Debt and Crisis in Latin America: The Supply Side of the Story* (Princeton: Princeton University Press, 1989). Not easily digested by the lay reader, this is still an important source. Reveals how big banks willfully fed the borrowing frenzy of the 1970s and skillfully badgered and manipulated Latin American countries after the 1982 bust.

Duncan Green, *Silent Revolution: The Rise of Market Economics in Latin America* (London: Cassell, 1995). A basic and readable introduction to global economic policies and the rise of international financial institutions such as the IMF. Green has a moral agenda, particularly evident in a chapter that "searches for alternatives."

Devesh Kapur, John P. Lewis, and Richard Webb, *The World Bank: Its First Half Century* (Washington, D.C.: Brookings Institution Press, 1997). A semiofficial history that should be approached with caution, it includes a chapter on the debt crisis in Latin America.

Chapter 10   Latin America in Perpetual Crisis

Paul Chevigny, *Edge of the Knife: Police Violence in the Americas* (New York: New Press, 1995). The author examines patterns of police violence in multiple urban areas throughout the western hemisphere.

Gilberto Dimenstein, *Brazil: War on Children* (London: Latin America Bureau, 1991). A brief account of the most violent years of "social cleansing" of street children in cities.

Jaime Malamud-Goti, *Game Without End: State Terror and the Politics of Justice* (Norman: University of Oklahoma Press, 1996). A human rights lawyer theorizes about the erosion of basic human rights in Argentina *after* the military regime.

Epilogue: A Strange World

Noam Chomsky and Edward F. Herman, *Manufacturing Consent: The Political Economy of the Mass Media* (New York: Pantheon, 1988). A classic study of media bias; identifies various double standards in coverage. The authors press their arguments far, charging that the media actually serve to bring public opinion into line with policy goals.

Robert W. McChesney, *Rich Media, Poor Democracy: Communication Politics in Dubious Times.* (Urbana, Ill.: University of Illinois Press, 1999). An examination of the profound changes in the U.S. news media over the past two decades, and the concomitant decline of a genuinely informed electorate.

Index

Abandonados, 178
ABC News, 111, 196
Academics, 111, 116, 164, 174
  methods and sources, 194–195,
    197–198
  and theories, 3–4, 8, 12, 16
  See also specific disciplines
Advertising, 177
Africans, 37–42, 63, 78
Agriculture, 7–8, 11, 62, 163, 168
  Inca, 24–25
  See also Land reform; *specific crops*
Alfonsín, Raúl, 157, 179
Allende, Salvador, 91
Alliance for Progress, 7, 9, 86, 91,
    118, 121, 155
Amnesty International, 183, 191
Andes, 24
ANL [National Liberation
    Alliance], 70–71
Apache helicopters, 35, 130
Apaches, 35
Araucanians, 35
Arawak, 28–30
Arbenz, Jacobo, 108
ARENA [National Republican
    Alliance (of El Salvador)], 127
Argentina, 8, 12, 54, 57, 59, 62, 157,
    175–176
  under Perón, 72–74
Arias Sánchez, Oscar, 105–106
Aristide, Jean Bertrand, 143–146

Asia, 165, 170–171
Atahualpa, 33
Atlacatl Battalion, 124, 128
Audiencias, 48, 50
Austerity, 163
Avril, Prosper, 144
Ayacucho, 137–138
Azcarraga, Emilio, 149
Aztecs, 21–22, 31–32

Baker, James, 158
Balboa, Vasco Núñez de, 30
Banfield, Edward C., 6
Banks, 139, 155–158, 169
Banzer, Hugo, 156
Baron Samedi, 42, 142
Batista, Fulgencio, 80–81
Battalion 3–16, 106–107
Bay of Pigs, 82
Bazin, Marc, 144–145
Belaunde, Fernando, 137
Benavente, Toribio de, 43
Bible, 115–116, 164
Black Legend, 30, 78
Bolívar, Simón, 52
Bolivia, 36, 52, 155–156
Bonds, 63, 81, 154, 169, 171
  See also Brady Bonds; *Tesobonos*
Bonner, Raymond, 125, 128
Border and (U.S.) Border Patrol,
    168, 190–191
Bourbon Reforms, 49–50

Bourgeois, Roy, 188–189
Boyacá (Battle of), 52
Bracero Program, 190
Brady Bonds, 176
Brasilia, 87
Brazil, 8, 57, 62, 77, 151, 158, 165,
    171, 178
    African slavery, 40
    economic crisis, 174–175
    military regime, 87–90
    in nineteenth century, 60–61
    under Vargas, 70–72
Brown, Ron, 166
Bucaram, Abdalá, 164
Buenos Aires, 51, 57, 59, 72–73,
    179
Bush, Sr., George (and
    administration), 92, 102, 167
Business, 140, 152, 166
    See also Banks; Corporations;
        Investments; Stocks and
        stockmarkets
Bussi, Domingo, 179

Cabildo, 48
Cajamarca, 26(map), 33
California, 59, 190
Calles, Plutarco, 67–68
Camdessus, Michel, 158–159, 170
Canada, 84, 167
Candomblé, 42
Cárdenas, Cuauhtémoc, 148, 181
Cárdenas, Lázaro, 68–70
Cardoso, Fernando Henrique,
    10–12, 174–175
Caribbean, 31, 40–42, 50,
    103(map), 186
    See also specific islands and nations
Carranza, Venustiano, 67
Carter, Jimmy (and administration),
    95–98, 110, 121, 156
Castro, Fidel, 7, 80–85, 157–158
Caudillos, 57
CBS News, 82,188

Cedras, Raúl, 145–146
Central America, 57, 95–96,
    103(map), 116, 193
    See also specific nations
Cerpa Cartolini, Néstor, 141
Chamorro, Pedro Joaquín, 96
Chamorro, Violeta, 97, 102
Chapultepec (Battle of), 59
Chase Manhattan Bank, 15
Chavez, Hugo, 152–153, 165
Chiapas, 129–130
Chichén Itzá, 23, 26(map)
Chile, 8, 90–92, 152
China, 186
Chiquita Brands (and United Fruit
    Company), 108, 186
Christian Base Communities,
    116–117
Christianity, 42, 144, 116, 163–164
    See also Bible; Church;
        Evangelicalism; Protestantism
Church (Roman Catholic Church),
    29, 39, 50, 54, 59–60, 65, 73,
    123, 138
    in colonial era, 43–47
    after independence, 56–57
    liberation theology in, 114–116,
        119–121
    and revolutionary Mexico, 67–68
    See also Christianity; Popes;
        specific clerical orders
CIA [(U.S.) Central Intelligence
    Agency], 82, 91, 111, 194
    and Contras, 99–101, 104–105
Científicos, 64
Citibank Corporation (and
    Citigroup), 155, 171
Ciudad Juárez, 66, 167
Claude, Sylvio, 143–144
Clinton, Bill (and administration),
    84, 112, 164, 169, 189–191,
    194
    and global economics, 166–167,
        169, 171, 187

Colóm, Alvaro, 112
Colombia, 130–131, 176–178, 181
Colonial era, 37–51
Colosio, Luis Donaldo, 149
Columbus, Christopher, 28–29
Columbus, New Mexico, 67
Commodities, 11, 61–62, 64
Communism, 8, 70–71, 88, 108, 116
  definitions of, 77–78
  See also Marxism; Soviet Union
Comte, Auguste, 61
Concientización, 116
Confederación General de Trabajadores [General Workers' Confederation (of Argentina)], 72
Conservatives and conservatism, 56–58
Constant, Emmanuel "Toto", 145–146
Constitutions, 50, 59–60, 65
Consumerism, 176–177
Contras. *See* FDN
Convents, 46
Corporations, 11, 87, 117–118, 139, 145, 171, 177, 194
  and global economy, 154, 161–162, 165–168
  control of media, 195–197 and stockmarkets
Corruption, 12, 156, 162
Cortés, Hernán, 31–33
Costa Rica, 99, 103(map), 104–106
Counterinsurgency, 86, 107–108
  in Peru, 138, 140
  as U.S.-guided strategy, 125–126, 130
Coyotes, 191
Crime, 178–181
Criollos, 49, 52–54, 60
Cristero Rebellion, 67–68
Cuauhtémoc, 32

Cuba, 7, 31, 103(map)
  revolution, 78–82
  and U.S., 82–85
Cuba Democracy Act, 84
CUC [Committee of Peasant Unity], 116–117
Currencies, 162, 165
  and devaluations, 168, 174–176
  See also specific major currencies
Cuzco, 24, 26(map)

D'Aubuisson, Roberto, 127
Dean, Warren, 12
Death penalty, 180
Death squads, 108–109, 119, 123, 127, 130, 138
Debt, 11, 154–160, 162–163, 184
  campaigns for relief of, 163–164
Dechoukaj, 143
Defense patrols, 110, 139
Déjoie, Louis, 143
de la Rua, Fernando, 175–176
Democracy, 65, 69, 135–136, 142, 144
  false nature of, 151–153
  *See also Media*cracy
Dependency theory, 10–12, 37, 115, 173
Desaparecidos, 93
Desegregation (racial), 81
Devaluations, 168–170, 174–176
Development (term), 3, 9–10, 155
Dias, Bartolomeu, 28
Díaz, Ordaz, Gustavo, 147
Díaz, Porfirio, 64–65
Diezmo, 47
Disease, 15
  in conquest, 32–33
Doctrine of National Security, 89–90
Dollar (U.S. currency), 14, 156, 158, 168, 174
Dominicans, 45
Drugs and drug trade, 101, 131, 139, 145, 148, 168, 181

Duarte, José Napoleón, 118, 122, 127
Duhalde, Eduardo, 179
Duvalier dictatorship, 142, 166

ECLA [(United Nations) Economic Commission for Latin America], 10
Economic nationalism, 68, 71, 161–162
in Cuba, 81–82, 86
Economics, 14–15, 61–63
global policies, 154–171
Economists and economics (discipline), 10, 14
Ecuador, 157, 164–165, 176
Education, 50, 59, 70, 99, 137, 163
EGP [Guerrilla Army of the Poor (of Guatemala)], 110
El Cid, 27
El Mozote, 124–125
El Salvador, 103(map), 117–129, 132, 135
Elections, 72, 79, 87–88, 99, 135–136, 151, 174
in El Salvador, 118, 127, 131–132
in Haiti, 143–146
in Mexico, 65–66, 70, 147–150
Embargos, 83, 102
Emphyteusis, Law of (Argentina), 54
Encomienda, 29–30
England. *See* Great Britain
English (language), 171, 177
Enlightenment, 50–52, 61
Environment, 167, 187
Estado Nôvo, 71
Europe, 99, 159, 164
Evangelicalism, 47, 101, 107, 109–110, 141
Exports, 62–63, 163, 168, 175

Faletto, Enzo, 10
FARC [Revolutionary Armed Forces of Colombia], 130–131
Fast-Track authority, 167, 171
FBI [(U.S.) Federal Bureau of Investigation], 69, 141, 181
FDN [Nicaraguan Democratic Force], or Contras, 95, 98–102, 105–106
FDR [Democratic Revolutionary Front (of El Salvador)], 122–123, 127
FECCAS [Federation of Christian Peasants (of El Salvador)], 117
Federal Judicial Police (Mexico), 181
Federal Reserve, 79, 171
Ferdinand, 27–29
Ferdinand VII, 51
Fernández de Cevallos, Diego, 150
Fincas, 108
First World (term), 1
Fischer, Stanley, 175
Flores Magón, Ricardo, 65
Florida, 82, 177
FMLN [Farabundo Martí Front for National Liberation], 123–125, 127–128, 131–132
Ford Motor Company, 93
Fort Bragg, North Carolina, 129
Fox, Vicente, 150
France, 41, 51, 60, 66, 99, 171
Franciscans, 45
Frank, André Gunder, 11
FRAPH [Front for the Advancement and Progress of Haiti], 145–146
Freire, Paulo, 116, 193
FSLN [Sandinista National Liberation Front], 96
Fujimori, Alberto, 139–141
Functionalism, 5

García, Alan, 139, 158
Gates, Bill, 193
GATT [General Agreement on Tariffs and Trade], 171
GDP [Gross Domestic Product], 169–170, 176, 193
Generation of 1837, 59
Gerardi, Juan, 112
Germany, 69, 71, 166
Globalization. *See* Economics
Goodwin, John, 82
Goulart, João "Jango", 87–88
Governments
   colonial, 47–50, 54
   See also specific nations
Great Britain, 41, 51, 92–93, 99, 166
   as model for development, 6, 11
Greenspan, Alan, 175
Guadalupe-Hidalgo, Treaty of, 59
Guatemala, 35–36, 103(map), 107–113
Guerrilla warfare, 80, 90, 93, 148
   in El Salvador, 123–124, 128
   in Guatemala, 107–109
   See also specific groups
Guevara, Ernesto "Che", 80, 82, 84
Gutiérrez, Gustavo, 115, 121
Goldman-Sachs Company, 166, 169
Gourgue, Gerard, 143
Gurría, José Angel, 170
Guzmán, Abimael, 137–139

Haciendas, 54, 64
Haig, Alexander, 123
Haiti, 41–43, 103(map), 142–146, 163
Harbury, Jennifer, 111–112
Harrison, Lawrence, 15
Havana, 26(map), 31, 81, 85
Heavily Indebted Poor Countries [HIPC], 164

Hernández, Roberto, 149, 151, 169–170
Hidalgo, Miguel, 52–53
Hispaniola, 29
Historians and history (discipline), 9–10, 16, 57, 93, 144, 194–195
   and theory, 12–13
Holland, 40
Holy Office of the Inquisition, 46, 53
Honduras, 103(map), 106–107
Huerta, Victoriano, 66
Hull, John, 105
Human rights, 89, 93, 177–183
   See also Massacres; Prisons; Torture
Huntington, Samuel, 9

IADC [Inter-American Defense College], 86
Iberia, 25–27
IFIs [international financial institutions], 159–161, 163–165
   See also specific institutions
IMF [International Monetary Fund], 157–165, 168, 170–171, 174–176
Immigration, 62, 146, 171, 189–191
Import substitution industries, 71, 161–162
Inca, 23–25, 33
Independence, 51–54
Indians, 19, 130, 165
   before encounter, 20–25
   and christianity, 44–45
   conquest of, 31–35
   Spanish treatment of, 30
   today, 35–36
   See also specific tribes and cultures
Industrialization, 3–4, 10–11, 15, 68, 71, 184

Inflation, 92, 102, 137, 140, 148, 156, 162, 169, 174
Intendants, 50
Inter-American Development Bank, 155
Internet, 130, 177, 197
Investments, 54, 56, 79, 87, 91, 159–161, 164–165
  in 'age of progess', 62–64
  and debt crisis, 154–156
  and economic crises, 169, 174–175
  See also Banks; MAI
Iran-Contra Scandal, 101
IRCA [Immigration and Control Act (of 1986)], 190
Isabella, 27–29
Israel, 110
Itrubide, Agustín de, 53

Jamaica, 41, 103(map), 180
Japan, 99, 140, 170–171, 184
Jesuits, 45, 50
  slayings of in El Salvador, 128, 189
Jews and Judaism, 164
João, 53
John Paul I, 120
John Paul II, 92, 120–121
Juárez, Benito, 59–60
Jubilee 200, 163–164
Judiciaries, 140, 180–181
Justiceiros, 178, 180

Kennedy, John F., 7, 82, 85
Keynes, John Maynard, 158
Khrushchev, Nikita, 82
Koehler, Horst, 159

la Cruz, Sor Juana Inés de, 46
La Prensa, 96
Labor, 65, 87, 90, 119, 161, 185, 193
  and populism, 68, 71–72
  repression of, 93, 147, 167
  See also Sweatshops
Ladinos, 108, 111
Lagos, Ricardo, 152
Land reform, 69, 81, 88, 99, 108, 122
Las Casas, Bartolomé de, 30, 43
Latifundio, 54, 69, 108, 136
Lautaro, 35
Lavalas, 144
Lavín, Joaquín, 152
Letters of Intent, 160
Liberals (nineteenth century), 54, 56–57, 59–60
Liberation theology, 114, 116, 143
Lima, 26(map)
Limbaugh, Rush, 188
Low Intensity Conflict, 126, 130–131

Machu Picchu, 24, 26(map)
Madeira Islands, 38
Madero, Francisco I., 65–66
Mahuad, Jamil, 165
MAI [Multilateral Agreement on Investment], 171
Malinche, 31
Malnutrition, 1, 14, 39, 102
Manigat, Leslie, 144
Mapiripán, 131
Maroons, 41
Martí, José, 78, 80
Martínez, Gustavo Alvarez, 107
Marxism, 13
Massacres, 33, 109, 130–131, 138, 147–148
  in El Salvador, 119, 124–125
  in Haiti, 143–145
Maya, 22–23, 45
  conquest of, 34
Mazorca, 57
Medellín Bishops Conference, 115

Media, 87–88, 104, 116, 130–131,
138, 165, 169–170, 189
and bias, 149, 195–198
and Central America, 100,
111–112, 125, 127–129
and Cuban revolution, 80–82
influence of, 151–153
See also Television; *specific news
sources*
*Media*cracy, 151–153, 178
Medina, Ofelia, 15, 19
Menchú, Rigoberta, 35–36, 111
Menem, Carlos, 175, 179
MERCOSUR [Southern Cone
Common Market], 175
Mestizos, 35, 52, 138
Mexico, 15–16, 19–23, 48,
129–130, 155, 190
conquests of, 30–32, 34
economic crisis, 168–170, 174
independence, 52–53
in mid-nineteenth century,
58–60
political processes, 146–150
revolution, 64–70
See also NAFTA
Mexico City, 7, 32, 44, 49, 53
Miami, 82, 85, 97–98
Middle class, 5, 67, 70, 136, 147,
152, 161
in Argentina, 93, 177
in Brazil, 89–90
in Central America, 98, 108, 118
in Chile, 91–92, 176–177
and crime, 179–181
and Cuban revolution, 80–81
MilGroup [(U.S.) Military Group],
126, 129
Militaries and militarism, 50, 57,
59, 71–72, 90, 93, 120, 130,
156, 163, 179
coups, 8, 73, 80, 89, 91–92, 94,
108, 122, 136

in El Salvador, 118–119, 121–128
in Haiti,1 43–145
in Peru, 136–141
regimes in twentieth century,
86–94
See also Counterinsurgency;
United States of America,
military
Minas Gerais, 53
Mochica, 24
Moctezuma II, 31–32
Modernization theory, 5–9, 118,
173, 176
revival of, 14
Monge, Luis Alberto, 105
Monterrosa, Domingo, 126
Montesinos, Antonio de, 30
Montesinos, Vladimiro, 140, 196
Montoro, André, 178
Moors, 26–27
Mothers of the Disappeared, 93
MRTA [Tupac Amarú
Revolutionary Movement],
139–141
Muisca, 25, 34
Mulattos, 42, 142, 146

Nader, Ralph, 183, 186
NAFTA [North American Free
Trade Agreement], 149,
167–168
Namphy, Henri, 143
National Guard (of Nicaragua),
96–97, 99, 105
Nationalism, 51, 68, 77–78, 80,
151, 154, 171–172, 175
Navidad, 26(map), 29
Neoliberal economics, 159–160,
166, 170–171, 174
Netzahualcóyotl, 21
Newshour (television show), 130, 196
Newspapers, 125
See also specific names

Newsweek, 100, 188
New York Times, 80, 105, 125, 195–197
Nicaragua, 95–102, 103(map)
Nobel Peace Prize, 35, 106, 111
Noche Triste, 32
Noirisme, 142
Nonoalca, 23
Noriega, Manuel, 101
North, Oliver, 101–102, 105
Nuclear warheads, 83–84
Nuevo Peso (Mexican currency), 162, 169
Nuño de Guzmán, Beltrán, 34

Obando y Bravo, Miguel, 103
Obregón, Alvaro, 67
Oil, 62, 165
    See PEMEX; Petrobrás
Olympic Games, 7, 147
Operação Bandeirantes, 89
Operation Gatekeeper, 191
Operation Mongoose, 83
Opus Dei, 120
Organization of American States, 86, 97
Orozco, Pascual, 66
Ortega, Daniel, 98
Ortiz, Diana, 110–111

Palmares, 40
Pampas, 62
PAN [National Action Party (of Mexico)], 68, 148–150
Pan American Union, 63
Panama, 26(map), 30, 103(map), 172
    canal, 63
Paramilitaries, 109, 130–131
    See also Death squads; Militaries and militarism
Paseo de la Reforma, 64
Pastora, Edén, 97, 104–105

Patti, Luis, 179
Pazos, Luis, 170
PDC [Christian Democratic Party (of El Salvador)], 118
Pedro I, 54, 60
PEMEX [Petróleos Mexicanos], 69–70
Pentagon. See U.S.-Military
Péralte, Charlemagne, 42
Perón, Eva (Evita), 72–73
Perón, "Isabelita", 92–93
Perón, Juan, 72–74, 92
Pershing, John J. "Blackjack", 67
Personalism, 4
Peru, 23–24, 33–34, 48, 52, 180–181
    in late twentieth century, 136–141
Peso (Argentine currency), 93, 175
Petrobrás, 71
Pinochet, Augusto, 91–92
Pizarro, Francisco, 33
Plantations, 39
Platt Amendment, 79
Pledge of Resistance, 100–101
Police, 64, 178–182, 187
Political culture, 5, 7
Political scientists and Political Science (discipline), 9, 14, 16, 151, 198
Pombal, Marquis de, 53
Popes, 29, 114, 164
    See also John Paul I; John Paul II
Population, 14, 55, 61
Populism, 68, 71, 73–74, 77
Porfiriato, 64
Portillo, Alfonso, 112
Portugal, 27–29, 38, 53–54
Positivism, 6, 61
Poverty, 1, 7, 9, 64, 72, 96, 117, 161, 176
    trends in, 14–15
    See also Malnutrition

PRD [Party of the Democratic Revolution], 148–150
Prebisch, Raúl, 10
PRI [Party of the Institutionalized Revolution], 146–150, 181
Prisons, 180
Privatization, 162–163, 165
Profit remittance, 71–73
Proposition 187, 190
Protestantism, 47, 110
  See also Evangelicalism
Psychological Operations (Psy Ops), 126–129
PTB [Brazilian Labor Party], 87, 89

Quadros, Jânio da Silva, 87
Quechua, 24
Quetzalcóatl, 31
Quilombos, 40

Race, 80–81, 136, 142
  See also Desegregation; *specific racial groups*
Radio Cuscatlán, 129
Railroads, 62, 64
Reagan, Ronald (and adminstration), 12, 95–96, 105, 110, 123, 156, 166
  and Nicaraguan revolution, 98–101
Real (Brazilian currency), 162, 174
Reconquest, 27
Regionalism, 54
Religion, 27
  of Africans, 42–43
  of Indians, 21–24
  See also Church; Protestantism
Residential Representative, 160
Rio de Janeiro, 51, 53, 88, 180
Rios Montt, Efraín, 109–110
Roberts, Cokie, 111
Romero, Oscar, 120–121, 127

Rondas. See Defense patrols
Roosevelt Corollary (to Monroe Doctrine), 63
Rosas, Juan Manuel de, 57–58
Rostow, Walt, 6
Royal Council of the Inides, 48
Rubin, Robert, 166, 169, 171
Rurales, 64

Saint Domingue. *See* Haiti
Salinas de Gortari, Carlos, 148–149, 170
Sandinistas. *See* FSLN
San Martín, José de, 52
San Martín, Ramón Grau, 79
Santa Anna, Antonio López de, 57–58
São Paulo, 71, 87, 180
SAP [Structural Adjustment Program], 159–165
Sarmiento, Domingo F., 59
SIN [National Intelligence Service (of Peru)], 140
School of the Americas, 129, 188–189
Seattle, 187–188
Sendero Luminoso, 137–140
Sepúlveda, Juan de, 43
Silver, 49–50
"Sixty Minutes" (television show), 111, 188
Slavery, 30, 38–41
Snuff tapes, 183
Social Scientists. *See* Academics
Somoza, Anastasio, 96–97
Soviet Union (and Russia), 1, 7, 82–84, 170–171
Sovereignty
  economic end of, 154, 160
Spain, 9, 26–27, 29, 43, 51, 92, 194
  and colonial government, 48–50
  and Cuba, 78–79

Sports, 64
    See also Olympic Games; World
        Cup
Stanley, Paco, 181
Stein, Barbara and Stanley, 37
Stewart, Bill, 97
Stocks and stockmarkets, 153,
    169–171
Subversion, 135, 140
    See also Counterinsurgency;
        Guerrilla warfare
Sucre (Ecaudoran currency), 165
Sugar, 37–38, 61
Sweatshops, 185–186
Sweeney, John, 166, 193

Tango, 62
Tariffs, 68, 161
Taxes, 163
Technocrats, 159–160, 170
Teleco, 145
Televisa, 149–150
Television, 7, 47, 81–82, 101–102,
    112
    and crime, 178–179, 180–181
    and El Salvador, 127–129
    in Mexico, 149–150
    in Peru, 140–141
    in U.S., 188–189, 197
    See also Media; *Media*cracy;
        specific networks
Tenochtitlán, 21, 26(map), 31–32
Teotihuacán, 20, 26(map)
Tesobonos, 169
Texas, 58, 66
Texcoco, 21
Theory, 3–14, 54, 173
Third World, 1, 2(map), 3
Tlatelolco, 147–148
Tlaxcalans, 22
Toltecs, 21, 23
Tordesillas, Treaty of, 29
Torres, Camilo, 115

Torture, 89, 93, 106–107, 110, 119,
    127, 138
    in El Salvador, 124–125
    and law and order, 179–183
Tourism, 85
Toutons Macoute, 142–144
Trade, 10, 28, 49, 51, 56, 61,
    167–168
    of slaves, 38–39
    See also MERCOSUR, NAFTA
Tranches, 160

U.S.S. "Maine", 78–79
Ungo, Guillermo, 118, 122–123
United Fruit Company. *See*
    Chiquita Brands
United Nations, 99, 107
United States of America, 4, 54, 56,
    62–63, 71, 74, 89–90, 131, 137,
    160–161, 193
    congress of, 95, 100–102, 105,
        123, 167, 189
    and Cuban revolution, 80–84
    dangers to wealth of, 77,
        135–136, 188–191
    and El Salvador, 121–123,
        125–129
    and global economics, 155–158,
        163, 166–171, 174, 183–187,
        191–192
    and Guatemala, 107–108,
        110–112
    and Haiti, 41–42, 142–146
    and Mexican revolution, 66–67,
        69
    military, 83–84, 86, 108,
        126–132, 135, 150–151, 157,
        188–189
    scholarship and media in,
        194–198
    and torture, 182–183
    See also Business; CIA; FBI;
        Investments; *specific presidents*

UNO (of Nicaragua), 102
URNG [Guatemalan National Revolutionary Union], 110
USAID [(U.S.) Agency for International Development], 15, 105, 193

Vargas, Getúlio, 70–72
Vargas Llosa, Mario, 165
Vatican II, 114–115
Velasco, Juan, 136
Venezuela, 152–153, 165, 176
Veracruz, 31–32, 66
Vespucci, Amerigo, 29
Viceroyalties, 47–48
Vietnam war, 126
Villa, Francisco "Pancho", 66
Villalobos, Joaquín, 124, 128, 132
Virgin of Guadalupe, 44
Voodoo, 42–43, 142

Wages, 11, 14, 145, 167, 170, 185–186, 193

Wall Street Journal, 128, 153, 195
Wallerstein, Immanuel, 12
Weber, Max, 6
White, Robert, 122–123
Wolfensohn, James, 159
Women, 40, 46, 93, 99, 148
    See also specific persons
World Bank, 155, 158–160, 163–164
World Cup, 93, 165, 177
World Systems theory, 12–13
WTO [World Trade Organization], 166, 171, 186–187

Yucatán, 23

Zapata, Emiliiano, 66
Zapatistas (of Chiapas), 129–130, 170
Zedillo, Ernesto, 149–150, 168–170, 181
Zombies, 43, 142
Zumbi, 42